THE MACROECONOMICS OF DEVELOPMENT FINANCE

Also published in association with the Institute of Social Studies

Richard Brown
PUBLIC DEBT AND PRIVATE WEALTH
Debt, Capital Flight and the IMF in Sudan

Geertje Lycklama à Nijeholt
TOWARDS WOMEN'S STRATEGIES FOR THE 1990s
Challenging Government and the State

Kurt Martin (*editor*)
STRATEGIES OF ECONOMIC DEVELOPMENT
Readings in the Political Economy of Industrialization

The Macroeconomics of Development Finance

A Kaleckian Analysis of the Semi-Industrialized Economy

E. V. K. FitzGerald
Professor of Development Economics
Institute of Social Studies, The Hague

M
St. Martin's Press in association with the INSTITUTE OF SOCIAL STUDIES

First published in Great Britain 1993 by
THE MACMILLAN PRESS LTD
Houndmills, Basingstoke, Hampshire RG21 2XS
and London
Companies and representatives
throughout the world

A catalogue record for this book is available from the British Library.

ISBN 0–333–56063–9

Printed in Great Britain by
Ipswich Book Co Ltd
Ipswich, Suffolk

First published in the United States of America 1993 by
Scholarly and Reference Division,
ST. MARTIN'S PRESS, INC.,
175 Fifth Avenue,
New York, N.Y. 10010

ISBN 0–312–08356–4

Library of Congress Cataloging-in-Publication Data
FitzGerald, E. V. K. (Edmund Valpy Knox), 1947–
The macroeconomics of development finance : a Kaleckian analysis of the semi-industrialized economy / E.V.K. FitzGerald.
p. cm.
Includes index.
ISBN 0–312–08356–4
1. Finance—Developing countries. 2. Economic development–
–Finance. 3. Kalecki, Michał. I. Title.
HG195.F56 1993
339.5—dc20 92–4715
CIP

For my mother

Contents

List of Tables and Figures

Tables

Figures

Preface

The general agreement that industrializing countries must maintain macroeconomic management regimes that simultaneously meet the constraints of monetary stabilization and adjust domestic prices to match a volatile world economy has by no means exhausted the development agenda. The greater part of the world's population still suffers from technological backwardness, low productivity, trade imbalances, lack of infrastructure and above all widespread absolute poverty. To these have been added more recently the fiscal consequences of financial insolvency, the loss of familiar policy instruments due to administrative failure and the implications of political emancipation for perceived consumption entitlements.

Most of my experience as a professional economist has been gained in the somewhat frustrating attempt to resolve in practice the conflict between planned basic needs provision and the macromanagement of financial balances in mixed economies. This book brings together the analytical approaches I have employed within an explicitly Kaleckian framework. During my doctoral studies at Cambridge in the early 1970s, a period now regarded as the golden sunset of Keynesianism, I was more impressed by the Kaleckian view of investment finance and production structures as reflections of market organization and fiscal behaviour than by post-Keynesian fascination with income distribution and growth models. Kalecki's approach to wagegoods requirements and enterprise investment seemed to me to be both relevant to semi-industrial economies which had begun to interest me, and to fit well with the concept of 'justice as fairness' which had recently been formalized by Rawles in his *Theory of Justice*. This outlook – unfashionable as it may be at present – informs the whole of this book.

This approach led quite naturally to two lines of enquiry. On the one hand, I have tried to contribute to an analytics of finance based on realistic institutional structures rather than the transfer of theory from industrialized societies. Inadequate macromanagement of mixed economies seems to me to have contributed not only to the collapse of ambitious state-led strategies to overcome rural poverty and industrial backwardness but also failure of policies designed to support national accumulation with natural resource rents. I reported results of this line of enquiry in *Financing Economic Development* in

1989. On the other hand, my work on the implementation of Third World socialist strategies has focused upon the necessity to reconcile the desire for collective basic needs provision and radical structural change with a production system responding largely to market forces – both from the international economy and from peasant and artisan firms. The failure to resolve this central issue has had disastrous consequences, which have been underlined by the subsequent experience of Eastern Europe. I discussed this line of enquiry in *Markets within Planning* in 1988.

My first debt of gratitude is to my fellow members of the Finance and Development Research Group, Karel Jansen and Rob Vos, for their support and friendship. I would also like to thank the staff of the ISS Publications Office for their help in preparing this book, and the editors of the *Cambridge Journal of Economics*, *Development and Change*, the *Journal of Development Studies* and *Oxford Economic Papers* for permission to make use of previously published material. The constructive criticism of my colleagues and students at Cambridge and The Hague has been invaluable in clarifying my ideas – I can only claim sole title to the errors. Above all I am indebted to my family who – like those of so many of my fellow development economists – bear a disproportionate share of the burden in our chosen field of enquiry.

E. V. K. FitzGerald

1 Kalecki and the Finance of the Semi-industrialized Economy

1.1 THE MACROECONOMIC ANALYSIS OF SEMI-INDUSTRIALIZED ECONOMIES

This book is about those 'semi-industrialized' countries which have passed H. Chenery's turning point 'at which the contribution of manufacturing to growth exceeds that of primary production'[1] and thus possess structural characteristics which distinguish them from both the poor agrarian societies on the one hand and the rich industrial nations on the other.

These semi-industrialized economies support about a third of the population of the Less Developed Countries (LCDs) and account for some four-fifths of its production.[2] After the socially costly experience of macroeconomic stabilization in the 1980s – largely achieved by the reduction of fiscal demand and wages – structural adjustment proper in these economies is proving far more elusive because it requires the reconciliation of the saving and investment decisions of distinct institutional sectors. That sound macroeconomic analysis should be based upon microeconomic understanding of such sectoral behaviour should be beyond dispute.[3] After all, the theory of the firm has always been a central concern of post-Keynesian economists[4] and has more recently been recognized as essential to a more realistic neoclassical approach, known as the 'New Institutional Economics'.[5]

In semi-industrial economies markets do not clear in a simple textbook manner but are conditioned by behavioural considerations such as firm survival, ownership concentration and political relationships – all of which strongly condition enterprise behaviour and impose endogenous constraints on government policy. Moreover, continued industrialization involves fundamental changes in the structure of production, trade and distribution – to be achieved through capital formation, new technology and modern administration. None the less the orthodox discourse of macroeconomics when applied to industrializing countries – as characterized by the World Bank (WB) and the

International Monetary Fund (IMF) – still bases its view of market behaviour on the simple pre-Keynesian tenets of Alfred Marshall. By implication, firms and households atomistically maximize profits and welfare, while market failure is explicitly attributed to 'distortions' brought about by misguided government intervention.[6]

This neglect persists despite recent advances in microeconomic analysis – ranging from the peasant household to the transnational enterprise – many of which have neoclassical foundations.[7] Recent work in model-building – particularly of computable general equilibrium models – to be found in the 'neo-structuralist' literature[8] allows these advances to be included in macroeconomic analysis, although so far these models have tended to express the microeconomic heterogeneity of developing countries by circumstantial rigidities or constraints. Above all, the failure to specify the behaviour of the enterprise sector is surprising when orthodox theory insists that private rather than public initiative is to be the motor of growth, while heterodox theory attributes market failure to business attitudes.

The macroeconomic analysis applied by the pioneers of modern development economics – among whom Michael Kalecki was a leading member – was explicitly derived from these observed behavioural considerations. Their work represents a continuation of the classical tradition of political economy, which itself originated in the Industrial Revolution and survived in Central Europe due to late industrialization there.[9] Indeed, neoclassical economics only emerged in the late-nineteenth-century Anglo-Saxon economies where the structural changes implied by industrialization were assumed (optimistically as it turns out) to be complete, so that only marginal changes in resource allocation were considered necessary in order to achieve optimal efficiency.[10]

The argument for returning to the work of the early development economists thus goes beyond a heterodox critique of the contemporary neoclassical paradigm of development economics. The issue is not merely that neo-orthodox stabilization policies and adjustment programmes do not take poverty criteria or national sovereignty into account, but rather whether the neoclassical description of how semi-industrial economies function is plausible at all. However, in order to produce an analytical method of some practical utility to policymakers, it is necessary to specify the 'operational rules' of the different institutional sectors which underpin the macro-structures of semi-industrialized economies. Chapter 2 suggests how this heterogeneity can be formally defined, measured and modelled through the use of the 'capital accumulation account' in the UN Standard National Accounts System. This permits the translation of general structuralist principles into analytical models which include recent advances in both economic theory and statistical measurement.

1.2 THE FOUNDATIONS OF MODERN DEVELOPMENT ECONOMICS

Development economics only became established as a distinct branch of economics after the Second World War, justifying its separate existence on the grounds that the technological and institutional structures of Third World economies were sufficiently different from those of the 'First World' to justify a distinct approach. Its intellectual origins can be found in the classical tradition in economics. Not only were Adam Smith, David Ricardo and Karl Marx clearly concerned with the experience of early industrialization, agrarian change, population pressure and social transformation – in other words, with the agenda of what would now be termed 'development' economics[11] – but also the rejection of the neoclassical paradigm of the smoothly functioning market economy in favour of a more institutional and structural approach to change which had much in common with that of economic historians.[12] The Keynesian revolution[13] had invalidated the optimistic belief in the capacity of the market to achieve automatic adjustment towards an optimal allocation of resources. Indeed, it was against the Old Orthodoxy of 'sound money' based on balanced budgets and the Gold Standard that J. M. Keynes himself had rebelled, and not against neoclassical theory as such, for there was much of Marshall's *Principles* in the *General Theory*. This macroeconomic foundation was strengthened by the experience of planning in the industrialized economies during the Second World War, and the Fabian project of welfare provision on the basis of citizen entitlement immediately afterwards.

Meanwhile, the Eastern European experience of 'late industrialization' in the inter-war period and that of the first attempts at comprehensive national planning in the Soviet Union led to a concern for intersectoral relationships, the problem of large firms, and the role of the peasantry.[14] This empirical and historical outlook was complemented by a strand of neo-Ricardian analysis (particularly evident in Kalecki) that attempted to translate Marx's reproduction schemes into a tractable model for economic policy and planning. This rich tradition of experience and thought was transferred to the West in general, and to the nascent UN in particular, by the mass emigration of Eastern European economists during and after the Second World War.

Significantly, in the immediate post-war years 'Southern' economists such as Arthur Lewis and Raul Prebisch began to construct models of the Third World economy based upon unequal trading relationships between North and South and technological heterogeneity within the Southern economies.[15] The former postulate led to new theories of international trade based on specific interpretations of price formation and demand patterns, and suggested that determinate intergovernmental action was required to overcome the trade barriers to growth posed by the external constraint in the 'dual-gap' analysis. The latter postulate produced a model of the domestic peripheral economy divided between a modern industrial sector (including agribusiness and minerals) of large modern enterprises and a technically backward sector of peasants and artisans; but which are articulated one with the other by the exchange of labour and commodities.

Meanwhile, the critique of neoclassical theory and the construction of an alternative theory reflecting the institutional reality of late capitalism, was taken up by 'post-Keynesians' in the North who could also count upon the earlier work by Kalecki–Sraffa on the macroeconomic analysis of a world characterized by monopoly, administered prices, and socially negotiated income distribution.[16] Despite this debate, economists in the 'classical tradition' working on the Third World (including Kalecki himself) did not devote much energy to formal macroeconomic theory. Rather, in the wake of post-colonial pressure for economic independence, they evolved development strategies based on the rapid transformation of a backward agricultural sector, the proletarianization of the peasantry, technology transfer and reintegration into the world trading system. Industrial development was widely regarded as essential for sustained economic growth, and thus the overcoming of poverty and the achievement of economic sovereignty, and also requiring considerable state involvement in common with the experience of other 'late' capitalist developers such as Japan and Italy. This approach became the accepted framework for the United Nations and development agencies around the world.

In the immediate post-war period, development economists generally regarded finance as being essentially an issue of state directed mobilization of resources in order to support an increased rate of industrial accumulation. This view represented a radical break with the Anglo-Saxon principles of 'sound finance' that had ruled in both the colonies and independent primary exporters before the Second World War, which had been based on free trade, adherence to the Gold Standard (or its equivalent in sterling), private investment criteria, and balanced budgets.[17] This new approach was consistent with contemporary Keynesian views and might be better regarded as a continuation of the Continental European tradition on industrial development,[18] and even the classical concept of economic surplus mobilization to support accumulation. As Lewis himself describes the view at the time: 'Where had the money come from to pay for modernization in the past? The short answer was that profits had risen relative to the national income, because productivity has risen faster than wages'.[19]

The resources required for the increased rate of accumulation in developing countries were to be both internal and external; that is, profits domestically generated or transferred from abroad. The source of the internal resources and the most appropriate means of mobilizing them was the subject of vigorous debate. Lewis (1954) explicitly identifies retained profits (that is, enterprise savings) as the main source of investment finance, and his point about 'unlimited supplies of labour' is that they hold down both nominal and real wages so as to maximize accumulation and growth. Nurkse (1953) suggests that if underemployed labour is used on public works, macroeconomic savings are generated because investment rises without consumption falling: a Keynesian advance on Lewis's more classical model. Kalecki (1976) argues that the reduction of non-essential consumption should effectively finance development if the government is to maintain a commitment to maintaining real wages and peasant incomes; while Kaldor (1959) takes a more pessimistic view of this argument, suggesting that inflationary government deficits generate aggregate savings by depressing real wages. However, their analysis was more concerned with macroeconomic aggregates, reinvested profits and budgetary balances than with bank deposits or interest rates. Even more specialized authors such as Prest (1962) and Hicks (1965) did not analyse financial intermediation in depth, on the assumption that banks in developing countries are mainly concerned with commercial transactions.

External resources were agreed to be necessary in order to raise foreign exchange availability and permit investment (largely based on imported capital goods) to take place, due to the difficulty of expanding exports sufficiently. Although some doubts were expressed as to whether internal and external savings were, in fact, complementary, the 'dual-gap' model became the basis for the standard approach to aid. For a given growth target, domestic savings levels were projected using a fixed coefficient applied to GDP, as was the investment requirement from the capital–output ratio: the difference was the required level of net external resource inflow for the plan period. This became the accepted approach for agencies such as the World Bank, and could be seen as being equivalent to the Harrod equations for a developing economy constrained by trade rather than labour supply.[20]

Within this tradition, financial theory unfortunately did not advance much from the original model laid down by the founding fathers in the 1950s, as even a collection as recent as that by Newlyn (1977) attests. If anything, the two-gap model was simplified by assuming exports and domestic savings to be fixed in the short term, and thus that growth could only be increased by more foreign loans. The work on financial intermediation (for example, Goldsmith, 1969) was confined to the banking sector, reflecting the common belief that the growth of bank deposits was equivalent to resource mobilization. Extensive household expenditure surveys revealed low rates of personal savings but were not complemented by studies of the enterprise sector. The important debate between Latin-American economists and the IMF over stabilization policies[21] involved key issues such as the origin of budget deficits, sectoral price formation and the 'monetary approach to the balance of payments', but did not elicit a plausible finance theory consistent with the canons of development economics.

In the 1970s, a separate strand of what might be termed 'developmental monetarism' emerged, adapting monetarist theory to the segmented economies of the Third World. A simplified form of the dual economy model was used to distinguish an 'informal' sector with a financial surplus which can be channelled towards a savings-starved corporate 'modern' sector. If capital markets worked properly, funds would move from the former sector to the latter, increasing efficiency, investment and growth.[22] Meanwhile, the IMF shifted its analytical and policy focus from fiscal and parity issues to monetary and exchange problems. The 'Monetary Approach to the Balance of Payments' was refined from its initially almost Keynesian emphasis on domestic credit control and devaluation into a fully-fledged monetary theory where product markets respond to monetary imbalances, and foreign trade reflects the supply and demand for the domestic currency relative to that for foreign currency.[23] These two advances in monetarist theory were combined with the contemporary neoclassical critique of post-war development economics to create the powerful

'New Orthodoxy' which, with the powerful support of the Bank and the Fund, rapidly pushed aside the received wisdom of development economics painfully built up by its predecessors on the basis of three decades of empirical research and experience.

Post-Keynesian economists have worked out a theory of finance for the industrial economies, which regards savings as being founded on enterprise profits that can be raised in line with investment plans by oligopolistic enterprises.[24] In this approach, money is seen as essentially passive, so that credit regulation (of which interest rates are little more than a symbol) has more to do with consumer demand than with investment. Compared with fiscal policy, the rate of interest is considered as an ineffective macroeconomic instrument. Although the limitations of this analysis for an open economy are clear,[25] the Keynesians and the post-Keynesians have been able to mount a reasonably effective counter-attack on monetarism in the North, by criticizing the theoretical and methodological assumptions upon which the New Orthodoxy is constructed, and paying particular attention to aspects of the real world, such as the heterogeneity of market structures, price formation systems, and self-financing of enterprises.[26] This critique also reaffirms the Keynesian position, effectively denied by neoclassical economists, that there is a concept of macroeconomics distinct from the simple aggregation of microeconomic decisions by atomistic and homogeneous individuals, where any deviations from pure market equilibria are 'distortions'. Rather, market clearing is the result of interactions between heterogeneous social groups, firms and states, each with its own associative power over the market as well as its own objective functions.

Such a theoretically advanced counter-attack has yet to be made by or on behalf of the Third World, although there have been many critiques of the neo-orthodox position from the standpoint of the problems raised by IMF-type stabilization policies and structural adjustment. On the one hand, authors such as ILO (1987) or Cornia, Jolly and Stewart (1987) argue that such policies lead to reductions in real welfare of the poor due to budget cuts, unemployment and lower real wages and that they prevent LDCs from industrializing by forcing them back into a subordinate position as primary exporters. The corollary is that the debt problem alone has forced poor countries to accept such prescriptions, so this should be resolved at source by international banking reforms. On the other hand, authors such as Thorp and Whitehead (1987) or Killick (1984) suggest that the problem with the prescriptions of the New Orthodoxy is not just that they are socially undesirable, but rather that such policies cannot succeed due to the nature of the external sector (inelastic exports, exogenous prices, producer goods imports, and so on) and the endogeneity of the money supply, which 'passes through' devaluations without contracting effective demand. The corollary is that any subsequent improvements in the balance of payments after such schemes are due to commodity cycles at best, and disproportionate declines in aggregate output at worst.

Unfortunately, financial and monetary issues are not addressed in much technical depth in either line of critique, except the institutional aspects of the relationship between borrowing governments and lending banks (Griffith-Jones and Sunkel, 1986). What is more, the policy alternatives offered are limited to improved loan conditions or greater expenditure on basic needs within the overall demand reduction. This, of course, is the strength of the New Orthodox position in crisis conditions: it does have immediate prescriptions for restoring credit-worthiness and halting inflation.

1.3 THE NEW ORTHODOX APPROACH

In principle, various policy instruments can be used in alternative ways in order to gain logical objectives such as competitiveness on world markets, balance-of-payments equilibrium or balanced sectoral growth patterns. However, adherence to an almost uniform approach has become a condition of international assistance. This policy model (IMF, 1987) is based upon:

(i) The lifting of exchange controls and the removal of tariffs and other protectionist trade barriers, which should lead to the adoption of world prices as market signals inside the economy;
(ii) Liberalization of domestic capital and labour markets: cheapening of labour costs to raise private profitability; reduction of fiscal deficits to halt inflation and external deficits; lifting of credit market controls to induce higher real interest rates to raise savings and force the efficient use of capital; and
(iii) A drastic reduction of the role of the state in the economy to allow the private sector (domestic and foreign) to expand, export and create employment as the long-run solution to social inequality.

In this substitution of market forces for development strategy, *finance is not simply an instrument of economic policy, but rather a vehicle for the liberalization of the economy*. These policy prescriptions are a logical consequence of the key assumptions on which the neoclassical theoretical framework of the New Orthodoxy is built:

(i) The market mechanism is the best mechanism for an efficient allocation of resources;
(ii) All economic actors are separate profit and utility maximizing subjects; and
(iii) All have perfect foresight, or at least 'rational expectations' about the future, according to neoclassical behavioural rules.

The exponents of the New Orthodoxy acknowledge that markets in developing countries are far from being neoclassically perfect and that their adjustment is mediated by institutional and technological factors. Nevertheless, they assume that these distortions are created by governmental intervention in the form of subsidies, tariffs and controls. Food shortages, trade deficits and inefficient industries are commonly explained as being the result of the failure of governments to induce the 'correct' price incentives. Even among those authors who recognize that the market does not always produce socially optimal solutions, the market mechanism still prevails as the 'second-best' solution, particularly because in state-led development strategies the experience of the 'failure of government' tends to be more devastating than the potential 'failure of the market' (see, for example, Lal, 1983), particularly where it turns capitalists and bureaucrats into speculators in a 'rent-seeking society' (Krueger, 1974, 1978).

Neo-orthodox analytical models prefer to aggregate all non-state actors into one homogeneous, competitive and profit-maximizing private sector. Consumption and production, investment and savings are independent decisions of individual actors guided by prices alone at the micro level. Ownership patterns, interest groups, and social organizations are not considered to affect the outcomes of the model except as 'distortions', as in the case of the financial repression school. The assumption of perfect foresight (or at least of rational expectations), is more often implicit than explicit in the New Orthodoxy. This may be because once Keynesian notions of uncertainty are introduced as a determinant of economic behaviour, the operation of the market becomes entirely different. Lack of market information and uncertainty about future developments may lead to market disequilibria and the balancing of supply and demand by rationing procedures and quantity adjustment, rather than by price clearing. It is possible, of course, to introduce risk and uncertainty considerations into the neoclassical analysis of credit and labour markets (see, for example, Stiglitz and Weiss, 1981), but in doing so the boundaries between the neo-orthodox and Keynesian or structural perspectives become blurred, to the advantage of the latter.[27]

There is little convincing empirical evidence available to support the claims by the New Orthodoxy that market-oriented solutions will lead to more efficient resource allocation, automatic stabilization and renewed economic growth. Historical studies of how economies have industrialized successfully (Gerschenkron, 1962; Lewis, 1986; Bradford, 1987) indicate that this has involved a high degree of state intervention in finance and technology, and deliberate management of external trade. What is more, those developing countries that have pursued heterodox stabilization policies appear to be no less successful than those proposed by the New Orthodoxy (Thorp and Whitehead, 1987; Taylor, 1988). Finally, there is no theoretical reason to believe that financial stability or even economic efficiency necessarily imply abandoning direct intervention in order to meet established social goals of national development such as health, education and nutrition (Toye, 1987).

Above all, New Orthodoxy is limited by the lack of specific treatment of the economic structure which underlies market forces.[28] At the microeconomic level, neo-orthodox assumptions about savings behaviour are based on the concept of the individual balancing present and future consumption. The behaviour of enterprises (which, as corporations or households, generate by far the greater part of savings in developing countries in the form of retained profits) is ignored. Moreover, the rate of interest is assumed to be a key determinant of these individual savings, which not only overlooks the wealth of empirical evidence that this is not the case (Gupta, 1984) but also confuses financial asset acquisition with savings at the macro-level. By the same token, investors are taken to be individual entrepreneurs; without reference to the specific behaviour of segmented ownership groups such as small farmers, state enterprises, foreign firms and domestic oligopoly groups. Investment decisions are supposedly made by comparing the expected rate of return with the rate of interest; ignoring the widespread evidence on foreign exchange and infrastructure bottlenecks on the one hand, and the limitations of domestic market size on the other, let alone difficulties of export market penetration and the uncertainties of labour relations.

It is symptomatic that, despite the evident importance of private investment within LDCs and its support by bodies such as the World Bank, there is little or no consistent survey data on corporate activities. However, what data there is on aggregate private investment functions indicates that it is mainly a lagged function of aggregate demand (Leff and Sato, 1980; Gupta, 1984). State investment, which commonly accounts for more than half of non-housing fixed capital formation in LDCs, is a function of perceived development strategy rather than of considerations of profitability (FitzGerald, 1978a). Similarly, multinational corporations have international strategies in which investment in one country is determined by factors such as input sourcing, regional markets, and intrafirm sales; not by the profitability of a single establishment or by the local interest rate (Dunning, 1981). Finally, households and small producers invest in housing, farm improvements or transport equipment as part of the expansion of their own productive income opportunities; and not merely as a portfolio choice (Jansen, 1990).

At the macroeconomic level, factor income distribution is not considered to be relevant by the New Orthodoxy, so the relationship between wage expenditure and consumption, and between profits and savings is left undefined. The relation between specific patterns of state intervention in support of the accumulation and distribution processes, and the fiscal or financial disequilibria that these can cause, is not made explicit, either. Modern sector (that is, corporate) enterprise behaviour is not rigorously or realistically specified, despite the fact that firms are clearly at the centre of private capital accumulation and modernization. What is more, households and enterprises are regarded in the New Orthodoxy as being quite separate, the former being seen as surplus savers and the latter as underfinanced investors, intermediated by formal or informal capital markets. Households are held to implement sophisticated life-cycle expenditure and asset acquisition strategies, despite the ambiguous statistical results from the household budget surveys on which these conclusions rest. Generally, such surveys show that household savings come from unincorporated enterprise activities or dividends from property; and thus, once basic household expenditure is imputed as the equivalent of wages, such savings come out of *profits* (FitzGerald and Vos, 1989).

The analytical separation of household savers from investing enterprises is a Keynesian notion and does not really apply to corporate capital, even in developed economies, where a major part of fixed capital formation is still financed out of depreciation and retained profits, price formation and profits of the corporate enterprise sector are based on average costs to provide the required investment funds and/or the repayment of credit. In developing economies, with a lack of long-term funding institutions and a narrow share market, this will hold to an even greater extent. Small enterprises, faced with credit rationing and high loan costs, tend to be self-financing; while larger businesses are usually organized in oligopolistic groups associated with a bank, which can guarantee the required liquidity on the basis of the profits of the group as a whole (Leff, 1976; Drake, 1980).

Neo-orthodox faith is still placed on the equilibrating and resource-allocation role of real interest rates, despite the lack of evidence of this in the real world (IMF, 1987). Available econometric evidence indicates that the income elasticity of demand for money is usually unitary (Ghatak, 1981): in other words, that it is fundamentally little more than the transactions demand as defined by Keynes in the *Treatise*. Firms do not behave in a neoclassical fashion, equilibrating the internal rate of return with the market interest rate. In consequence, the New Orthodoxy is unable to specify savings functions realistically, or even the demand for money, and thus cannot detect the consequences of specific macroeconomic policies for income distribution or external trade.

1.4 TOWARDS A KALECKIAN ANALYSIS OF THE SEMI-INDUSTRIALIZED ECONOMY

The renewal of interest in the work of Michael Kalecki reflects to a great extent the shortcomings of orthodox macroeconomic theory when faced with the structural disequilibria of industrialized economies,[29] while his writing on development economics has yet to be properly revalued despite the fact that he was a pioneer in the field.[30]

However, my reason for basing my analytical approach to developmental macroeconomics on the work of Kalecki[31] is not entirely straightforward. He did do some work on planning in LDCs, but his role as a pioneer in the subject[32] is mainly based on his theoretical work on development finance which forms the basis for the models in Chapters 3 and 6. Unfortunately, Kalecki does not seem to have seen the need for a complete macroeconomic analysis of demand management in the developing economy,[33] his central point being that LDCs are 'not capable of absorbing all available labour . . . the main problem here being the deficiency of productive capacity rather than the anomaly of its underutilization'. In this approach, the rapid buildup of capacity is limited by insufficient private investment (but not by profits), investment goods supply (that is, import capacity) and supply of wagegoods for the new employment therefrom. Kalecki's policy recommendations included public investment to affect both volume and composition of capital formation, taxation of profits and land reform to increase food supply; although he considered that political obstacles would probably render them unattainable.

In my opinion the value of Kalecki to the construction of the macroanalytics of the semi-industrialized economy (SIE) does not lie mainly in his writing on development. In her introduction to the collection of Kalecki's papers on development economics,[34] Joan Robinson argues that Keynes had to struggle out of the neoclassical framework to regain the classical tradition, while Kalecki worked in the European political economy tradition, which is in effect Ricardian. As Robinson points out, Keynes' microeconomics was still Marshallian, while Kalecki's concept of the market was based on imperfect competition between firms. Thus, for example, Keynes' households save after satisfying a psychological propensity to consume, while the Kaleckian savings process is part of the firms' disposition of profits.

In effect, Kalecki worked out the effect of the accumulation behaviour of firms (rather than households) in different sectors (particularly raw materials, producer goods and wagegoods production) as a result of their oligopolistic behaviour, and the consequences for price formation. He provides a simple yet rigorous policy framework where the mechanics of the relationship between producers and the state are made explicit by specifying the effect of government expenditure in terms of employment and wagegoods demand generated thereby, and the impact of taxation on the functional distribution of income. Above all, Kalecki places investment decisions by the state and businessmen and the consequences for income distribution at the centre of his macroeconomic analysis; both in terms of corporate generation of profits (the mark-up determining distribution within industry), the distribution of these between investment and dividends (for households), and the effect on demand patterns on the one hand, and the conflict between social classes over wages, prices and government policy on the other.

The main weaknesses of the Kaleckian model from the point of view of advanced capitalist economies is its relative structural rigidity, which makes phenomena such as household financial asset acquisition, competitive imports or endogenous technological change difficult – but not impossible – to handle. However, these lacunae are not so problematic from the point of view of the SIE, where productive and financial structures are simpler. Kaleckian theory as a whole does have the microeconomic foundations[35] required to construct a macroeconomic theory for the SIE because it has a clear vision of enterprise behaviour, price formation within the modern sector (including the real exchange rate) and relations with other sectors, particularly small-scale production – both urban and rural[36] – and the world economy.

Kalecki also wrote extensively on the post-war problems of industrialization in Eastern Europe, and the way in which he tackles problems of growth, technological change and labour productivity are of relevance to any SIE. His approach to the problem of adequate utilization of labour reserves and the fulfilment of citizen entitlements to basic needs provision in planned economies is probably even more relevant to a democratic society facing industrial restructuring. The central problems of economic planning posed by Kalecki – such as the wagegoods supply constraint and the proportions between the 'departments' required for balanced investment – are still relevant to socialist economies today, although, as they move towards some form of 'mixed economy', central control must be exercised by financial means. Kalecki's well-known paper on 'intermediate regimes' is suggestive in this context, although it is probably best seen as an early contribution to the 'relative state autonomy' debate[37] in peripheral capitalism. Instead, Chapter 8 combines his work on socialist economies with that of Kornai to analyse the reform process.

The close reading of the two published versions of Kalecki's seminal paper *Financing Development* in Chapters 3 and 6 from two different points of view – the short and long run – suggest that they provide the basis for an analytical model of the semi-industrialized macroeconomy, which can be complemented by specifications of enterprise behaviour derived from his work on industrial economies. Most evaluations of Kalecki's work on development economics[38] undervalue his contribution because they reduce the model to one of the food supply constraint on real wages. In fact, Chapter 3 demonstrates that implicit in *Financing Development* is a complete two-sector (wagegoods and producer goods) short-run macroeconomic model from which output, prices, profits, wages, employment, and peasant incomes can all be derived once the algebra is properly specified. The model can be constructed formally by imputing appropriately Kaleckian rules for price formation (mark-up pricing in industry and demand-set prices for food) and defining the accounts for each institutional sector. Although Kalecki did not work out a monetary theory elsewhere in his work, he does provide here some indication of how not only the fiscal but also the banking balances might be handled in an economy, without capital markets. Chapter 3 contains a simple specification of the financial system along these lines as well, which allows the balances for government, banks, enterprises and households to be fully defined and thus the demand for and supply of money to be satisfactorily specified. The resulting model thus represents a considerable advance on previous post-Keynesian analysis of the dual economy such as that of Kaldor.[39]

The Kaleckian macroeconomic framework derived in Chapter 3 for the semi-industrialized economy should be applicable to debates on stabilization policy, particularly because it allows income distribution criteria to be included in a formal model. It is often suggested that orthodox (that is, Bank-Fund inspired) policies neglect income distribution. This seems to me to be a misplaced criticism because all stabilization policies (or any other economic policy for that matter) involve a measure of income redistribution; and the ability of particular social groups to impose (or resist) such a redistribution is central to the success of economic policies as well as to their desirability. The Bank and the Fund are doubtless well aware of this; although their models do not explicitly include factor income distribution[40] they do argue *ex hypothesi* that the recovery in private investment and growth will eventually compensate for short-run welfare losses.

To make my Kaleckian model suitable for comparison with orthodox stabilization policy analysis, a more precise model is required. To allow a critique of the neo-orthodox model from the point of view of welfare effects, an analytical framework which clearly links the two must be constructed. In Chapter 4 the familiar Hicksean IS-LM model is replaced by an IS-XM model based on the capital accumulation account set out in Chapter 2 with a flexible export sector and clear specification of wages, profits, trade, investment, taxes and government expenditure. The equilibrium solution to this model allows the implications of monetary and fiscal policies to be derived through comparative statistics. The chapter contains three main conclusions: that stabilization requires some means of enforcing the corresponding redistribution of income; that active tax policy is required in order to achieve equilibrium without increased poverty; and that public investment is a more effective instrument of demand management than monetary policy.

The redistribution of resources in order to finance the industrial capital formation required for continued industrialization takes place within a specific institutional framework. The early development economists took it for granted that such accumulation would be centred on the public sector and that public works were the ideal method of absorbing surplus labour. However, the subsequent literature has been critical of this proposition, citing factors such as the opportunity cost of government wages; the systemic fiscal imbalance generated by state support for industrialization; and the impact on private investment of public-sector borrowing. The modern methodology for the appraisal of public investment was set out by Little and Mirrlees (1974) and adopted by the World Bank shortly afterwards. Although based on neoclassical trade theory for its determination of economic costs and benefits, the new methodology contained Lewisian assumptions about a dual labour market and about the positive effect of low wages on profits, savings and growth.

Chapter 5 sets out to challenge these assumptions by constructing a model of a labour market with formal, urban–informal and rural sectors, where the generation of modern urban jobs leads to further internal migration through the increased wage-demand for informal services. This increases the supposed 'shadow wage' (that is, opportunity cost) of unskilled labour used in public works. However, the existence of a constrained supply of wagegoods also implies, in Kaleckian fashion, that the real wage falls with increased employment. The effect of these modifications of the standard model is tested for illustrative data for Peru,[41] and the effect is shown to be substantial. The establishment of 'objective' resource valuation criteria for mixed economies based on world prices also requires some method of revaluing 'non-traded' goods and services. The neo-orthodox approach suggests that this can be done by decomposing prices into (traded) input costs, but this is not, in fact, so: an implicit set of governmental behavioural rules is concealed in the proposed methodology.

The model for planning in a mixed economy, which Kalecki intended to construct on the basis of his analysis of growth and intersectoral balance in *Financing Development*, is weakened by his failure to specify a (peasant) food supply function. In Chapter 6, the internal terms of trade affect peasant savings and investment in productive capacity, which implies that attempts to 'squeeze' the peasantry in order to finance industrial investment (through low wage costs and high profits based on depression of the internal terms of trade) will, in fact, have contradictory results in the longer term. The Kaldor model also includes reinvestment in the two sectors, but the Kaleckian formulation in terms of price formation is more satisfactory regarding the clarification of the distributional implications. Chapter 6 goes on to suggest that a similar 'response function' should also be applied to the industrial sector, where low wages will prevent worker productivity from rising despite greater capital investment financed by the profits they generate. In other words, higher rather than lower internal terms of trade and industrial wages may turn out to be more conducive to growth than a regressive factor income distribution.

The literature on the balance between production sectors in the long-term industrialization framework implied by a Kaleckian 'perspective plan' employs the two classical 'departments': production of the means of production (Department I); and production of the means of consumption (Department II). These are conventionally identified as state industry and peasant agriculture respectively,[42] which conflates production sectors with institutional forms of organization. In practice, however, the primary sector still produces most of the foreign exchange necessary to import producer goods in the semi-industrialized economy; which implies two important differences from the paradigm – that exports are, in effect, a considerable part of Department I, and that these come from agriculture. During the 1980s, debates on the contradictions of Third World socialist economies as specific social formations[43] paralleled those on the Centrally Planned Economies (CPEs) themselves.[44] Particular attention was paid to systemic imbalances arising from the behaviour of the state and peasant producers. The last two chapters of this book are concerned with the experience of centrally planned semi-industrial economies: they focus on the systemic 'crowding out' of consumption and petty production by state investment on the one hand, and the limited room for macroeconomic manoevre available to semi-industrialized Third World societies in their frustrated attempt to construct socialism on the other.

The implications of this redefinition of the planned 'peripheral' economy are explored in Chapter 7.[45] The constraint on growth is foreign exchange and not the supply of labour or wage goods as such: in consequence the possibilities for accumulation depend on international resource rents, and thus the depression of consumption by peasants and workers does not, in fact, contribute much to the rate of growth. Moreover, the existence of a 'mixed economy' in the sense that world markets determine prices in Department I, while much of Department II is in the hands of small producers or community organizations, means that state accumulation is limited by the response of other institutional sectors. The analysis of macroeconomics and intersectoral disequilibria in peripheral socialist economies is extended in Chapter 8, in an attempt to systematize the institutional context of the Kaleckian reproduction scheme in Chapter 7. The perceptive model of state behaviour constructed by Kornai for the 'shortage economy' in Eastern Europe is adapted to the semi-industrialized economy with a considerable small-scale sector and subordinated to the world markets. This reformulation suggests that macroeconomic policy in a 'reform period' in such economies will be closely constrained by heterogeneous production forms, fiscal crisis, severe external resource constraints and social pressure for basic needs satisfaction. Current events in Eastern Europe itself, as well as in planned Third World economies seem to confirm this conclusion.

2 The Structural Approach to the Semi-industrialized Economy

2.1 THE SEMI-INDUSTRIALIZED ECONOMY

H. Chenery, in his benchmark study for the World Bank, defines the transitional status of semi-industrial economies in terms of specific 'shifts in internal demand, exports and production from the primary sector to manufacturing'.[1] In fact, such economies broadly correspond to those countries categorized by the IBRD as 'middle-income' economies. Their dimension relative to 'low-income' (largely primary) and 'high-income' (industrialized) economies is indicated in Table 2.1.

Table 2.1 World economic structure,[a] 1988

	Primary ('low-income') economies	*Semi-industrial ('middle-income') countries*	*Industrial ('high-income') countries*	*World total*
Population (millions)	2984	1068	784	5101
GNP per capita (US$)[b]	320	1930	17080	3470
GDP (US$ trillion)[b]	0.89	2.20	13.87	17.02
Energy use per capita[c]	0.32	1.09	5.10	1.29
Number of countries	42	54	25	121

Source: IBRD (1990).
[a] Reporting members of World Bank only; except in the case of population, which includes non-reporting members.
[b] At 1988 prices.
[c] Tons of oil equivalent consumed.

Chenery establishes the characteristics of 'semi-industrial' economies in part *ex hypothesi* and in part from the observed dispersion of the world's economies themselves: 'The most essential are indexes of the shifts in internal demand, exports, and production from the primary sector to manufacturing. The principal benchmark used . . . is the point at which the contribution of manufacturing to growth exceeds that of primary production. Supplementary benchmarks are a minimal per capita GNP (as a proxy for domestic demand for manufactures) and a minimal share of manufactures in exports and production' (1986, p. 85).

According to Chenery (1986), in the 1950s, this category included eleven countries: Spain, Portugal, Israel and Yugoslavia in the Mediterranean; Argentina, Mexico, Brazil and Uruguay in Latin America; Japan and Hong Kong in Asia; and South Africa. There were 37 members by the mid-1970s: 27 economies had joined, but only Japan had made a clear transition out of the group into full industrial status during the intervening decades. As Table 2.2 below indicates, by the mid-1980s the semi-industrial category broadly corresponded to the 'middle-income economies' (MIE) in the *World Tables* (IBRD, 1988), which fulfil the Chenery criteria (1986, ch. 4), in terms both of his main benchmark of the manufacturing contribution to growth and his 'minima'. This category contains both the 'upper middle income' (UMI) countries group, which includes the so-called NICs and most of Eastern Europe; and the 'lower middle income' (LMI) countries group, which includes a wide range of economies from Liberia to Lebanon.

Table 2.2 Chenery criteria for semi-industrial status, 1988

	Manufacturing contribution to GDP growth[1]	*GNP per capita*	*Manufacturing value-added share of GDP*	*Manufactured share of exports*	*Number of countries*	
					in the group	*meeting all criteria*
Original Chenery Criterion	> 50%	> $650[2]	> 18%	> 25%		
Group Means						
Lower-middle income economies	61%	$1 380	25%	46%	37	25
Upper-middle income economies	82%	$3 240	23%	80%	17	12
Middle income economies	73%	$1 930	24%	69%	54	37

[1] Defined as $= r_m Y_m/(r_m Y_m + r_a Y_a)$ where r is the 1980-88 sectoral growth rate and Y is sectoral share of GDP in 1988; subscripts refer to manufacturing (m) and agriculture (a).

[2] Original 1976 figure, given in Chenery (1986) adjusted for US inflation 1976–88.

The structural characteristics of incomplete industrialization employed as 'stylized facts' in this book can be seen as an expression of these Chenery shifts:

(a) Industry (manufacturing, construction and utilities) makes a larger contribution to GDP than the primary sector (agriculture, livestock and mining) and the productivity differential between the two is still very wide compared to the primary economies;
(b) The primary sector itself no longer employs the greater part of the workforce, the population having become largely urbanized although only in part absorbed into the formal (that is, 'employed') sector;
(c) Industry still relies to a significant extent on imported producer goods but does not itself yet generate sufficient exports for growth once debt service is taken into account, so that capital formation still depends on primary exports;
(d) Most domestic consumption requirements and basic intermediate inputs can be provided by domestic industry, but techniques of production are still largely exogenously determined and incorporated in imported equipment;
(e) The primary sector presents a constraint on industrialization in terms of the provision of foreign exchange and wagegoods – although *not* in terms of labour supply;
(f) International trade takes place at prices determined on world markets and foreign exchange availability (including loans rationed by international banks) places an effective constraint on economic expansion;
(g) Wages and world prices are linked through the real exchange rate, which determines the profitability of the export sector and the ratio of prices between the traded and non-traded sectors; and
(h) Savings and investment largely take place in the public sector and private enterprises (including unincorporated family firms), while household savings and investment are mainly limited to housing.

2.2 THE STRUCTURAL APPROACH

The structural approach is not easy to define because it is embedded in historical situations, but can be considered to embrace three basic premises, in line with the classical tradition in development economics:

(i) Economies are built up from economic agents such as firms, governments and households whose *behaviour* reflects the particular context of the institutions (laws, production organization or social class) in which they operate;
(ii) Product and factor markets 'clear' through both quantity and price adjustment according to various *systemic* patterns of institutional behaviour, market power, imperfect information and class interests; and
(iii) The institutional setting and related market formations are basic *structural* features, but these are not unchangeable over time; rather the process of industrialization both conditions and is conditioned by such structures.

The neo-orthodox characterizations of structuralism as 'eclectic' (Dornbusch and Fischer, 1984), or as an overestimation of the inflexibilities and costs of economic adjustment processes (Little, 1982), or simply as a doctrine of market failure (Arndt, 1985) are all incorrect. Structural economics is based on the premise that all economies have a determinate (albeit mutable) structure of institutions and technology. The institutional framework refers above all to ownership, but also to the organizational form of enterprise, social group organization and state intervention. The historical setting of

Table 2.3 Comparative structure by industrial category

	Primary economies	*Semi-industrial economies*	*Industrial economies*
Agricultural share of GDP	33%	12%	5%
Industrial share of GDP	27%	40%	35%
Urban share of total population	25%	58%	78%
Exports/GDP	19%	27%	21%
Debt service/exports	24%	22%	n.a.
Investment/GDP	18%	25%	22%
Employment share:			
Agriculture	72%	43%	7%
Industry	13%	23%	35%
Fiscal (/GDP):			
Taxation	16%	13%	24%
Current expenditure	12%	15%	17%

Source: IBRD (1990).

these characteristics condition the way in which resources are allocated and markets eventually clear. Macroeconomics should be built up from the microeconomic level by studying the behaviour of the agents and the markets in which they operate (sometimes known as the 'structure–conduct performance' approach) which then leads on to a macroeconomic structure which includes banks, government and foreign trade. Production structures are seen as relatively inflexible in the short run as they embody a determinate technology, which can only be changed over time by investment. However, macroeconomic equilibrium *ex post* means that the inventions of agents *ex ante* are necessarily changed in (inverse) proportion to their market power.

Thus, phenomena such as market clearing by quantity as well as price, excess demand and underemployment, or chronic balance-of-payments deficits are seen as systemic; unlike the neoclassical view of such imbalances as distortions or the result of unwise government policy. In sum, structuralism is not merely a matter of low supply elasticities or pricing rigidities; rather it is based on the empirical observation of economic behaviour in conditions of technological, organizational and social heterogeneity. There is no suggestion in structural economics that markets are in some sense 'bad' or that state planning is 'better', as some critics (for example, Little, 1982) suggest. The central position is distinct: that markets work in ways quite different from those which neoclassical theory suggests, and that state intervention of some kind is required for any market to function at all – a postulate with which even Adam Smith was in complete agreement.

The importance given to institutional and technological rigidities in the functioning of the economy does not imply, however, that these structural features are considered invariable over time. Sectoral shifts of the labour force may be accompanied by technological change and changes in producers' attitudes, such as that from subsistence food farming to commercial export farming. Financial intermediation can be a positive vehicle through which such institutional change is brought about; but excessive money supplies in situations of commodity shortages may produce shifts towards production for black markets or lead to a labour resource reallocation out of the peasant sector and into urban informal activities. Structural analysis would and should include the analysis of the driving forces behind such sectoral changes and bring out the implications for economic behaviour and the macroeconomic balance. Further, in economies that are consciously engaged in processes of institutional reform, a structural approach is required to be able to monitor and manage the process of transition.

The macroeconomic implications of the structural approach are not dissimilar to the post-Keynesian analysis of industrial economies, in so far as the *ex post* equilibration of *ex ante* savings and investment plans made at the firm or household level relate to income distribution and output levels determined at the aggregate level. Savings in LDCs relate to income distribution and they tend to be principally generated by self-employed incomes (through household 'firms') and corporate enterprise profits. A typical case is that in which profits are determined by the mark-up on enterprise costs in the factory sector, while the internal terms of trade are the crucial variable in determining incomes of small-scale producers. In the corporate enterprise sector, wages tend to be negotiated collectively, while in the small-scale sector there is a market-clearing wage; but overall, its real value depends on the price and supply of wagegoods in a Kaleckian fashion. Wage-earners show low savings rates in developing countries once household incomes are disaggregated to separate out the profits of unincorporated enterprise. Thus profits and wages adjust through the process of aggregate market equilibration, as do the internal terms of trade, giving macroeconomic underpinning to the functional income distribution.

Investment by small-scale producers is closely related to their savings capacity, but large-scale producers may rely on a significant share of self-finance (that is, retained profits). In both cases, such savings can be increased: in the former by raising output and in the latter by raising prices. Whether businesses invest or not depends upon confidence about their entitlement to future profits, which are in turn dependent on the availability of infrastructure, skilled labour, markets and imported inputs. Investment demand in LDCs does not appear to depend to any great extent on the rate of interest as such, which is more often an element of production costs (and thus of inflation through the mark-up pricing rule) than a resource allocation mechanism. Credit constraints on investment demand are biased by the segmentation of the domestic credit market: corporate enterprises usually have better access to bank credits than do small-scale producers, and the latter tend to suffer from 'credit squeezes' accompanied by high interest rates.

Savings and investment do not easily clear at an aggregate level in LDCs because the macroeconomic equilibrium tends to be constrained by the external sector, which constrains the markets for consumption and capital goods. On the one hand, developing country exports are highly vulnerable to technological or institutional changes in the economics of the industrialized nations, while imports are linked by technical coefficients to domestic production and accumulation.

External finance, on the other hand, is constrained by credit-rationing rules applied by the international banking system or by donor stringency in the case of development aid flows. Internationally, the vulnerability of developing countries requires the state to negotiate their trade and credit relations directly with foreign companies, international banks and other states. This fact logically implies a very different definition of economic efficiency from the neoclassical one. Such a definition is based not so much on profitability at current world prices (that is, 'comparative advantage'), but rather is defined in terms of effective contribution to long-term goals of basic needs satisfaction and technological absorption (PREALC, 1987).

Indeed, it might be said that in the structural view of LDCs, income distribution and the trade balance underpin macroeconomic analysis in the same way that the IS-LM curves do in the Keynesian analysis of industrialized market economies. State intervention in the economy is regarded by structuralists as problematic, but inevitable if the economy is to function at all. This is partly because of the political dimension of competing social claims on resources, but mainly because industrialization requires structural transformations which individual firms will not or cannot carry out.

During the three decades since this paradigm of development economics was established, structural analysis has advanced along a broad front of an essentially sectoral or microeconomic nature. On the one hand, the causes and consequences of domestic phenomena such as poverty, underemployment, agricultural and industrial enterprise behaviour, migration, tax reform, and infrastructure bottlenecks were analysed in depth, yielding elaborate models and methods of sectoral and project planning. On the other hand, detailed analyses of international phenomena such as technology transfer, international commodity markets, and multinational corporations have allowed a more detailed picture of the insertion of developing countries into the world economy to emerge.

2.3 STRUCTURALIST MACROECONOMICS

Unfortunately, more recent work on structuralist macroeconomics has been based on considerations of production and consumption at best – and response to the New Orthodox agenda at worst – rather than on an explicit theory of the firm and the household. The scheme for resource mobilization set out by Lewis and Kalecki was not worked out rigorously so as to specify enterprise profits or savings behaviour, although foreign trade (and thus the external savings gap) was well specified in models of the interaction of production sectors, price formation and functional income distribution.

Eshag (1983), for instance, applies Keynesian and Kaleckian concepts to LDCs, placing fiscal and monetary policy within a strategic framework of resource mobilization. He argues that monetarism is a simplistic bankers' approach, and ultimately stagflationary because it is the supply of necessities that constrains growth, rather than the supply of labour and the wages as in industrialized countries. Eshag holds that money is passive in LDCs, in the sense that the Central Bank must act as lender of last resort to the government and to the commercial banks, while investment does not depend on interest rates but rather upon market prospects for business and government infrastructure decisions. The author concludes that savings is essentially a matter of macroeconomic adjustment, and its insufficiency a question of 'unwillingness, or inability, to take the necessary measures to restrain the growth of public and private consumption' (Eshag, 1983, p. 122) basing himself on Kalecki's concept of restrained consumption of non-essentials as 'the gist of the problem of financing development' rather than Keynes' adjustment of savings to *ex ante* investment through variations in national income. Although he does introduce aggregate demand analysis into development economics, Eshag lacks the analytical rigour needed to define market clearing mechanisms or derive the functional income distribution.

Taylor (1983, ch. 1) is one of the few economists who has attempted a rigorous analysis of 'structural' macroeconomic analysis as such, as opposed to the empirical analysis of particular constraints (for example, Chenery, 1975) which might be subsumed under neoclassical theory as a 'second best' description of institutionally constrained markets, or even 'market failure'. Taylor gives a Keynesian content to his definition when he criticizes the 'standard approach to theory' for 'routinely supposing that markets clear by price; and that getting prices right assures a Pareto-efficient allocation'. In contrast, he argues that structuralism is concerned with the process by which equality between savings and investment is reached: whether prices or quantities adjust to do this; whether the response is on the supply or demand side; how wages and income distribution are related to social conflict; and how the external dimension to this equality is expressed in terms of variations in the current and capital account of the balance of payments. Thus, for Taylor, 'structuralist models incorporate ... [these] technical and behavioural relationships. They focus attention on how the income distribution and output levels vary to satisfy the major macrobalance in the short run. Longer-run developments depend on the reactions of gainers and losers to these initial adjustments' (Taylor, 1983, p. 7).

Taylor's main contribution is in his innovative model building in the structural tradition, building on previous work linking income distribution to consumption demand patterns through household budget modelling (Lluch, Powell and Williams, 1977), and from these patterns to the production structure through the input–output matrix. This represents a considerable methodological advance in the reflection of economic structure and income distribution in macroeconomic analysis resulting in the creation of multisectoral, computable general equilibrium models (CGEM) for LDCs (Taylor *et al.*, 1980; Dervis, de Melo and Robinson, 1982). Data problems in the estimation of such CGEM models have been resolved in many cases by the use of a Social Accounting Matrix (SAM), which links income distribution to consumption demand, on the one hand, and to the production structure through factor incomes at the branch level on the other (Pyatt and Thorbecke, 1976; Pyatt and Round, 1985).

The theoretical detail of such modelling varies, and the outcomes very much depend upon the 'closure rules'; in other words, the way in which prices and quantities finally adjust to achieve the required *ex post* balance (Taylor, 1979). Typically, savings, finance and accumulation play a minor or derivative role in these models, and flow-of-funds matrices are rarely integrated into SAMs (Vos and Barreiros, 1990). This impedes the explicit modelling of finance, and the establishment of a direct link between short-term monetary variables such as inflation, interest rates and budgets, and the long-term real variables such as the structure of production, income and wealth. Although the primary elements for modelling such a link were established by R. Stone some time ago[2], they have not yet been applied to developing economies, despite the fact that with simpler institutional structures, narrow capital markets and relatively good financial statistics, the task should not be such a difficult one.

Traditionally, economic growth in LDCs has been considered to be constrained by the availability of foreign exchange. In the literature on economic development this characteristic forms the centre of the widely used 'Two-Gap' growth model (Chenery and Bruno, 1962) which reflects the 'elasticity pessimism' of the Prebisch–Singer hypothesis of uneven world economic development between North and South. Because certain raw material inputs and capital goods can only be obtained from imports, a lack of import capacity may be the binding constraint on growth, rather than any limit on the capital stock, population or domestic savings. With buoyant commodity prices and world markets or easy access to foreign capital, foreign exchange receipts might be large enough to allow for all required complementary imports; in which case, the economy is considered to be savings constrained. However, most LDCs are still exporters of primary commodities and net importers of manufactured goods. The empirical evidence indicates that the former have a lower income elasticity (Goldstein and Khan, 1982) than the latter, so that, assuming price-clearing commodity markets, world economic growth will tend to lead to declining terms of trade and chronic trade deficits for primary exporters. When the 'two-gap' approach modifies the Harrod–Domar model of growth, foreign capital is assumed to complement domestic savings, so that capital transfers to developing countries raise their investment and hence their growth rate. This simple model clearly needs considerable modification, because foreign capital may be used to finance consumption (Griffin, 1970; Weisskopf, 1972), and capital inflows may affect domestic relative prices by changing the sectoral balances of the economy and thus income distribution and related savings patterns (De Melo, 1987).

The gradual liberalization of world financial markets, and the explosive growth of lending by private creditors to developing countries in the 1970s, cast doubts upon earlier views on foreign-exchange-constrained growth in the South. With higher income levels and more industrialized economic structures, it appeared that access could be gained to private capital markets and thus concerns about foreign exchange constraints seemed unjustified, so long as domestic macroeconomic policies were 'sound'.

The shortcomings of this optimistic view soon became apparent. Borrowing countries had to face severe liquidity problems after the unexpected increase in real interest rates in the early 1980s, in which the fiscal and monetary policy mix in the Northern economies played a key role. Debt servicing problems created fear of massive default among lenders, followed by a revulsion against bank lending to Southern borrowers, leading to net capital transfers from South to North. In most indebted countries, these resource transfers have been financed by a reduction in investment. Such an adjustment might be reasonable in the face of a short-term disturbance, but has serious consequences for economic development in the longer run, particularly the decline in productive investment and the loss of labour skills.

These recent developments indicate the continuing relevance of the 'two-gap' model of foreign exchange bottlenecks on Southern growth. However, the external constraint should now be more widely defined than before, going beyond export markets and trade elasticities (FitzGerald, Jansen and Vos, 1989). LDCs face credit rationing on world capital markets: low-income countries that have no access to private capital markets and rely on external finance from official sources; and the semi-industrialized countries that have potential access to international private loan markets, but which appear to international lenders as a particular risk class of borrowers. External financial conditions have differed between both groups of countries over the past two decades. The supply of external finance has been fairly stable for 'official borrowers', although commodity prices and export earnings have been highly variable for this group of countries. Semi-industrialized 'private' borrowers have access when the availability of international finance is high, but may be 'rationed out' of finance by higher indebtedness or international illiquidity.

2.4 A DISAGGREGATED ACCOUNTING FRAMEWORK[3]

An integrated and consistent system of accounts, covering national income and expenditure as well as financial flows, forms the indispensable quantitative basis for the macroeconomic analysis of any economy. The balance between savings and investment – known technically as the 'accumulation account' (UN, 1968) – is the overall macroeconomic accounting identity which integrates the balances for two principal categories of transaction that take place within an economy: commodity transactions (that is, production and acquisition of goods and services) and financial transactions – in other words, the acquisition of financial assets and the use of sources of investment finance.

The 'financial programming' models of the New Orthodoxy apply such accounting rules as well, but they tend to restrict their macroeconomic analysis to the very aggregate level, distinguishing at best four sectors: the government sector, the private non-financial sector, the banking sector and the foreign sector (for example, IMF, 1987). Within the private sector, consumption, savings and investment decisions are assumed to be strictly independent, while the sectoral origin and destination of savings and investment play no role. From the analysis in the previous sections, it will be clear that a structural approach requires a more disaggregated accounting framework, which allows for the proper analysis of macroeconomic and financial relations between economic actors that can be distinguished by differences in behaviour and institutional context. These differences may relate to market-based and non-market-based decision-making, to differences in access to commodity and capital markets, price formation and so on. Although the accounts of commodity and financial transactions for each of the actors, institutional sectors and economic sectors must sum to zero *ex post*, their *ex ante* claims on resources will meet system constraints that are crucial to the determination of the characteristics of equilibrium in the economy. The institutional setting of each agent will determine how their adjustment to system constraints (such as foreign-exchange availability) or systemic characteristics (such as pricing rules) comes about.

This need for an adequate disaggregation of commodity and financial transactions is fully recognized in the United Nations Standard National Accounting system (SNA) (UN, 1968). The investment-savings or *accumulation balance* is one of the four balances in the SNA system, the other three being the balances of production (sales of goods and services and gross income payments or value added); consumption (income and consumption outlay accounts); and external transactions (balance of payments account). All four accounts are integrated into one system, and in fact any one can be derived from the other three: a fact which is central to the Kaleckian models which will be described in Chapters 3 and 6. The SNA takes the accumulation balance as the centre of financial analysis and builds up the rest of its macroeconomic system with the other three balances, which is the approach used throughout the present volume.

Each institutional sector in the SNA has its own accumulation balance of investment and savings, including the acquisition of financial liabilities and assets. The SNA points out that these cannot be simply aggregated at a national or international level as though an economy were made up of homogeneous economic individuals:

> In any national accounting system transactors are necessarily grouped; it would be impossible and also useless to treat every individual transactor separately. But they need not be grouped in the same way in all parts of the system and indeed, it is not desirable that

> they should be . . . In the analysis of production we are mainly concerned with workplaces, or establishments, in which most operating decisions are taken. In the analysis of finance, on the other hand, we are mainly concerned with the frequently much larger units in which most financial decisions are taken. For example, a business corporation may control a number of establishments producing similar or very different commodities and so assignable to the same or different industrial categories. And the corporation may itself be only one of a number, all of which are controlled by a giant business enterprise . . . However, not all productive activity is organized in corporations. There are also unincorporated enterprises, own-account workers, peasant farmers and so on; and in some countries the greater part of production is in such hands. The production accounts of these unincorporated producers are merged with the production accounts of corporate establishments in the same kind of production. But the operating surplus from these activities is, in each case, simply part of the income of the proprietor's household and is merged with other forms of income, such as income from the employment of family members, from investment or from pensions, to provide a basis for household decisions on spending and saving. (UN, 1968, p. 71)

The accumulation balance for the economy as a whole can be set out in its most aggregate form as the familiar balance between domestic investment (I) and domestic savings (S), on the one hand, and the external trade balance of exports (X) and imports (M), on the other. Clearly, for any given level of investment (I), one or more of the other variables must adjust in order to 'finance' it:

$$I - S = M - X \tag{1}$$

This can be expanded in different ways. In the case of an analysis of the sectoral balance between industry and agriculture in the closed economy, the *ex ante* savings gap can be expressed as the excess demand (D_a) for agricultural goods (food) and that for non-agricultural goods (D_{na}) in relation to the respective output volumes (Q_a, Q_{na}). A crucial determinant is then the price relation between the two sectors ($\theta = P_{na}/P_a$); and the accumulation balance can be rewritten as:

$$I - S = (D_a - Q_a) + \theta(D_{na} - Q_{na}) \tag{2}$$

where all variables are expressed in real terms of the price of the agricultural commodity (P_a). In the case of the open economy, the external balance is added. For example, *if* the agricultural good is exported at the world market price (P_x), the domestic price ($P_a = eP_x$) being set for a given exchange rate (e) and imports consist of non-agricultural goods used in domestic production and consumption, *then* the accumulation balance will reflect real import-capacity (M_{na}), for a given capital inflow, and the export volume (E) arising from the sectoral imbalances. The relevant relative price is now the external terms of trade ($\theta* = P_{na}/eP_x$). We can now write equation (2) as:

$$I - S = \theta * M_{na} - E_a \tag{3}$$

Savings and investment decisions take place in different institutional contexts and are made on the basis of different income-generation situations. As I have argued above, profits are the major source of savings in semi-industrialized economies, for two reasons. Firstly, systems of voluntary wage-savings such as pension funds, contractual savings accounts, personal mortgages and so on, are not a characteristic of LDC financial systems; while social security funds tend to function as an extension of the fiscal system. Secondly, the profits of self-employed income generated in unincorporated firms usually organized as household production units constitute a major source of domestic savings in many LDCs. It is therefore useful to build the appropriate institutional breakdown into the macroeconomic balance equation:

$$\begin{aligned}(I_g - S_g) + (I_c - S_c) + (I_{uc} - S_{uc}) &= (D_a - Q_a) + \theta(D_{na} - Q_{na}) \\ &= \theta * M_{na} - E_a\end{aligned} \tag{4}$$

where the subscript g is used to identify the public sector, c stands for corporate enterprise and uc for unincorporated enterprise.

A now-standard approach to the analysis of the open economy (Dornbusch, 1980) is to distinguish between excess demand and output in a traded (t) and a non-traded (nt) sector. This framework can be useful to study effects of external shocks on sectoral adjustment and finance. 'Windfall gains' such as an unexpected improvement in the external terms of trade (for example, an oil price increase for oil exporters or booming coffee prices) can be considered as an income transfer which leads through spending and resource reallocation effects to an expansion of non-traded goods sectors. The latter clearly include infrastructure and government services, but may also embrace potentially tradeable goods sectors, such as import substituting industries which – being accustomed to high levels of protection – cannot easily redirect production from domestic to world markets. The different nature of and balance between traded and non-traded goods sectors will be important in the management of the external account. Falling export oil prices or deterioration of other elements of the external account (for example, an increase in interest rates with a high level of external indebtedness) may force domestic sectoral adjustment. The accumulation balance can be rewritten to yield:

$$\begin{aligned}(I_g - S_g) + (I_p - S_p) &= (D_t - Q_t - F_f) + \theta t(D_{nt} - Q_{nt}) \\ &= \theta_t * M - E + iF\end{aligned} \quad (5)$$

where the relative price index now reflects the 'real exchange rate' ($\theta_t = P_{nt}/P_t$). The corporate and unincorporated enterprise sector having been aggregated into one private sector, the fiscal ($I_g - S_g$) and private sector savings balances ($I_P - S_P$), now clearly result from the *ex post* balancing of traded and non-traded goods markets. The demand for goods and services will be a function of national income, domestic value-added plus income transfers from abroad and less net factor payments: $Y = Q_t + \theta_t Q_{nt} + F_f$, where F_f includes 'enclave' (for example, oil) revenues less interest payments on foreign debt (iF).

In this way, the disaggregation of the accumulation balance permits the analysis of savings and investments to be built up from the specification of the behaviour of each sector, institution or economy, rather than being attributed to aggregate IS and LM curves with anonymous elasticities in the Keynesian tradition, or to the simplistic aggregate asset demand functions of the monetarist school. It also allows the consequences of macroeconomic stabilization policies to be traced through the economic structure via the clearing of major product and factor markets, yielding specific consequences for output, employment, foreign trade and income distribution.

2.5 FINANCIAL BALANCES AND THE INSTITUTIONAL STRUCTURE OF THE SEMI-INDUSTRIALIZED ECONOMY

The SNA provides a framework within which financial variables can be built into the same system of socioeconomic classifications, but only few LDCs dispose of flow-of-funds data that are consistent with and at the same level of disaggregation as national accounts data. However, in recent years, the construction of Social Accounting Matrices (SAMs) for a wide range of LDCs has provided a quantitative basis for the analysis of income formation, distribution and spending of disaggregated production units and socioeconomic groups. Financial relations logically 'close' such a system of accounts, matching sectoral and institutional savings surpluses and deficits, but, unfortunately, very few SAMs have elaborated flow-of-funds blocks.[4]

Here we shall outline the financial accounting structure that will be used in succeeding chapters. The first institutional division is undoubtedly that between the public and private sectors. Using the same nomenclature as before, we have the accumulation balance as:

$$I - S = F \tag{6}$$

which can also be expressed in terms of the corresponding changes in assets and liabilities brought about by investment, savings and credit decisions. These involve changes in fixed capital (K), in domestic financial assets (A_d) and liabilities (B_d), and external assets (A_f) and liabilities (B_f) held by domestic agents. Thus (6) becomes:

$$\Delta K - \{\Delta A_d - \Delta B_d\} = \Delta B_f - \Delta A_f \tag{7}$$

which can be rearranged as changes in the 'national balance sheet' (leaving aside technical problems of depreciation and revaluation) as:

$$\Delta K + \Delta A_f = \Delta B_f + (\Delta B_d - \Delta A_d) \tag{8}$$

For the public sector, we have investment (I_g) and savings made up of the difference between current fiscal income (T) and current expenditure (G). The balance (which we assume for expositional convenience to be negative) is covered by net public foreign borrowing and transfers (F_g) plus the net transfer of funds from the domestic private sector (Z), which includes bank credits, monetary creation and so on, and is in practice the balancing item:

$$I_g - (T - G) = F_g + Z \tag{9}$$

For the private sector, we have as uses of funds, investment (I_p) and the transfer (voluntary or otherwise) to the public sector (Z). Private saving in semi-industrialized economies, for reasons indicated above and discussed again below, is generated almost entirely by profits (R); complemented by net foreign finance (F_p) in the form of loans or direct equity investment, although in many cases this inflow may well be less than the outflow of 'flight capital' (ΔA_f):

$$(I_p + Z) - sR = F_p \tag{10}$$

The sum of (9) and (10) becomes once again the familiar accumulation balance (6), albeit in disaggregated form:

$$\{I_p + I_g\} - \{sR + (T - G)\} = \{F_p + F_g\} \tag{11}$$

The interaction of the two accounts is complex, but the implicit assumption of the New Orthodoxy (IMF, 1987; IBRD, 1983; Dornbusch and Helmers, 1988) that the private sector accumulation balance (10) is stable – in the sense that any increase in Z leads to a compensating increase in F_p (and thus in F) – or that at least private savings is stable (so that private investment is 'crowded out') seems implausible in both theory and practice. Theoretically, there is no reason to believe that projects (R) will remain stable in the face of major macroeconomic changes – or that private investment and savings decisions will move in the same direction, particularly when foreign asset acquisition ('capital flight') is an available alternative. In practice, the experience of the semi-industrial countries as a whole (FitzGerald, Jansen and Vos, 1988) over the last two decades is of quite violent fluctuations in the private sector accumulation balance. For example, stabilization efforts since the 'debt crisis' have not led to commensurate budget deficits (due to rising interest costs (5)), despite reduced external finance, leading to a so-called 'transfer problem':

$$\Delta\{I_g - (T - G)\} < \Delta F_g;\ Z > 0$$

Meanwhile, private investment rates have fallen, but private savings have risen sharply, in order to cover not only the 'transfer problem' but also increasing capital flight:

$$\Delta\{sR - I_p\} > \Delta Z;\ F_p < 0$$

Clearly, therefore, we need to know much more about private savings and investment decisions *as enterprise activities* to go beyond the concept of a simple market for funds cleared by the interest rate, or savings as the inverse of the consumption function and determining investment.

Semi-industrialized economies have quite complex institutional structures, but in practice it seems useful to distinguish between five main economic actors, the first four of which disaggregate the private sector:

Wage labour households

In this category the basic source of income is wages. These wages are almost entirely consumed, not saved (particularly when consumer durables and housing are counted as deferred consumption), which is a phenomenon quite distinct from the developed economies. Wage labour can be divided between two groups. Firstly, the poor and unskilled, whose wage income is spent entirely on wage goods and who face a fairly competitive labour market. With little or no access to means of production, they must sell their labour power for what they can get. Secondly, skilled and administrative workers, with greater control over their wage level (through trade union action) and a capacity to acquire consumer durables. The savings (and investment) of this latter group is mostly confined to the purchase or direct construction of housing.

Small household production and trade units

Also classified as unincorporated enterprises, this category embraces a wide range of activities by peasants, artisans, petty traders and so on and which take place in competitive markets. Their main source of income is the profit earned in the small enterprise, including the imputed incomes of the own-account worker and the family labour he or she employs. Consumption, production, savings and investment decisions take place within the same unit on the basis of the total household income; while investment largely takes the form of purchasing equipment or expanding labour employment in order to enhance production and income. This investment is limited by available resources, which typically consist of their own surplus income (savings) plus credits from informal money-lenders and some rationed amount of government credit channelled through state–owned development banks. Their main relation to the formal banking system, if any, is as depositors.

Private corporate firms

This category consists of privately-owned enterprises which have a legal corporate status. In practice this category mostly refers to companies applying modern, large-scale production techniques. They may have the market power to influence prices to some significant degree, but may encounter market size limitations on output (unless exporting). They finance their investment mainly out of depreciation and retained profits of the group. Bank credit can easily be obtained, though it may largely be used for working capital needs. Their easy access to bank credit may be even more extensive as, in many LDCs, non-financial corporate enterprises also tend to have close ties with (family-owned) domestic banking groups (see, for example, Leff, 1976). Thus their investment is not usually limited by savings (moreover, the state usually extends fiscal incentive for all fixed investment) but rather by expected profitability in the medium term based on projected sales volume and confidence as to asset tenure, exchange rates and so on.

Foreign firms

This category may not only include multinational corporations, but also establishments of international banks with global investment or credit rationing rules; both rely to a great extent on some degree of price control (for example, through intragroup sales or local oligopoly) to maintain their mark-up. These rely to a great extent on retained profits and local bank credit (for which they are preferential clients) but can always gain access to international bank credit to achieve steady investments. By definition, of course, we expect gross profits to exceed investment costs (that is, a positive cash flow) over any but the very short term.

The state sector

The government administration, central bank, state-owned development banks and public enterprises form the (well- or badly-managed) state sector in LDCs, jointly constrained through the fiscal balance. Controlled prices of public enterprise output put a burden on the central government budget deficit; but public enterprise investment may largely be financed from either the budget or low-cost state bank credits. Fiscal deficits can be financed by raising taxes or foreign borrowing, though both may be limited due to political resistance by tax payers and credit rationing by international banks or aid donors. In the last resort, expenditure need not be constrained to the extent that new money can be created. Thus public investment is not limited by public saving as such, but rather by the perceived consequences of fiscal deficits for macroeconomic instability.

This institutional breakdown and the wide definition of 'enterprise' it implies is crucial to our analysis, because the income category relevant for savings is typically profits. In the case of corporate enterprise, savings relate to retained profits, while in the case of the self-employed, savings are generated from income associated with household production and are reinvestible in the own firm. It is our basic contention that the analysis of the generation and expenditure of profits is not only a central – albeit neglected – aspect of finance but the whole macroeconomics of the semi-industrialized economy.

In principle, at least five channels through which the accumulation balances achieve equilibrium might be distinguished. The relative importance of each of these channels may vary, of course, from one case to another.

(a) Intermediation through the formal banking system, involving deposit holdings for household transaction and savings purposes and enterprise working capital needs, on the one hand, and credit supplies to investors, on the other hand.
(b) Finance channelled through the informal or unorganized money markets, involving a variety of financial arrangements not legally institutionalized, ranging from rural savings and loan associations to usurious urban money-lenders. The unorganized money markets are used largely by households and institutions that do not have (sufficient) access to formal bank credits and which do not have bank accounts, usually because the individual institution does not have the 'correct' social and financial standing.
(c) Government bonds and money creation to finance fiscal deficits may also affect the private financial balance. Treasury and parastatal bond markets tend to be underdeveloped in LDCs and thus have less potential to channel private savings directly into the government sector. Bond markets can be replaced to some extent by high obligatory reserve requirements imposed on commercial banks or deficit financing by drawing on central bank credits (in other words, money creation) may 'force' private savings adjustment through inflationary pressures.
(d) Direct capital transfers may take place between private institutions, directly and outside financial markets. LDC equity and

bond markets tend to be marginal to company finance, for apart from a high degree of self-finance, firms may fund a significant part of their capital needs directly from equity investment by the owners or member firms of the same 'group'.

(e) External financing may also take various forms, but access may be restricted to a small number of domestic institutions and be limited by the country's creditworthiness, the government's relations with governments of donor countries, the economy's attractiveness to foreign companies, and so on.

At the national and international level, the problem of financing economic development thus relates to the transfer of and command over resources which takes place so that the *ex ante* decisions of the various actors to save and invest come into overall equilibrium and the accumulation balance holds *ex post* at both national and world level. This is a broad definition of finance, which goes beyond strictly banking activities, to embrace sectoral balances, income distribution, fiscal activities and external markets. Investment decisions may be restricted for some actors by credits and other sources of finance; for others, savings and available finance may not act as a constraint on investment. Savings may be voluntary and lead to financial asset acquisition, but there may also be involuntary reductions in consumption, 'forced' through the effect on commodity markets of private sector mark-ups or public sector deficit financing. How the overall *ex post* accumulation balance is established, therefore, depends on how the different actors behave within the financial system as I have defined it.

3 The Macroeconomics of the Semi-industrialized Economy

3.1 KALECKI'S APPROACH TO DEVELOPMENT FINANCE

Financing Development[1] is undoubtedly Kalecki's most influential contribution to development theory: it goes beyond monetary flows to the implications of higher investment and growth for income distribution and savings[2] on the one hand; and treats wagegoods supply – which he calls 'necessities', and which are now known as 'basic needs' – as central to macroeconomic analysis rather than as an additional welfare issue.[3] On key issues such as wage determination and the sources of saving Kalecki had very different views from his contemporaries such as Lewis (1954) and Nurkse (1953), while his treatment of the foreign exchange constraint goes beyond the consideration of constraints on output growth in Chenery (1975) to accumulation and income distribution. Unfortunately, Kalecki's argument has been all too often reduced by those authors who cite him to the somewhat obvious proposition that if food supply from backward agriculture grows less rapidly than demand generated by population growth and rising per capita income, then inflation will reduce the wage share in national income.[4] This may be due to the fact that *Financing Development* is written in Kalecki's familiar laconic prose but without his customary algebraic clarification, while at several points the analysis is neither fully worked out nor entirely consistent. In this chapter I will reconstruct his implicit model of a semi-industrialized macroeconomy by applying the analytical method used by Kalecki when writing on developed industrial economies.

3.2 THE 'GIST OF THE PROBLEM OF FINANCING DEVELOPMENT'

The first 'comparative-statics' version of *Financing Development* (Kalecki, 1976, pp. 41–63) is less well known than the second 'growth' version published some two decades later (which will be discussed in Chapter 6), but it is analytically rather more interesting because the interaction of economic agents is better defined. Three social classes are defined: capitalists, small proprietors (peasants, artisans, small shopkeepers, and so on) and workers. Only capitalists save, while others consume their income. There are two output branches: investment goods (Department I) and consumption goods (Department II). Kalecki then develops an argument similar to that of his model of industrialized economies, based on the 'expanded reproduction schemes of Marx', where it is shown that savings – national income (the sum of output in the two Departments), less consumption (that is, output of Dept. II) – are automatically equal to investment (that is, output of Dept. I). Thus 'investment finances itself' once production decisions are made: these savings can take the form of either reinvested profits or bank credit derived from the deposits of firms' liquid reserves (p. 43). Kalecki concludes 'there are no financial limits, in the formal sense, to the volume of investment. The real problem is whether this financing of investment does, or does not, create inflationary pressures . . . the crucial point . . . [being] the possibility of expansion of supply of consumer goods in response to demand' (p. 44).

Kalecki looks next at the cases of inelastic and elastic supply response to demand in Department II. In the former case, inflation results from increased investment due to the increased wagegoods demand from Department I, leading to 'forced savings' from higher prices and profits but also to a wage–price spiral as workers react to a falling real wage. With elastic Department II supply, wagegoods output responds and there is no inflation, while increased 'normal' profits finance the new investment without altering the factorial distribution of income. Government investment is also, by the same logic, self-financing through the increased profits it generates in Department II, which can be channelled to the budget in the form of loans from the private to the public sector without 'crowding out' private investment.

Kalecki argues that in underdeveloped countries Department II contains both an elastic supply of manufactured consumer goods (industry has excess capacity) and inelastic supply of food, constrained by pre-capitalist ownership patterns in agriculture. A rise in investment generates greater employment and wagegoods demand, which is reflected in higher food prices and lower average real wages. If the peasants benefit from the higher food prices, then they will demand more industrial consumer goods, and non-food consumer-goods capacity will be utilized. However, if 'the benefits of higher food prices accrue to landlords, merchants or money lenders then the reduction in real wages . . . will not have as a counterpart an increased demand for mass consumption goods on the part of the countryside; for increased profits will not be spent at all, or spent on luxuries' (p. 47).

Kalecki recognizes that this is a special case (albeit still fairly widespread in the Third World of the 1950s) but it does reflect his belief that sectoral accumulation is constrained by ownership forms. He clearly believes that increased prices might work their way through to peasant incomes, but this would require institutional changes 'from land reform and cheap bank credit for peasants to improvements in the method of cultivation, small-scale irrigation and cheap fertilizers' (p. 48). This implies that an improvement in the internal terms of trade could increase food supply, although he does not consider the effect of a larger supply of consumer goods (as opposed to inputs) upon the marketable surplus. Indeed, he fails to distinguish between output and marketable surplus at all. None the less, his central proposition linking real wage determination to institutionally constrained food supply is clearly sound.

It is worth noting here that Kalecki explicitly dissents from two common 'structuralist' positions. One is the suggestion that migration to towns will release a peasant food surplus which is then marketed to feed the new urban workers; Kalecki argues that this will only raise on-farm consumption (pp. 46–7). The other is the underconsumptionist thesis that market size limits industrial growth in developing economies; Kalecki argues that increased investment will generate matching demand for consumer goods from the wages fund (pp. 47–8).

To complete the foundations of his model, Kalecki examines the effect of increasing productivity in the non-agriculture sector. This reduces employment (and the wagebill) proportionately for a given output level while industrial prices fall; real wages rise to some extent but 'so will peasant incomes' (p. 49). This is contrasted with the labour-absorbing, declining real wage path examined previously.[5] As in his analysis of industrial economies, he doubts whether the distribution of income between workers and capitalists will remain unchanged with rising productivity. On the contrary 'in the course of economic development, there will be a tendency towards increased concentration in industry, a rise in the degree of monopoly', reinforced by foreign investment, where 'the final result will be a shift in the distribution of income from wages and agricultural incomes to industrial profits' (p. 50).

The opening of the model to foreign trade is deceptively simple. 'Export industries' are introduced and placed in the previous departmental framework so that 'Department I will include, in addition to the industries producing investment goods, export industries which produce exports of equal value to the imports of investment goods' (p. 51), and similarly for Department II. What export industries Kalecki is thinking of are not at all clear; presumably he is not thinking of exports of capital goods. The logical answer would be mining or plantation 'enclaves' separate from the rest of his structure; but obviously there is no need for them to be allocated *ex ante* between departments, even though it is analytically convenient and draws attention to the fact that to a considerable extent such activities can act as if they were a producer goods sector.[6] By implication, imported inputs can be treated in the same way.

The supply of industrial goods (and employment) in Kalecki's model depends not only upon productivity but also on the external terms of trade; their improvement would allow investment to rise without inflationary pressure. He suggests that trade will represent a permanent constraint on growth in the semi-industrialized economy, as it is difficult to increase exports fast enough to match aggregate growth targets; due to both the lack of appropriate projects and the difficulties of penetrating foreign markets. Obtaining loans to purchase capital goods abroad also allows a lower level of savings (and higher wages) for a given level of investment; this holds good for imports of consumer goods too, from the supply side. A number of arguments against overseas borrowing and foreign investment are reviewed,[7] suggesting that improvements in the terms of trade and prevention of capital *outflows* are far more beneficial for long-term growth.

Kalecki introduces fiscal analysis[8] (pp. 52–3) by considering taxes (both direct and indirect) levied on each Department in order to finance a balanced budget made up of administrative expenditures on salaries. The investment–savings balance is maintained, and 'the process of investment again automatically creates a counterpart in savings. Production of consumption goods or their prices will be pushed up to a point where the surplus of consumption goods in Department II, equivalent to taxes paid there and the savings of capitalists of that department, will equal the demand for consumption goods coming from Department I and government officials' (p. 53). Thus real wage rates will be lower the larger the budget, whatever the form of taxation; so that lower administrative expenditure (even with a balanced budget) will mean less inflation and thus 'benefit the process of development' (p. 54).

So far, Kalecki assumes that public investment is covered by domestic loans; these can be replaced by foreign borrowing, but higher taxation can be introduced as an anti-inflationary measure. Positive budgetary savings are shown to reduce private savings by an equivalent amount: 'investment will always generate the saving necessary to finance it in excess of taxation and imports of capital' (p. 59). However, such government savings do not necessarily reduce real wages unless they are based on taxes borne by workers: they could be derived from lower capitalist consumption or a shift of their savings into taxes. Reduced capitalist consumption will not directly lessen demand pressure on Department II, but there will be less incentive to invest in non-essential (that is, luxury) industries. Financing investment through increased taxation also reduces liquid financial assets and thus speculative demand pressure on prices, as do credit restrictions.[9] None the less, 'the primary inflationary pressure experienced in the course of rapid economic development is, as shown above, the result of basic disproportions in productive relations. Thus these pressures cannot be prevented by purely financial devices' (p. 62).

The second and better-known version of *Financing Development* (Kalecki, 1976, pp. 98–115) has the apparent advantage of being cast in dynamic form, but in so doing leaves out much of the original macroeconomic detail. Inelastic food supply becomes the central proposition of a deceptively simple growth model. The 'departmental' structure is conflated to a two-good model ('necessities' and 'non-essentials') where the former are the basis of the wagegoods basket with staple foods as the 'chief item'. Kalecki examines the conditions under which maximum growth national income can be attained without food price inflation or taxation of the poor; yielding thereby a 'warranted' growth rate.[10] In his notation, this is the growth rate (r) which produces a growth of demand for necessities – the product of income per capita arising from population growth (q) and income elasticity (e) – so as to balance exactly the (exogenous) rate of expansion of supply of necessities (c_n):

$$c_n = q + e(r - q)$$

This 'can be considered as the approximate value of the rate of increase of supply of necessities which warrants the rate of growth of national income . . . without infringing our basic assumptions' (p. 101). The rate of growth of *total* consumption consistent with the warranted growth rate is that which 'makes a sufficient allowance for the investment required for the expansion of national income'; so non-essential consumption must be restrained by 'appropriate taxation of higher income groups and non-essentials must be devised'. He sums up his argument with the celebrated remark: 'This seems to me to be the gist of the problem of financing economic development in a mixed economy' (p. 104).

Although this second version of *Financing Development* concludes with an analysis of the trade balance and taxation rates required in order to maintain equilibrium growth, the results are essentially the same as those in the first version. Moreover, the later version does not have the clear definitions of classes or production sectors of the first, nor are the investment–savings mechanism and real wage system defined.

The Kaleckian analysis of the financing problem thus implies a macroeconomic model of some complexity and interest. The rest of this chapter is devoted to setting out this model formally, and attempting to resolve some of its inconsistencies while remaining faithful to its author's overall approach. I shall employ the comparative statics of the first version but the results can be extended without great difficulty to a growth model.[11]

3.3 THE BASIC MACROECONOMIC MODEL

The objective of this section of the chapter is to set out as clearly as possible a formal linear model implicit in Kalecki's view of the comparative statics of the open semi-industrialized economy, discussed above. The algebra is set out in the Appendix at the end of the chapter, references being to the section and equation numbers (for example, [A1, p. 1]). By so doing, some lack of clarity in Kalecki's arguments is resolved and some interesting new solutions derived.

We start with a closed two-good economy in the short run, where there is no investment and given (or planned) output levels. Necessities[12] are principally composed of food, produced by peasant farmers who provide a determinate amount to the market at a flexible clearing price. With the cash income therefrom, they purchase industrial goods. The industrial sector produces a set volume of consumer goods (that is, 'non-essentials'), and also creates 'formal' wage employment from a given, technologically determined, level of labour productivity. Industrial prices are formed by a mark-up on variable production expenses, which in this case are only labour costs at an institutionally set nominal wage. The Kaleckian concept of monopoly power is particularly appropriate to semi-industrialized LDCs where there is a high degree of branch concentration. A proportion of these wages (in our case, a linear parameter instead of Kalecki's elasticity) are spent on food.[13] It is assumed that all profits, farm incomes and workers' non-food budgets are spent on industrial goods. These definitions for the two product markets constitute the system of price formation, which admits of a simple solution in two equations and two unknowns (A1).

Kalecki's main concern in *Financing Development* for income distribution is focused on the behaviour of real wages. His own explicit result is that real wages (that is, consumption levels in the formal sector) vary inversely with the growth of industrial output (and thus employment) for a given demand elasticity and food supply growth. The general result towards which Kalecki was implicitly heading (A2:8), is that the real wage depends not only upon output composition, but also on labour productivity and the degree of monopoly. The central theme of *Financing Development* – that if the ratio between the two sectors is increased by industry growing faster than food output, then workers' incomes will fall – is essentially a 'Ricardian' scheme of real wage determination by food supply per capita. Even here, however, the relevant divisor is *industrial* employment, which itself is the product of manufacturing output and labour productivity. Moreover, it will only be strictly true when food is the *sole* wagegood (A2:9), which Kalecki does not, in fact, propose. As the proportion of food in workers' consumption declines,[14] we return to the familiar Kaleckian scheme for the industrialized economy, where the real wage depends on productivity and the mark-up. Industrialization would then involve the gradual shift from one wagegoods scheme to another, due to the changing demand pattern as real wages rise, rather than the exhaustion of surplus labour, as in Lewis (1954).

Kalecki largely ignores the effect of price changes upon peasant incomes, which is unfortunate. He assumes that increases in food prices generally accrue to landlords and merchants, and fails to specify how the farmgate price itself is determined. In fact, the solution for the internal terms of trade (A2:7) is of considerable interest, because it turns out to be a function of not only the ratio of food to manufactured output (and thus of the balance between the supply of necessities and aggregate production) and workers' propensity to consume food, as argued by Kalecki, but also of the industrial mark-up itself. This new result implies that on the one hand, the internal terms of trade are independent of the nominal wagerate, while on the other, they are inversely related to capitalist profits. In other words, the political economy issue in income distribution is *not* one of conflict of interest between workers and peasants (as might appear from Kalecki's formulation) but rather between both of these and capitalists, including state enterprises. On the assumption that peasant farmers receive all the proceeds from sales of food (A2:1), their aggregate incomes, when appropriately deflated by industrial prices, thus turn out to be not only a function of food output and the consumption propensities, but also inversely related to the mark-up. To this should be added the imputed value of their own food consumption.

To complete the picture of income distribution, it is necessary to examine the level of real profits. Industrial profits are simply defined in terms of the mark-up (A1, p. 4), but the size of the margin accruing to merchants and landlords due to their ability to retain what is in effect a scarcity rent on food (or at least its means of production such as land, storage and transport) is not so clear. So far, we have assumed that the market-clearing price for food all accrues to peasant farmers: if the farmgate price were fixed (as Kalecki implies) the margin would be easy to determine, but he gives no basis for such a system; and in any case it is difficult to see how the market price would have *no* influence. Of course, in the case of a mixed agrarian economy (Caballero, 1984), farmgate prices could be derived from mark-ups on costs in capitalist farms. It would seem more consistent with Kalecki's approach to attribute a degree of local monopoly power to landlords and merchants; in which case a proportion of food sales would be added to overall national profits (A2:11). Deflating these profits by industrial prices (capitalists do not eat!) yields a result for real profit income dependent on the two mark-ups and industrial output. The significance of this result is that income distribution is now explicitly linked to profit generation and employment – in other words, to capitalists' production decisions; and not just to the somewhat mechanistic balance between population and food supply.

Kalecki, as we have seen, has a fixed food supply (or at least a fixed growth thereof) which, while rather implausible, was a common view in the 1950s (see, for example, Lewis, 1954). All the evidence points towards a considerable response (at least of *marketed* food supply) to variations in the internal terms of trade. Kalecki is not unaware of this, but holds his ground by assuming that all the variations are absorbed by merchants and landlords; this is clearly not very realistic either. In my schematic representation (A3), marketed supply becomes a linear function of the internal terms of trade; which means that at equilibrium, the latter becomes a function of industrial output and the mark-up. In other words, once peasant supply response is included, then the 'Ricardian' scheme for wage determination is no longer valid, even in poor economies with a high propensity to spend wages on necessities. The significance of this result is quite different from that intuited by Kalecki himself; although he probably would have been quite sympathetic to it.

In his 'fixed food supply' formulation, profit rates can be raised in order to finance accumulation without affecting the real wage too much, because the cost is borne by peasants through the deteriorating terms of trade. However, once we allow marketed food supplies to respond to the internal terms of trade[15] – which could involve administered food prices – then higher profit (accumulation) rates and consequently deteriorating terms of trade will prejudice workers as well as peasants. In other words, an improvement in the internal terms of trade is favourable for workers to the extent that it leads to a better food supply per capita; it is unfavourable for capitalists as they must, in effect, supply more manufactures in order to feed their labour force. This not only brings Kalecki's model into line with the lessons of historical experience on the subject,[16] but also yields an interpretation more attuned to his political economy.

In the first version of *Financing Development*, a separate capital goods sector ('Department I') is defined and aggregate accumulation balances are discussed. However, the link to income distribution and pricing is not specified, while in the second version, investment is reduced to an unspecified requirement for output growth, and savings to the compression of non-essential consumption. Moreover, in the second version, it is implied that the manufacturing sector can be switched from capital goods to non-essentials.

The fundamental accumulation balance (that is, the *ex post* investment–savings equality) can, in fact, be found (A4) from Kalecki's argument by specifying the demand for manufactures (which now includes capital goods) as that from peasants' cash income, workers' non-food expenditure, capitalists' consumption, and investment. This yields an automatic balance between savings out of profits[17] and the level of physical investment. This level of investment is regarded by Kalecki as 'planned', by which in a mixed economy he presumably means autonomous private investment plus complementary public investment to bring it up to the required amount. As usual, government expenditure (or any other autonomous expenditure, for that matter) can be substituted for investment in the short-run analytics. The necessary level of investment can simply be derived from the warranted rate of growth – which as we have seen, depends on population growth and the autonomous increase in the supply of necessities – by assuming a stable capital–output ratio (A4). This then works back through demand to profits and wages. We thus have an accumulation balance underpinned by the familiar Kaleckian determination of income distribution by investment. The problem is then to ascertain how the clearing mechanism (that is, adjustment of price and/or output) works in the manufactured goods market. Kalecki provides, at various points in the two versions of *Financing Development*, three different solutions.

The best-known solution to this problem is that given in the second version of Kalecki's paper, where price stability and inflexible supply of manufactures are assumed. In this case, the accumulation account would only balance if by coincidence the savings rate had the correct value, but Kalecki holds that it is likely to be too low so that a special tax must be levied on 'non-essential' (that is, capitalist) consumption. To model this, we can make the assumption that this additional tax would be used to fund the public portion of investment required to raise growth to the warranted rate. The resulting tax rate is entirely a function of what might be called 'enterprise parameters' (profit retention rate, mark-up and industrial growth) and thus neither the real wage nor the internal terms of trade need be depressed to obtain a new and higher rate of investment. This optimal tax rate corresponding to the warranted growth rate in the plan is a powerful concept, but hardly realistic. Kalecki himself qualifies his conclusion by pointing out political difficulties due to 'the influence of vested interest upon the government and because of the difficulty of overcoming tax evasion', even though in practice 'the low rate of expansion of agriculture resulting from agrarian conditions' will be the binding constraint and that the resulting national growth target 'will not usually be so high as to present an insuperable problem of financing investment by taxation' (1972, p. 152).[18]

However, in the first version, two other possibilities are considered – adjustment in manufacturing output, and inflation – both of which would raise profits and allow savings to come up to the investment level in the way familiar from Kalecki's other work. The former is obviously more attractive, although presumably imported inputs would constrain such expansion, a point to which we will return in the next section. If the mark-up remains stable the accumulation balance will yield the level of manufacturing output required to generate sufficient savings and bring about market equilibrium (A5:21–3). Determinate solutions for the real wage and the internal terms of trade now emerge as functions of the level of investment. The terms of trade (and thus peasant incomes) *improve* with higher investment, so long as manufacturing output can rise in response. The converse is true of the real wage, which declines with higher investment levels. Thus the distributive effect is asymmetric; particularly since capitalist consumption will also rise in real terms along with profits.

The third alternative is price adjustment, which also raises nominal profits towards the required level. This implies that the mark-up is no longer stable: in Kalecki's terms, that the degree of monopoly increases. This is technically feasible because this parameter depends not only upon industrial concentration, but also upon trade-union bargaining power. 'This is the case which is sometimes called in economics writings "forced savings". The reaction of workers to the reduction of real wages will be a demand for higher money wages, and thus a price–wage spiral will be initiated' (p. 44). In fact, there does exist an equilibrium ratio of wages to prices (whatever their absolute level) implicit in the *ex-post* accumulation balance (A5:24–6); and both the internal terms of trade and real wages decline at the higher level of investment. The social distribution of the cost of accumulation depends upon specific parameter values (and particularly the propensity to consume food), but generally the burden[19] on workers as a class appears to be less than upon peasants (A4) because the latter compete more directly with capitalists for industrial goods.

In the second version of *Financing Development*, the composition of industrial output is left unclear and the role of foreign trade is reduced to imports which supplement domestic supplies of necessities or non-essentials. Kalecki does not pursue the argument beyond making the logical point that food imports would allow the warranted rate of growth to be higher. Full specification of the model yields more interesting results. For instance, experience of commodity aid indicates that food imports impede the expansion of domestic supply, particularly by holding down the internal terms of trade; moreover the logical consequence of such imports in his model is to maintain profits. In the first version, the production pattern is more clearly specified. Department I serves not only for 'the production of investment goods for the sake of replacement and expansion of plant and equipment, but also for the accumulation of inventories even of consumption goods' (p. 42), although Kalecki does not explore the intersectoral transactions involved. He implies that Department I would also include public works such as roads.[20] The investment supply conditions are not defined, although apparently they are largely based on import capacity, because he later argues that a 'rise in investment will require considerably higher imports of capital goods which cannot be produced at home' (p. 52).

For the supply of consumption goods from Department II, the food component (IIa) is inelastic; but the manufactured component is 'elastic because considerable reserves of productive capacity exist' (p. 46). However, even in the latter case, it is also true that 'the increase in total industrial production will involve higher imports of foreign raw materials and semi-manufactures' (p. 52). The behaviour of the export sector required to finance those imports of capital goods and raw materials is not specified by Kalecki, beyond allocating imports between the Departments. This expositional device is convenient because he assumes that exports are exogenously determined by supply constraints and foreign market conditions. Typically 'enclave' activities are probably what he has in mind, which do not interact with the national economy except as a source of foreign exchange. If, however, the internal macroeconomic balance were to affect export volumes, then his model would have to be considerably modified.[21]

None the less, these clarifications do enable us to set out a more rigorous linear model (A6), with three 'production' branches: an autonomous (that is, fixed in the short run) supply of food; a variable supply of manufactured consumer goods determined by domestic demand but requiring foreign inputs with a fixed import coefficient; and a supply of capital goods, entirely imported but using local labour in construction and installation. Imports are obtained at a standard world price with the exchange rate set at unity for expositional convenience. Total net export income is fixed in the short run; the domestic or foreign resource inputs to exports need not be recorded in the model as they too are fixed. An exogenous level of net foreign finance is also included.

The manufacturing price formation system now includes imported raw materials in prime costs; and while the market-clearing balances for the two consumer goods are similar to those for the closed-economy case, the capital goods supply (imports) is set by 'physical' investment plans. The external constraint now acts as closure for the model in a structuralist fashion (Chenery, 1975), with six equations (A6:27–32) and six unknowns: three domestic prices; two domestic consumer goods supply levels; and profits. The external constraint replaces the internal accumulation balance. The investment–savings balance condition is still satisfied because *ex post* the profits equation is redefined in terms of clearing prices in each market, without fixed mark-ups (A6:33). Savings from profits then turn out to be equal to investment expenditure plus the external trade balance (A6:34).

This derivation of the accumulation balance from the clearing of product markets is a standard Kaleckian formulation of the way in which investment determines savings and income distribution: it is quite simple to prove his propositions as to the positive effect of increased external receipts (whether from exports or credits) on the supply of manufactures, and thus on real wages (A6:36) and profits. The internal terms of trade now also reflect the influence of the *external* terms of trade (A6:35) rather nicely; with a deterioration of the latter depressing the former through the impact on manufacturing costs. Wages now form only a part of industrial costs, so peasant incomes can actually rise if wages are increased, due to the demand effect outweighing the cost effect. An increase in investment will still lead to a deterioration in the internal terms of trade because the peasant sector is 'starved' of industrial consumer goods as investment uses up more scarce foreign exchange. Curiously, however, there will occur an *improvement* in the real wage when investment rises because employment falls with the level of import-constrained manufacturing output by more than the contraction in wagegoods supply.[22] Finally increments in the nominal wage will now lead to an increase in the real wage, as occurs in Kalecki's model for industrialized economies once raw material inputs are introduced.

3.4 MACROECONOMIC MANAGEMENT

Kalecki holds that 'there are no financial limits, in the formal sense, to the volume of investment' (p. 44). He sees financial balances as essentially *passive*, reflecting the 'real' macroeconomic savings process. As in the case of taxation, he regards bank deposits as ultimately being about restraining non-essential consumption. Nevertheless, he does provide the elements for a useful approach to fiscal and monetary policy analysis in developing economies.[23]

As we have seen, Kalecki does not believe that finance as such can act as a constraint on investment. The macroeconomic adjustment process itself generates sufficient profits to finance planned investment, either as reinvested funds or as loanable bank deposits. 'If investment is financed out of the liquid reserves of the entrepreneurs concerned, the process will result in a shift of deposits from those entrepreneurs to other capitalists. If investment is financed by bank credit, the savings accruing in the form of deposits will be available for absorption of the issue of debentures and shares by the investing entrepreneurs' (p. 44). Thus, within the macroeconomic investment–savings balance he inserts a process of financial intermediation, where firms (as a sector) spend a certain proportion of profits on capital goods almost immediately and deposit the rest in the banks; these are then lent to firms and (by implication) to the government. Kalecki does not specify the exact intermediation mechanism, but there are in fact at least four ways in which this might occur. Firstly, profits retained by firms themselves might all be used to purchase capital goods, the dividends being deposited by shareholders in the banks. Secondly, firms may need working capital in the form of bank deposits or loans as a complement to fixed assets. Thirdly, the two-way flow could just be the result of aggregating a pattern of surplus and deficit firms. Fourthly, firms can logically hold both financial assets *and* liabilities as part of their own liquidity management system.

The increment in bank liabilities (A7:37) can thus be modelled as a stable proportion of saved profits, reflecting capitalists' portfolio preferences. The increment in bank assets are new loans to firms, which are the difference between fixed investment and reinvestment of own profits by firms (A7:38). It can easily be demonstrated that, in fact, the equilibrium between the assets and liabilities of the banking system will thus be assured by the same aggregate price and quantity adjustments that determine the accumulation balance (A7:39). Government expenditure financed from loans has the same compensating effect on savings and balance deposits as changes in investment. In the case of foreign loans, the accumulation balance is itself modified; but so are bank liabilities by an equal amount (A7:41), so the balance sheet is once again secure (A7:40).

This seems to be a plausible description of semi-industrialized economies without stock exchanges or proper money markets, where controls over interest rates and negligible savings out of wages are also commonplace. Peasant saving could also be included. Kalecki's model of bank intermediation is also novel in that it explicitly links deposits to profits, and thus the supply of credit to income distribution.

Kalecki sketches the outline of a fiscal analysis based on his accumulation model, which contains valuable insights but is somewhat vitiated by his expositional device of classifying the source of taxation as the departments themselves – 'i.e. by capitalists, small proprietors and workers of [each] department' – in his equations, although his discussion refers to classes. The aim of his analysis is twofold: firstly, to show that government current expenditure is ultimately financed by reduced real wages; and secondly, that although profits will always adjust to cover all investment, public investment can better be financed by taxing capitalist consumption in order to sustain real wages.

Kalecki's fiscal analysis starts with a balanced administrative budget where expenditure is on the wages of the government labour force. This can be modelled as an addition to industrial employment (A7:, p. 42–3). Tax rates correspond to the effective incidence of direct and indirect taxes on the two income classes (A7:44). Once the basic model for the clearing of product markets is appropriately redefined to include both taxation and government wage expenditure (A8:45–9), the accumulation account emerges with separate balances for the government and private sectors (A8:50) which is useful for policy discussion. This allows us in turn to examine the effect of budget deficits (which Kalecki does not explore), indicating that profits will be larger, due to excess demand driving up manufacturing output or – more probably – prices, than in the case of a balanced budget. From this it is clear that an increased rate of profits tax will result in a higher profit level being generated in order to finance a given level of investment; the adjustment mechanism being the upward pressure of administrative *wage* expenditure on prices. This will depress real wages but raise peasant incomes.

Thus Kalecki is correct to propose that *ceteris paribus* the higher government expenditure and revenue are, the lower will be real wages after taxation. This is not only so in the case where the taxes are paid directly by workers or in the case of indirect taxation, but is 'true even in the case of direct taxes paid by capitalists' (p. 53). A different result holds if taxes are imposed to cover a part of (public) investment, for in this context they are 'an anti-inflationary measure . . . it is easy to show that the amount of savings corresponding to a given level of investment (private and public) will be reduced by the amount of the original taxation' (p. 58). In effect, this is equivalent to running a budget *surplus* on current (that is, government saving), in which case post-tax retained profits need not be so large. The logical way to achieve this desirable outcome is by raising profit taxes which will not, in this case, reduce total savings (to which the budget now adds) nor depress real wages. In the first version of *Financing Development*, Kalecki was quite optimistic on this theme: 'Financing public investment by taxation of profits appears to be sound policy. It should be noticed that in this way only such profits would be taxed away as are in fact created by public investment' (p. 60). However, fifteen years later he was rather more cautious: 'The other, strictly financial, problem of levying taxes on the higher income groups and non-essentials is also very grave because of the influence of vested interests upon the government and because of the difficulty of overcoming tax evasion' (pp. 105–6).

When the model is extended to include a fiscal sector, the banking system will still adjust passively because the budget deficit will indirectly generate extra bank deposits (from increased private profits) equal to the amount of loans needed by the government (A8:52). Kalecki is thus correct in arguing that if 'the government finances investment initially by loans from the banking system, the disbursement of the respective sums will generate an equal amount of liquid savings, which will then be available for taking up government securities and thus make possible the funding of the loan' (p. 45). There is no 'crowding out' by profit taxes, because 'savings and profits generated are such as would be obtained if there were no public investment' (p. 60). In other words, any increment in the money supply cannot be considered as a source of government finance. New treasury debt would be absorbed automatically by the increase in the (current account) deposits of entrepreneurs who receive government payments. Any increase in output or in prices would have been generated by the *initial* (for example, budgetary) expenditure effect itself, not by monetary creation. There is no need, therefore, for a separate supply–demand relation for money in order to determine prices; nor for fear of 'crowding out' of private by public investment.

In sum, monetary policy is strictly 'passive' in the sense that the authorities need only respond to increased transactions' demand for money, whether due to increases in output or prices. In the case of developing economies, 'imported' inflation (through rising import prices or devaluations) would also be perfectly consistent with his approach. None the less, inflation is the result of the wage–profit struggle and structural factors, particularly the food supply and the degree of monopoly, in Kaleckian theory. Taking the wagegoods 'basket' as the relevant cost-of-living indicator (A1:8), then inflation can be generated by industry (and thus employment) growing more rapidly than agriculture or by wage pressure without modification in the degree of monopoly. As we have seen, inflation can also be initiated by an increase in investment which, under constrained supply conditions, allows the mark-up to rise as part of the macroeconomic adjustment process through 'forced savings'. In fact, any autonomous demand increment such as government expenditure can be treated in the same way. In the longer run 'the inelasticity of supply in agriculture and the monopolistic tendencies in industry emerge as important factors underlying inflationary effects in the course of rapid economic development' (pp. 50–1). However, 'the primary inflationary pressure experienced in the course of rapid economic development is . . . the result of basic disproportions in productive relations. Thus these pressures cannot be prevented by purely financial devices. The solution of the problem must be based on economic policies embracing the whole process of development' (p. 62).

However, Kalecki does argue elsewhere[24] that a 'crude quantity theory' can apply under conditions of hyperinflation. This situation, where price expectations themselves generate anticipatory price and wage adjustment, is considered to be of 'theoretical interest because this happens to be the only case where the quantity theory of money finds its full application' (1962, p. 276). The velocity of circulation becomes a function of anticipated rate of price inflation, and as output is capacity-constrained, the monetization of a given budget deficit (which Kalecki takes as fixed in real terms) will generate an ever-increasing supply of high-powered money (A9). He goes on to argue that if the rate of inflation is lower than expected then the velocity of circulation will fall and the economy stabilize. If the reverse occurs then 'galloping inflation' builds up until there is a radical change in the management of the economy or the currency collapses.

Hyperinflation thus involves a change in the basis for price formation from production cost to speculative expectations. Consequently, 'in view of the fact that the course of prices under hyperinflation is fully determined by the above factors, changes in money wages will not affect prices provided that the real value of its budget deficit plus banking credit to private business remains unchanged' (1962, p. 280). Thus, wages *can* rise faster than prices, although institutionally they usually lag behind, and result in 'enormous profits of entrepreneurs in general and big business in particular'. But, as the indexing mechanism improves, big business ceases to support it and: 'it is at this point that there usually emerge stabilization schemes which put a stop to hyperinflation' (1962, p. 281). An all too familiar story in Latin America today.

Kalecki states that restrictions on bank credit as an anti-inflationary measure would only be effective 'when directed against the hoarding of commodities . . . [however] such a system may be rather difficult to operate . . . [an alternative is] maintaining the real value of deposits, government bonds and banking credits by revaluing them constantly' (p. 61). However, even such asset indexing can only reduce *secondary* speculative inflation; the underlying causes are to be found in the product markets and are not a monetary phenomenon at all.

3.5 CONCLUSIONS

This chapter contains an attempt to systematize the mass of analytical insights contained in the few pages, written over thirty years ago, of *Financing Development* and to extend its logic into a formal algebraic construct encompassing recognizable 'stylized facts' about semi-industrialized countries on the periphery of the world economy. We have concentrated on the domestic economy, and upon the short run; leaving aside the issues of the external sector and stabilization policy, on the one hand, and growth dynamics and planning on the other. The key policy conclusion is that the taxation of profits, rather than restrictions in wages or government expenditure, is the key to macroeconomic management.

As in all Kalecki's work, the central insight relates to the distributional effect of investment and output decisions made by capitalists, and the impact of government policy upon the resultant equilibria. Accumulation is funded by reductions in the real wage and, to a lesser extent, by deterioration in peasant income through the internal terms of trade; the mechanism being based on the maintenance of a determinate degree of monopoly (mark-up) in the industrial sectors and scarcity rents arising from food supply or foreign exchange constraints.

I have found it necessary to extend Kalecki's model in order to allow for a price-responsive peasant supply of food; the result of which was to modify his results but not the underlying logic of his approach. None the less, I have kept to Kalecki's assumption that labour productivity is unaffected by the real wage level. In practice this is not so: a high investment rate based on low wages may not improve labour productivity because work intensity falls at the same time as capital intensity is increased. This effect is strengthened in economies where there exist alternatives to wage labour (such as the 'informal sector') or where there is a social commitment to support labour incomes directly through citizen entitlements.[25]

In sum, *Financing Development* clearly provides the basis for a viable theory of 'development macroeconomics' with clear parallels to Kalecki's analysis of industrial economies, even if he appears to have thought it unnecessary to set out a formal model himself.

APPENDIX

This algebraic appendix follows the argument in the text step by step, the separate sections being identified at each point.

1 Price Formation

In the simple closed-economy model, employment (L) is determined by industrial output (Q_2) and labour productivity (b), a constant:

$$L = Q_2/b \tag{1}$$

and the wagefund (W) by the nominal wagerate (w):

$$W = wL \tag{2}$$

Industrial prices (p_2) are formed from a mark-up (g) on labour costs, the only input:

$$p_2 = (1 + g)w/b \tag{3}$$

and profits (R) are thus:

$$R = \frac{gw}{b} Q_2 = gwL \tag{4}$$

Food prices (p_1) are endogenously determined by the interaction of demand generated by the proportion (a) of wages spent on food and a given supply (Q_1) by peasant farmers:

$$Q_1 p_1 = awL \tag{5}$$

Demand for manufactures comes from the expenditure of all profits (R), peasant money incomes ($Z = awL$) and workers' non-food expenditure:

$$R + awL + (1-a)wL = wL + gwL$$
$$= (1+g)\frac{w}{b}Q_2$$
$$= p_2Q_2$$

From (1) and (5) we have:

$$p_1 = \frac{aw}{b} \cdot \frac{Q_2}{Q_1} \tag{6}$$

2 Income Distribution

The internal terms of trade (T) are:

$$T = \frac{p_1}{p_2}$$
$$= \frac{a}{(1+g)}\frac{Q_2}{Q_1} \tag{7}$$

The wage deflator reflects the whole wagegoods basket weighted by the proportion of food (a) and non-food ($1-a$) items in it, so the real wage is defined as:

$$\bar{w} = \frac{w}{ap_1 + (1-a)p_2}$$
$$= \frac{b}{a^2\dfrac{Q_2}{Q_1} + (1-a)(1+g)} \tag{8}$$

From (8) we have:

$$a \rightarrow 1 \; ; \; \bar{w} \rightarrow \frac{Q_1}{L}$$

$$a \rightarrow 0 \; ; \; w \rightarrow \frac{b}{1+g} \tag{9}$$

Real peasant income ($\bar{Z}$) is given by:

$$\bar{Z} = \frac{p_1Q_1}{p_2}$$
$$= \frac{a}{1+g}Q_2 \tag{10}$$

The level of real profits ($\bar{R}$) can be derived directly as the sum of industrialists' profits and landlord and merchants' margins (f) on food sales deflated by manufacturing prices:

$$\bar{R} = \frac{(p_2Q_2 - wL) + fp_1Q_1}{p_2}$$

$$= Q_2\frac{(g + fa)}{1 + g} \qquad (11)$$

For ease of exposition, from now on we deal with a single category of industrial profits (that is, $f = 0$).

3 Food Supply

We now relax the assumption of fixed food supply. The marketed portion (Q_1) of total food output (E) is a function of the internal terms of trade (T) such that:

$$Q_1 = Q_1(E, T) \qquad (12a)$$

where $\partial Q_1/\partial E > 0$ and $\partial Q1/\partial T > 0$

Because E is presumably also a positive function of T we can reduce this to:

$$Q_1 = Q_1(T)$$

where $\partial Q_1 > \partial T > 0$ and $\partial^2 Q_2/\partial T^2 < 0 \qquad (12b)$

The simplest expression for food supply would be:

$$Q_1 = cT \qquad (13)$$

Substituting (13) into (7), we derive a new solution for the equilibrium value of the internal terms of trade (T):

$$T = \left\{\frac{aQ_2}{(1 + g)c}\right\}^{1/2} \qquad (14)$$

We must also modify (8) in order to derive the real wage again. Substituting (14) into (8) leads to the rather clumsy expression:

$$\bar{w} = \frac{b}{a^{3/2}\left\{\frac{Q_2(1 + g)}{T}\right\}^{1/2} + \{(1 - a)(1 + g)\}} \qquad (15)$$

Note, however, that now that food supply response is included, the simple 'Ricardian' deterioration of wages is no longer valid. Even in the extreme case where wagegoods are mainly food, wages are still a function of profits (that is, the mark-up) because as $a \rightarrow 1$,

$$\bar{w} \rightarrow ba^{3/2}c^{1/2}\{Q_2(1+g)\}^{-1/2}$$

replacing (8) as the real wage equation.

4 Investment and Savings

We now introduce investment and derive the accumulation balance. The demand for manufactures is now made up of the expenditures of peasants and workers, plus capitalist consumption and investment, respectively:

$$p_2Q_2 = p_1Q_1 + (1-a)wL + (1-s)R + Ip_2 \tag{16}$$

for a given savings rate (s) out of profits (R), and an exogenous level of physical investment (I). In Kalecki's formulation the 'necessary' level of investment ($I*$) can be derived from the warranted rate of growth ($r*$) of course, on which see also Chapter 6. For a current level of capital stock (K), known rates of growth in population (q) and food supply (c_n), and a given value of the income elasticity (e):

$$\begin{aligned} I* &= r*K \\ &= K\{c_n - q(1-e)\}/e \end{aligned}$$

The *ex post* accumulation balance can be found by substituting (5) and (1) into (16). As profits (R) are:

$$R = p_2Q_2 - wL \tag{17}$$

we *derive* the accumulation balance as:

$$sR = Ip_2 \tag{18}$$

A tax (t) on capitalist consumption is used to fund the public portion of investment, so from (3) and (18):

$$\frac{g}{1+g}Q_2\{s + (1-s)t\} = I \tag{19}$$

and by rearrangement the tax rate required to finance investment without inflation is given by:

$$\frac{\dfrac{I}{Q_2}\left(1+\dfrac{1}{g}\right) - s}{(1-s)} \tag{20}$$

5 Two Variants

In the earlier version of *Financing Development*, two other variants are considered. In the first of these variants, the mark-up remains stable (g) and thus the accumulation balance (18) can be expressed as:

$$sQ_2\frac{g}{1+g}=I$$

$$Q_2=sI\left(1+\frac{1}{g}\right) \tag{21}$$

This yields solutions for the real wage ($\bar{w}$) and the internal terms of trade (T) as functions of the level of investment. Substituting (21) into (7):

$$T=\frac{a}{1+g}\frac{Q_2}{Q_1}$$

$$=\frac{as}{g}\frac{Q_2}{Q_1} \tag{22}$$

The real wage ($\bar{w}$) is found by substituting (22) into (8):

$$\bar{w}=\frac{b/(1-g)}{aT+(1-a)}$$

$$=\frac{b}{1+g}\left\{\frac{a^2s}{g}\frac{I}{Q_1}+(1-a)\right\}^{-1} \tag{23}$$

In the second variant, price adjustment in response to excess demand raises profits towards the equilibriating level. The corresponding price (and thus wage) level is found from the accumulation balance (18) and the profit definition (17):

$$p_2=\frac{w}{b\left(1-\frac{1}{sQ_2}\right)} \tag{24}$$

which now yields the equilibrium terms of trade (T) inversely related to the rate of investment (I):

$$T=\frac{a}{sQ_1}(sQ_2-I) \tag{25}$$

The real wage ($\bar{w}$) is derived by substituting (24) and (4) into (6), to yield:

$$\bar{w} = b\left\{a^2\frac{Q_2}{Q_1} + \frac{(1-a)}{\left(1 - \frac{I}{sQ_2}\right)}\right\}^{-1} \tag{26}$$

which is also inversely related to investment rates.
Note that the burden of investment on workers' income (W) is less than on that of peasants (Z) because:

$$\frac{\partial Z}{\partial I} = -\frac{1}{s}$$

while

$$\frac{\partial W}{\partial I} \rightarrow -\frac{1}{s} \text{ when } a \rightarrow 0 \text{ and } \frac{\partial W}{\partial I} \rightarrow 0 \text{ as } a \rightarrow 1.$$

6 The Open Economy

The model is now expanded to three 'production' branches: an autonomous supply of food (Q_1); a variable supply of manufactured consumer goods (Q_2) determined by domestic demand but requiring foreign inputs at a fixed import coefficient (m_2); and a supply of capital goods (Q_3) imported at a fixed coefficient (m_3) using labour for installation. Imports are obtained at a single world price (p_4) for which the exchange rate is set at unity for expositional convenience. Total export income (X) is fixed, net of domestic or foreign resource inputs. The manufacturing price formation equation now includes imported raw materials:

$$p_2 = (1+g)\left(\frac{w}{b_2} + m_2 p_4\right) \tag{27}$$

as does that for investment goods:

$$p_3 = (1+g)\left(\frac{w}{b_3} + m_3 p_4\right) \tag{28}$$

while the market clearing balances for the two domestic goods are essentially as before, and the demand for investment goods (Q_3) is expressed in terms of 'physical' investment plans (I):

$$p_1 Q_1 = aw\left\{\frac{Q_2}{b_2} + \frac{Q_3}{b_3}\right\} \tag{29}$$

$$p_2 Q_2 = p_1 Q_1 + (1-a)\left\{\frac{Q_2}{b_2} + \frac{Q_3}{b_3}\right\} + (1-s)R \tag{30}$$

$$p_3 Q_3 = I p_3 \tag{31}$$

The external constraint is that imports (M) should be equal to or less than the sum of exports and net foreign finance (F):

$$M = (m_2Q_2 + m_3Q_3)p_4 \leq X + F$$

On the assumption that domestic demand management is such that manufacturing output (Q_2) rises to meet the external constraint (31), substituting (30) yields, for a given investment level (I):

$$Q_2 = \frac{1}{m_2}\left\{\frac{X+F}{p_4} - mI\right\} \tag{32}$$

This last equation acts as the 'closure' of a model of six equations ((27) to (32)) and six unknowns ($Q_2, Q_3, p_1, p_2, p_3, R$). The external constraint (32) has a role corresponding to that played by the internal accumulation balance (18) in the closed-economy model. The investment–savings balance condition is still satisfied because into (30) we now substitute the (redefined) profits equation:

$$R = \left\{p_2Q_2 - \left(w\frac{Q_2}{b_2} + m_2Q_2p_4\right)\right\} + \left\{p_3Q_3 - \left(w\frac{Q_3}{b_3} + m_3Q_3p_4\right)\right\} + X \tag{33}$$

from which the savings/investment equality emerges *ex post* once more as:

$$\begin{aligned} sR &= X - p_4(Q_2m_2 + Q_3m_3) + Q_3p_3 \\ &= Ip_3 + (X - M) \\ &= Ip_3 - F \end{aligned} \tag{34}$$

The internal terms of trade (T) now reflect the influence (m_2p_3) of the external sector through (27) and (28),

$$\begin{aligned} T &= p_1/p_2 \\ &= \frac{aQ_2/Q}{(1+g)\left\{1 + \left(\frac{b_2m_2 + b_3m_3}{w}\right)p_4\right\}} \end{aligned} \tag{35}$$

and are inversely related to the rate of investment:

$$\partial Q_2/\partial I < 0;\ \partial T/\partial Q_2 > 0;\ \partial T/\partial I$$

Substitution of (35) into (8) yields a new formulation for the real wage, which varies positively with the external terms of trade:

$$w = b\left\{a\frac{Q_2}{Q_1} + (1-a)(1+g)\left(1 + \frac{mp_3b}{w}\right)\right\}^{-1} \tag{36}$$

7 Banking

Firms spend a certain proportion (α) of their reinvested profits (sR) on capital goods immediately, depositing the rest in banks. The increment (A) in bank liabilities is thus defined as:

$$A = (1 - \alpha)sR \tag{37}$$

while the increment (B) in bank assets is new loans to firms (the difference between fixed investment and reinvestment of own profits):

$$B = Ip_3 - \alpha sR \tag{38}$$

It can be shown that the equilibrium of the banking system ($A = B$) will be assured by the same aggregated price and quantity adjustments that secure the accumulation balance itself. Substituting (18) into (38):

$$\begin{aligned} B &= sR - \alpha sR \\ &= (1 - \alpha)sR = A \end{aligned} \tag{39}$$

Government expenditure (G) financed from domestic bank loans has the same effect as changes in investment. In the case of foreign loans (F), the accumulation balance is modified to give:

$$Ip_3 = F + sR \tag{40}$$

while bank liabilities and assets become:

$$\begin{aligned} A &= F + (1 - \alpha)sR \\ B &= Ip_3 - \alpha sR = F + (1 - \alpha)sR = A \end{aligned} \tag{41}$$

so the banks' balance sheet is again kept *automatically* in equilibrium *ex post*.

8 Fiscal Sector

A tax-funded administrative budget (G) spent upon government employees (L_4) at the single domestic wage rate (w) adds to the modern sector labour force (L):

$$G = wL_4 \tag{42}$$

$$L = L_2 + L_3 + L_4 \tag{43}$$

Tax revenue (N) is made up of levies on profits (t_w) and wages (t_r) such that:

$$N = t_w W + t_r R \tag{44}$$

Profits (R) and the national wagebill (W) are now given by:

$$R = (p_2Q_2 - wL_2) + (p_3Q_3 - wL_3) \tag{45}$$

$$W = wL \tag{46}$$

The clearing condition for the market for industrial consumer goods (Q_2) is again:

$$p_2Q_2 = W(1 - t_w) + R(1 - t_r)(1 - s) \tag{47}$$

while that for investment goods (Q_3) is:

$$p_3Q_3 = I \tag{48}$$

Substituting (42), (43), (44), (45), and (46) into (47) yields:

$$p_2Q_2 = (p_2Q_2 + p_3Q_3) + (G - N) - sR \tag{49}$$

so that rearranging and substituting (48) finally yields an accumulation balance that distinguishes between government and the private sector in the way outlined in Chapter 2:

$$I = (N - G) + sR(l - t_r) \tag{50}$$

Note that in the case of a current budget deficit ($N < G$), profits (R) will be larger (due to excess demand driving up Q_2, or more probably P_2) than in the case of a balanced budget ($N = G$). In the latter case, (50) reduces to the familiar:

$$I = s(l - t_r)R \tag{51}$$

The banking system is also equilibrated by the same mechanism. From (37) we have the increment of bank liabilities (A), and substituting in (51), we get the increment in bank assets (B), the sum of business borrowing ($Ip_3 - \alpha sR$) and new government credits (D):

$$\begin{aligned} A &= (l - \alpha)sR \\ &= (Ip_3 - \alpha sR) + D = B \end{aligned} \tag{52}$$

9 Hyperinflation

Under hyperinflationary conditions the monetary demand function (37) is no longer stable, and the propensity to hold bank deposits (α) becomes an inverse function of the anticipated rate of price inflation ($p*$). For Kalecki (1962) the crude quantity theory of money becomes applicable in this situation because output is capacity-constrained ($Q \leq \bar{Q}$). The stock of circulating money (H) and the price level (p) move together; while the velocity of circulation (v) depends on the subjective outlook of businessmen ('business confidence'):

$$H.v(\dot{p}*) = p.\bar{Q} \tag{53}$$

and the increase in money in circulation per unit of time (dH/dt) is generated by the monetization of the budget deficit ($\bar{D}$) which Kalecki takes to be set by the government in real terms:

$$dH/dt = p\bar{D} \tag{54}$$

The actual rate of change of prices ($\dot{p}$) is found by differentiating (53) and substituting (54) into (55) to yield:

$$\dot{p} = v(\dot{p}*)\frac{\bar{D}}{\bar{Q}} \tag{55}$$

4 The Analytics of Stabilization Policy

4.1 STABILIZATION IN THE SEMI-INDUSTRIALIZED ECONOMY

In this chapter, elements of the central arguments presented in Chapter 3 are expressed in an analytical model of short-run adjustment in a semi-industrialized economy, allowing financial flows to be revealed as a reflection of the relationship between accumulation balances in different institutional sectors. For practical policy applications such a model must obviously be country-specific rather than general for all developing economies. None the less, once the methodological approach is demonstrated for a reasonably typical structure, the way in which such models might be built for economies with alternative structures should also be clear.[1] In the short run, productive capacity can be taken as given, and current investment does not affect current output directly. In Chapter 6 we will examine the question of intersectoral allocation of investment affecting income distribution from the supply side, and thus long-term resource mobilization. Not only Kalecki but also Keynes placed the relationship between exports and growth, and thus imports and accumulation, at the heart of the stabilization problem in the longer run.[2] It is therefore necessary to make these explicit in a short-run model too.

The aim here is to model realistic commercial relationships between sectors of the economy from which the functional income distribution emerges and affects demand. The accumulation balance emerges as the key 'closure' in the macroeconomic equilibrium, and constitutes the context in which financial policy actions designed to maintain or restore external (balance of payments) and internal (price) stability may be properly analysed. In contrast to the New Orthodox approach to finance, such an accounting framework and sectoral price-formation rules allow savings and inflation to be defined in relation to the production process itself. An alternative neo-structuralist approach based on the extension of the 'two-gap' model can be found in Bacha (1990).

I argued in Chapter 1 that the 'IMF' (or monetary) theory of stabilization – upon which see IMF (1987) and Khan *et al.* (1989, 1990) – is a central element of the New Orthodox approach, and is based on a somewhat superficial interpretation of the accumulation balance where the domestic private sector is assumed to be stable by definition, and thus all external (balance-of-payments) and internal (monetary) disequilibria are due to fiscal mismanagement and, ultimately, excessive state involvement in the economy. However, as the behaviour of the private sector is not specified, the analysis remains *ex hypothesi.*[3] What is more, as employment and income distribution are not included in such models, these issues are relegated at best to the 'trickle-down' of the benefits from renewed output growth in the long run. Here we attempt to overcome both these limitations, so that the effects of fiscal/monetary variables can be fully appreciated, through correctly specified accumulation balances. Such an approach also allows the demand for, and supply of, money to be explicitly linked to the real variables in the economy, rather than relying upon dubious regressions on GDP,[4] while a full flow-of-funds analysis is made possible, based on sectoral uses of liquidity.

Recent 'Keynesian' approaches do imply a greater specification of the composition of demand, allowing for differential price behaviour in traded and non-traded sectors, and can be adapted to include the effect of functional income distribution upon savings.[5] 'Structural' theory yields a greater specification of foreign trade as part of the production process, itself limited by capacity bottlenecks, and the analysis of the effect of functional income distribution upon demand for various categories of goods.[6] However, progress has been slow[7] in the formal application of such approaches to the financial sector in developing economies. My aim in this chapter is to make a modest advance on such 'structural–Keynesian' theory by bringing together the elements just mentioned in a specifically financial model of stabilization; the inspiration for which may be traced to Kalecki.[8] I shall proceed in five stages. Firstly, I shall establish the basic model of the 'real side' of the economy, covering production, external trade, market clearing, investment, saving and income distribution. Secondly, I shall examine the macroeconomic stabilization conditions in relation to the external sector, particularly changes in world prices, foreign credit and the exchange rate. Thirdly, I shall turn to the foundation of stabilization policy itself: the control of wage levels, autonomous expenditure and the exchange rate. I shall then come to explicit financial questions, introducing the fiscal sector as a fourth step; to be finally followed by the inclusion of a banking/monetary sector to complete the model.

4.2 THE BASIC MODEL

The basic model is that of a semi-industrialized economy possessing a relatively simple production and ownership structure; this will underlie the market, financial and distributive processes under discussion. The basic model has two productive sectors (agriculture and industry), to which two 'non-productive' sectors (government and the financial sector) are subsequently added. There exist only two social classes, capitalists and workers, although other classes (such as peasants) could be included. The economy is heavily dependent on foreign trade for its operation, exporting much of the output of the primary sector and importing all material inputs for the secondary sector supplying the domestic market: in this sense it is 'semi-industrialized'.

The primary sector is agriculture. It produces from a combined endowment of land and capital, which is given in the short run and is working at full capacity. However, with this endowment, it can produce either export commodities or supply the domestic (food) market; and can shift between the two at the margin with relative facility from one year to another.[9] This is a traded sector, where prices are set according to world (border) prices, mediated by the exchange rate. The demand for exports is infinitely elastic from the country's point of view, but increased domestic demand for food will shift agricultural resources (or products, as the case may be) away from exports.[10] This approach differs from that of the 'traditional' structural model (which has constrained exports separate from food supply)[11] and probably reflects more closely the prevailing situation in most developing countries where world markets have now penetrated the agricultural sector and governments no longer artificially depress crop prices. None the less, those two sectors of agriculture could be handled separately.[12] Production is organized in business enterprise in this basic model (which may, of course, be small firms) so as to permit the analysis of the effect of the wages level and the exchange rate on farm profits as well as on industry.

The secondary sector in the basic model is manufacturing industry and construction. It employs labour and capital to produce all the domestic non-food requirements of the economy: consumer goods and investment goods. Producer goods for the agricultural sector are not included in this model, for the sake of simplicity.[13] Investment goods are locally-'produced' in the sense that even imported plant and equipment must be installed by the domestic construction industry. Output is constrained by foreign exchange availability for imports as secondary or 'industrial' production is homogeneous in our model, there is a single import coefficient determined by prevailing technology and insensitive to world price.[14] The level of industrial output will 'clear' in the domestic market with a domestic price determined by effective demand from consumption and investment requirements, as it is a non-traded sector.

Income distribution is made up of two categories: wages and profits. Nominal wages are negotiated institutionally, and employment depends upon the level of output with given technical coefficients. Profits depend upon prices and costs. These are exogenous in the agricultural sector, but in the industrial sector a degree of monopoly exists, permitting administered prices with a determinate mark-up, although when the foreign exchange constraint binds on production (as it does in the situation examined here), then excess domestic demand pressure will determine industrial prices. The inverse case, where there is mark-up pricing in industry and endogenous market-clearing prices in agriculture, has been discussed in Chapter 3.

This basic model can be set out as a system of six equations in six endogenous variables. The primary sector market balance is made up of: firstly, supply determined by investment decisions in previous periods (Q_1) at an exogenous world price (p_1) and policy-determined exchange rate (e); and secondly, demand made up of exports (E), again at world prices, and domestic requirements generated by the national wage bill (W) and the propensity to consume food (a) which is a parameter. Note that only workers consume food, and thus exports are effectively a residual after their demand (depending on employment and real wages) is met.[15]

$$ep_1Q_1 = aW + ep_1E \qquad (1)$$

The market balance for industrial products, is given by output (Q_2) at the domestic endogenous price (p_2) on the one hand, and by demand on the other. Demand is made up of three elements: the non-food component of wage expenditure; that part of profits (R) which are not saved under the given propensity to save (s); and the investment requirement (I). This definition implies that only capitalists save, as argued in Chapter 2; although by 'capitalist' we mean both corporations and informal enterprises, including household firms.

Investment volume is determined by decisions made by capitalists in previous periods, due to the lag between project decision and completion, which means that it may be taken as given in the short run:

$$p_2Q_2 = (1 - a)W + (1 - s)R + p_2I \tag{2}$$

Employment (L) is determined by the level of output (Q_1, Q_2) in the two productive sectors, with given employment coefficients (l_1, l_2) as technology is also fixed in the short run. No labour supply constraint is imposed, because the services sector (particularly the urban informal sector) acts as the effective labour reserve, although we do not model this explicitly:[16]

$$L = l_1Q_1 + l_2Q_2 \tag{3}$$

The wage bill (W) is determined by a single national nominal wage rate (w). Clearly, this can be modelled with separate wage rates in each sector, but this would only complicate the algebra without adding any relevant insights. We assume that this nominal wage rate is set institutionally by bargaining between trade unions, employers and the government:

$$W = wL \tag{4}$$

Profits (R) are generated in each of the two production sectors (which, for the moment, I have assumed to be homogeneous in savings behaviour) depending upon costs and prices in each sector. Costs of land and capital are ignored for agricultural profits (R_1) as this is a short run analysis. The import price (p_3) does enter into industrial costs, via a fixed import coefficient (m) and the exchange rate (e).

$$R_1 = ep_1Q_1 - wl_1Q_1$$

$$R_2 = p_2Q_2 - (wl_2 + ep_3m)Q_2$$

$$\begin{aligned} R &= R_1 + R_2 \\ &= (ep_1 - wl_1)Q_1 + (p_2 - ep_3m - wl_2)Q_2 \end{aligned} \tag{5}$$

Finally, the external balance of the economy is given by the flows of exports (p_1E), imports (p_3mQ_3) and net foreign finance (F), all expressed in terms of a suitably-weighted foreign currency basket. The 'net foreign finance' term is assumed to be exogenous in the short run and includes disbursements of foreign credit, direct investments, donations and so on; net of outflows corresponding to servicing of external liabilities, and any other monetary movements, particularly capital flight. The external balance is derived from the reasonable assumption that industrial output (Q_2) will be raised up to the limit of foreign exchange availability by policy-makers:

$$F + p_1 E = p_3 m Q_2 \tag{6}$$

This gives us a system of six equations with six endogenous variables (E, Q_2, p_2, W, L, R), which for linear formulations such as this will have an unambiguous solution. The Jacobian for this kind of model are discussed in Taylor (1983). We have two key policy variables (e, w) and five structural variables (a, m, s, l_1, l_2). There are two exogenous price variables (p_1, p_3) set by the world market; and two quantity variables (Q_1, I) which, because they are determined by investment decisions made in previous periods, can also be taken as being exogenous.

4.3 THE CONDITIONS FOR STABILITY

The solution of this six-equation system is found via the way in which the three markets clear, through which the articulation of investment and savings is brought about. Firstly, the external balance (6) effectively determines the level of industrial output as a positive function of exports and foreign finance, from the 'supply side'

$$Q_2 = \frac{F + p_1 E}{p_3 m} \tag{7}$$

Secondly, the substitution of equation (3) into (4) and this latter into (1) yield an inverse relationship between industrial output and exports, from the 'demand side', as food demand affects exports:

$$Q_2 = \frac{p_1 e}{a w l_2}(Q_1 - E) - \frac{l_1}{l_2} Q_1 \tag{8}$$

The intersection of these two relationships (see Figure 4.1 on page 76) determines the levels of domestic output and external trade. The key result in this case being the equilibrium level of industrial activity (Q_2'):

$$Q_2 = \frac{(ep_1 - awl_1)Q_1 + eF}{(awl_2 + ep_3m)} \tag{9}$$

Thirdly, the substitution of equations (8) and (3) into (4) yields the wage bill now that employment (L) is known. Substituting (1), (4), (5) and (6) into (2) determines the equilibrium value of the domestic price for manufactures (p_2'), which is crucial in determining the income distribution:

$$p_2' = \frac{s(1-a)W - (1-s)eF}{sQ_2 - I} \tag{10}$$

From this solution we can also immediately find the profit level from (5). The key distributional variable is the real wage ($\bar{w}$), which can be derived by defining the consumer price index as the weighted mean of food and manufactures prices,

$$\bar{w} = \frac{w}{ap_1e + (1-a)p_2} \tag{11}$$

The inverse relationship between export volume and the level of the real wage becomes clear by substituting (11) into (1):

$$E = Q_1 - a\bar{w}L\left\{a + (1-a)\frac{p_2}{ep_1}\right\} \tag{12}$$

However, from my point of view the most important derivation is that of the accumulation balance itself, both because this underpins my financial analysis and because it becomes the effective 'closure' of my basic model. In fact, the balance between investment and savings does not have to be defined independently as a 'market for funds': it emerges as the *resultant* from the clearing of product markets and the functional income distribution. As investment is determined *ex ante* in the short run, savings must adjust *ex post* at the macroeconomic level. As the level of aggregate activity is constrained by the external sector, this adjustment cannot be 'Keynesian'; rather it is a 'Kaleckian' route through output composition and income distribution, where differential sectoral price movements have a crucial role to play.[17]

Finally, therefore, substituting (2), (3) and (4) into (5), yields total profits (R) as a function of industrial output and prices (Q_2, p_2), which have already been determined by the market clearing mechanism:

$$R = \frac{1}{g} e(p_1 E - p_3 m Q_2) + p_2 I \tag{13}$$

So that by substituting the result from our market-clearing process (7) we have the equality of savings (external and domestic) and investment:

$$eF + sR = p_2 I \tag{14}$$

From the point of view of financial analysis, it is important to stress that the process by which this accumulation balance is reached is to be found in the product markets. Because the price mechanism adjusts profits at the market-clearing stage, there is no need for a separate clearing of the 'savings' market *at the aggregate level.* In other words, sufficient savings are always available to finance planned investment in the Kaleckian approach because they result from the product market equilibrium itself.

Figure 4.1 summarizes the market clearing procedure. The north-east quadrant represents the two main constraints on the economy: the upward-sloping trade constraint (7) and the downward-sloping food-constraint (8). In the north-west quadrant, we have a hyperbola (9) expressing what is, in effect, the savings function. For any given Q_2 this is the value of p_2 that clears the market, and also generates sufficient profits such that savings match investment. The origins of this balance in my model can be expressed in terms of the Hicksian model of macroeconomic balance: the equivalent of the 'IS curve' is represented by accumulation balance (12); but (7) takes the place of the 'LM curve' in terms of the demand for foreign currency rather than domestic liquidity. The south-west quadrant is merely the definition of the real wage (11); while the south-east quadrant links exports to the real wage (12).

The stabilization problem can be usefully explored by looking at the effects of various 'shocks' arising from changes in external circumstances, before turning to the effect of the policy variables themselves.

(a) If primary-sector output (Q_1) is smaller than expected, and no other policy instruments are used; then (8) moves inwards towards the axis of Figure 4.1. The inverse clearly obtains for an increase

Figure 4.1 Market clearing in the semi-industrialized economy

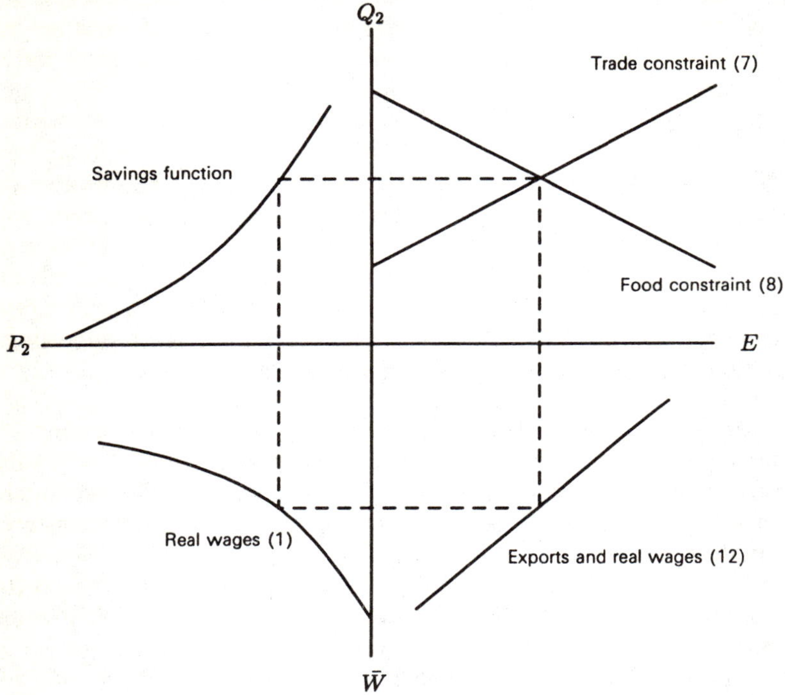

in Q_1. The domestic price level (p) rises as manufacturing output (Q_2) declines, and its prices (p_2) rise, in the market-clearing process. Both real wages (w) and employment (L) fall in what might be called a classic post-Keynesian case of 'stagflation'; while primary sector profits decline, even though secondary sector profits will be maintained.'[18]

(b) A deterioration in the external terms of trade (p_1/p_3) yields a similar but not identical logic. The slope and intercept of the external constraint (7) fall, but the domestic food constraint (8) is unchanged, so secondary output (Q_2) falls (as do real wages and employment) but exports (E) rise as domestic consumption declines. This process of 'natural' adjustment is, in fact, produced by a combination of the Engel-effect, from changing real incomes caused by relative price changes within the wagegood basket, and the shift in income distribution. For the economy as a whole, this effect is accompanied by higher secondary sector prices (p_2) and thus also stagflation. Neo-Ricardian trade theorists would see this is a characteristic feature of peripheral primary exporters and as constituting, in effect, a 'backward sloping supply curve'.[19]

(c) Foreign borrowing or 'aid' possibilities (F) allow the intercept of the trade constraint (7) in Figure 4.1 to move upwards, and the price curve (10) to move inwards. This generates a lower internal price level and higher real wages; so employment also rises with secondary output. However, the new equilibrium also leads to lower exports (E) and, as a result, profits in both sectors and domestic savings *decline* (13). This result reflects the structural view that 'external' savings may substitute for, rather than being a complement to, internal savings.[20]

It should be noted that these three external shocks, although they all have an equivalent immediate effect upon the external balance (greater or smaller foreign exchange availability) do not have the same impact on the domestic balances. In other words, they are not symmetrical. In consequence, a combination of, say, (b) and (c) – that is, borrowing abroad to compensate for terms of trade deterioration in the short run – will have perverse distributional effects in the short run, quite apart from the long-run consequences of accumulated debt.

4.4 THE FOUNDATIONS OF STABILIZATION POLICY

The policy variables in the model so far defined are the nominal wage rate (w) and the exchange rate (e), both of which were held constant in the previous section. These could be combined as a 'real' exchange rate as Dornbusch and Helmers (1988) do. Expansionary state expenditure policies can also be explored at this stage in my argument by looking at an autonomous increase in investment (I), although I shall later introduce taxation and current government expenditure.

An increase in investment (I) will shift the IS schedule (10) in the north-west quadrant of Figure 4.1 outwards, but will not affect the equilibrium in the north-west quadrant. In consequence, prices (p_2, and thus also p) will rise because of increased demand in the market for secondary sector goods (the supply of which is constrained by the trade balance) and thus real wages ($\bar{w}$) will fall, even though employment (L) is maintained. Secondary sector profits rise, generating a higher level of domestic savings (sR) to match exactly the increased investment. This is, of course, the canonical 'post-Keynesian' analysis of forced savings.[21] From the point of view of stabilization policy, it implies that a reduction in the rate of investment will not of itself reduce pressure on the external account because consumption will have a balancing effect upon demand. The implication for financial balances is that increased domestic saving, the counterpart of which is reduced consumption, will require a redistribution of income away from wages and towards profits. In terms of the accumulation balance (14) any reduction in external savings F will be met by increased savings (sR) for a given investment level; but this adjustment will come about because of the clearing mechanism of the domestic commodities market discussed in the previous section – 'shock (c)' – of this chapter.

The exact symmetry of this result depends to some extent upon the assumption of homogeneous production coefficients in the secondary sector for investment goods and consumer goods. However, it is reasonable to assume that the import coefficient for investment goods production (especially if this 'production' is, in fact, little more than installation) will be higher than that for consumer goods, and the employment coefficient will be lower. In other words, in Figure 4.1 the trade constraint curve (7) will be shifted downwards by the increased import coefficient (m) and the food constraint curve (8) will be shifted upwards by the reduced secondary employment (L_2), with even stronger effects on the real wage ($\bar{w}$) and employment (L) than if these coefficients remained unchanged.

The irreducible import component implicit in investment and consumption is one of the central elements in the structural interpretation of stabilization policy. In general, it is argued that attempts to rectify an imbalance in the external trade constraint by cuts in manufacturing output (Q_2) or real wages (w) will require a disproportionate recession in output and/or an unacceptable deterioration of income distribution.[22] Such an assertion can only be tested by reference to relevant parameter values, but it is clear that low values of the coefficients for consumption of imports (m) and food (a) will raise the elasticity of the relationship which expresses the required adjustment of the secondary sector to external (that is, Q_2, p_1) shocks. In the limiting case where there is no external credit ($F = 0$) or food consumption ($a = 0$), the elasticity would be effectively determined by the import coefficient alone.

Equation (9) can also be usefully expressed in terms of a 'real' exchange rate ($\bar{e} = e/w$), which yields the interesting result:

$$Q_2 = \frac{(\bar{e}p_1 - al_1)Q_1 + \bar{e}F}{(al_2 + \bar{e}p_3m)} \tag{15}$$

where the positive effect of an increase in the real exchange rate (that is, shift of income from wages to profits) on the level of industrial output consistent with the external constraint becomes evident.

The implications of this result are considerable, and even somewhat ironic. The process of import substitution will reduce the import coefficient (m); in which case the 'elasticity' will rise and adjustment via recession (that is, the reduction in Q_2 necessary to balance a given reduction in p_3/p_1) will be much more severe. Only when manufactured imports are either truly competitive producer goods or non-essential consumer goods can they be cut without disproportionate effects on domestic industry and employment. A lower food consumption coefficient (a) will also increase external vulnerability, as real wages have to be cut disproportionately in order to provide surplus products for export. Only when a strong manufacturing export base has been built up will reductions in real wages (that is, an increase in the real exchange rate) have a proportional and positive effect on exports as well as on imports. In sum, stabilization may well be much 'easier' (in terms of the required variations in real wages and employment) in either non-industrialized or fully industrialized economies, than in semi-industrialized ones.

In practice, however, stabilization policy has traditionally involved adjustments of the exchange rate in order to improve the trade balance (B):

$$B = p_1E - mp_3Q_2 \tag{16}$$

The direct effect of real exchange rate variation on exports may be found from (1) and (3), and the positive 'price elasticity' arises in fact from the effect of variations in food prices *and* industrial output on wagegoods demand:

$$E = Q_1 - \frac{a}{p_1\bar{e}}\,\{l_1Q_1 + l_2Q_2\} \tag{17}$$

$$\frac{\partial E}{\partial \bar{e}} = \frac{aL}{\bar{e}^2} - \frac{al_2}{p_1\bar{e}}\cdot\frac{\partial Q_2}{\partial \bar{e}} > 0 \tag{18}$$

In effect, I argue that in a foreign exchange-constrained economy, where domestic prices are determined by demand pressures rather than costs, the effect of devaluation on imports will be set by the level of industrial output, so *ex hypothesi* any change in exports will be matched by an equal change in imports as industrial output adjusts to foreign exchange availability. Differentiating (16) and substituting (7) yields:

$$\frac{\partial B}{\partial e} = p_1 \frac{\partial E}{\partial \bar{e}} - mp_3 \frac{\partial Q_2}{\partial E} \cdot \frac{\partial E}{\partial \bar{e}} = 0 \tag{19}$$

In other words, real devaluation may not affect the net trade balance (as in the standard structuralist models) but it does have a significant positive impact on exports and industrial output in this model. The impact arises, however, from the redistributive effect of the change in the real exchange rate, and the consequences of this for profits, rather than a neutral supply-response as in neoclassical models. The effect of a devaluation (that is, a higher e) is higher food prices, which reduce real wages and increase exports. This then allows industrial output to rise[23] due to greater import capacity, unless, of course, the newly released funds have to be allocated to service external debt (in other words, if F is reduced) or reserves are built up ($B > 0$). It is generally clear from inspection of the profit function (5), that devaluation (that is, raising the value of e) has the effect of increasing agrarian profits (R_1). The effect upon industrial profits (R_2) is more complex: if imports are not allowed to rise then production (Q_2) is stable, while demand (and prices) remain the same, so that profits fall through increased costs. Real wages will fall in either case, of course, as prices (p) rise. Differentiating (5) for fixed Q_2 yields:

$$\frac{\partial R_1}{\partial e} = p_1 Q_1 \tag{20}$$

$$\frac{\partial R_2}{\partial e} = -p_3 m Q_2 \tag{21}$$

Not only does the differential impact on the two sectors plausibly reflect the well-known conflict between farmers and industrialists on exchange-rate policy,[24] but also the net effect of devaluation on profits is in fact *negative* when export income is less than import expenditure, reflecting the overall decline of domestic expenditure.

$$\frac{\partial R}{\partial e} = p_1 Q_1 - p_3 m Q_2 = -F \tag{22}$$

This positive result of currency devaluation on the balance of payments depends crucially upon the nominal wage rate (w) remaining constant or at least the real exchange rate ($\bar{e} = e/w$) being raised. If wages are adjusted due to, for instance, trade union response to the sort of 'stagflation' generated by external shocks of the type analysed in the previous section, then there will be an upward shift in domestic demand, which will lead to an increase in industrial profits, because the price (p_2) inflation will outweigh the increased wage costs. The effect on primary sector profits will be obviously negative;[25] and the overall result will be a reduction in profits. Differentiating (5) after substituting (9) yields:

$$\frac{\partial R}{\partial w} = -\frac{a}{s} L \tag{23}$$

The higher nominal wage rate will lead to further external disequilibrium if prices (p_2) are not allowed to rise to choke off imports, but will also reduce export availability by shifting (8) downwards in the north-east quadrant of Figure 4.1. Real wages will fall, as will employment; but the real wage will still be above its previous level because food prices are not affected. Thus, while the industrial sector is relatively 'protected' from variations in wage rates and exchange parities, the primary sector profits are highly vulnerable to both. The interplay between these three variables is, therefore, a central concern of what might be termed the 'political economy of stabilization'.

In practice, reaction to pressure on profit margins in the export sector is usually the factor which forces a government into devaluation, either because of political protest (a form of 'monopoly power') or because producers shift out of exportable (Q_1) production to other, more profitable, activities. We can express this by adding an additional constraint to our model, in terms of the minimally acceptable primary sector profit rate (r_1) for exporters, so that:

$$e p_1 \geq (1 + r_1) w l_1 \tag{24}$$

In this case, there will clearly exist a determinate minimum value for the real exchange rate ($\bar{e}$), which will vary with world prices (p_1) and labour productivity in the sector (l_1), and thus may change considerably over time:

$$\bar{e} \geq (1 + r_1)\frac{L_1}{p_1} \tag{25}$$

This will in turn determine the upper value of the real wage (w) from (11), although it should be noted that the effect becomes progressively less important as the food share (a) in the wagegoods consumption basket declines, as is expected to occur during industrialization. However, in practice, even this maximum real wage is not easily reached, for each nominal wage rise is countered by business pressure for a devaluation. Thus it is necessary for the government to set the two simultaneously in order to avoid a continuous wage-parity spiral – unless, of course, it is willing either to freeze wages or subsidize exporters. Unless a new real exchange rate can be set so that solution (15) is reached without difficulty, so to speak, then an inflationary spiral (exacerbated by budget deficits) can easily become acute enough to be classified as 'hyperinflation'. At this point, any redistributive impact in favour of profits is outweighed by the effect of uncertainty on planned investment, and as Kalecki (1962) points out, direct political realignment is usually required in order to stabilize the situation.

4.5 FISCAL POLICY

The next step is to introduce the fiscal sector into my analysis. I am particularly interested in elucidating not only the macroeconomic incidence of budget imbalance, with its implications for financial and monetary policy, but also that of fiscal income and expenditure themselves. This I shall do by expanding my definition of the accumulation balance.

The expansion of the model involves the definition of taxation (T), current government expenditure (G) and public investment (I_g). Firstly, we define the level of activity, or 'service output', of the government (Q_3). The overall employment level (L) is now redefined from (3) to yield, for a given government employment coefficient (l_3):

$$L = l_1Q_1 + l_2Q_2 + l_3Q_3 \tag{26}$$

I assume planned public investment demand (I_g) is determinate in the short run and costed at the domestic industrial price level (p_2), so total government expenditure (G) is thus:

$$G = Q_3 w l_3 + p_2 I_g \tag{27}$$

The tax system is defined as being made up of two categories: tax rates on wages (t_1) and on profits (t_2). Each rate includes both direct income taxes and indirect taxes on consumption, in terms of effective incidence: that is, the proportion of factor income actually paid in tax (FitzGerald, 1978b). In the case of profits tax (t_2) I apply the rate only to that part which is not reinvested by firms. There is, therefore, a tax income (T) of:

$$T = t_1 W + (1 - s) t_2 R \tag{28}$$

Equation (1) for the primary goods market must be redefined to allow for post-tax wage expenditure, remembering that employment (L) now includes the government (26):

$$e p_1 Q_1 = a W (1 - t_1) + e p_1 E \tag{29}$$

Equation (2) for the clearing of the market in secondary sector goods must also be expanded, allowing for investment by the government (I_g) as well as in the private sector ($I_p = I_1 + I_2$):

$$p_2 Q_2 = (1 - a)(1 - t_1) W + (1 - s)(1 - t_2) R + (I_g + I_p) p_2 \tag{30}$$

From this formulation it is immediately clear that any particular level of E and Q_2 imposed by the external constraint (equation (7) in the north-east quadrant of Figure 4.1) is now in principle compatible with any desired income distribution.[26] In effect, three new equations (27) to (29) have been added into my six-equation system, but so have six new variables (T, G, Q_3, I_g, t_1, t_2). Even if expenditure commitments (Q_3, I_g) are set according to a development plan or even a structural adjustment programme, two degrees of freedom remain in order to set the two tax rates (t_1, t_2). There is no technical reason, therefore, why a stabilization programme should necessarily lead to a reduction in real wages or in government expenditure; appropriate dividend taxes (t_2) could be applied in order to stabilize aggregate demand. This is what

Kalecki holds to be the 'gist of the problem of financing development'.[27] Savings would not be reduced thereby, and although long-run private investment perspectives might be altered, strategic investments could enjoy special tax incentives or be replaced by state investment. Political considerations with respect to income distribution are another matter, needless to say. This tax structure could, of course, lead to a budgetary balance ($D = T - G$) which could be either positive or negative, depending on the macroeconomic and distributive balance desired.

From (29) it is also clear that, in principle at least, any required level of government activity is compatible with given stability conditions, with the same proviso as before. By the same token, such stability need not necessarily bear down on real wages by increasing industrial prices (p_2). At the very least, it may be concluded from this analysis that a stabilization policy package must contain explicit and progressive tax provisions, if poverty criteria are to be applied – an aspect which is generally absent from current neo-orthodox stabilization packages.[28] It is unfortunate, therefore, that the tradition of public sector development economics and the debate on tax reform (which used to be conducted under the aegis of the World Bank and the IMF themselves) appears to be dormant.[29]

However, expanded government activity on current account (Q_3) will raise demand for primary sector output (in other words, food) through an increased aggregate wage bill (W) due to greater public sector employment. Thus the balance of payments will be negatively affected by expanded state expenditure even if the budget is in balance, unless taxes on wages (t_1) are raised sufficiently in order to keep the overall wage bill stable.[30] Taxes on profits would not achieve this result, as capitalists are assumed not to consume food (that is, exportables), or at least to have a much lower propensity than workers to do so. From (29) we have:

$$\frac{\partial E}{\partial Q_3} = \frac{\partial L}{\partial Q_3} = \frac{al_3}{p_1\bar{e}}(1 - t_1) \tag{31}$$

As before, the higher the degree of primary sector integration to world markets, the greater the balance-of-payments impact of budget *size* (Q_3); and thus the rate of wage taxation (t_1) required to counteract it. In other words, it is very difficult for a highly open primary-exporting economy to maintain a commitment to basic needs provision through public-sector expenditure.

An optimal tax policy to achieve budgetary balance *and* preserve macroeconomic equilibrium depends upon the impact on aggregate demand of the component parts of the budget. Specifically, a macroeconomically neutral budget requires private sector demand for the two commodities to be reduced by the same amount as government expenditure increases them, so that both

$$at_1w(L_1 + L_2) = awL_3(1 - t_1) \tag{32}$$

and

$$(1 - a)t_1(L_1 + L_2) + t_2(1 - s)R = (1 - a)wL_3(1 - t_1) + I_gp_2 \tag{33}$$

'Optimal' tax rates (t_1*, t_2*) can now be derived in the sense of those rates which secure both budgetary balance ($T = G$) and leave the balance of payments (B) and domestic inflation (p_2) unchanged, for a given level and composition of government expenditure (Q_3, I_g). Thus from (32) and (33):

$$t_1* = \frac{Q_3L_3}{L}; \; t_2* = \frac{I_gp_2}{(1 - s)R} \tag{34}$$

In other words, the government wagebill should be financed from wage taxes and investment from taxes on distributed profits.

It is true that a compensating change in the tax structure (that is, t_1/t_2) could have been applied at the same time as the deficit was generated, in order to correct the income distribution. However, if this had been feasible, then it would presumably have been more rational to have restored the fiscal equilibrium in the first place.

The accumulation balance (12) must now be redefined because (33) has replaced (2) as the expression for industrial demand. This gives us again, as the result of the clearing of the two product markets, the familiar savings–investment relation:

$$eF + sR = p_2I_p + (G - T) \tag{35}$$

In the case where external credit (F) is given and the exchange rate (e) stable; then, in the short run, the impact of an increased fiscal deficit is to raise profits through inflation, in the manner discussed above for autonomous expenditure, and to reduce exports (and thus imports and industrial output) by increased wagegoods demand. Supposing that a certain proportion (g) of total government expenditure (G) is allocated to current expenditure, then:

$$\frac{\partial E}{\partial D} = -\frac{ag}{ep_1}\ ;\ \frac{\partial Q_2}{\partial G} = -\frac{ag}{emp_3}$$

Simultaneously, of course, the exchange rate (e) may have to be adjusted upwards in order to maintain capacity utilization in the primary (exportable) sector (24). This result indicates that a lesser degree of trade openness (higher 'a' in the sense that most exportables are consumed locally) or reduced access to foreign credits (low 'F') clearly makes the required exchange rate adjustment to budget deficits (with the consequences for income distribution between classes and between sectors that we have already discussed) more acute, with clear consequences for domestic price levels. In other words, the net effects are highly 'stagflationary'.

Last, but not least, we turn to the complete impact of the fiscal deficit on the external balance when external credit *is* freely available (that is, F becomes an endogenous variable). Although such an analysis is often framed in terms of the Monetary Approach to the Balance of Payments, it can be expressed just as well in terms of the accumulation balance (35). At first sight, an increased fiscal deficit would yield an equal increase in the need for foreign finance, suitably adjusted by the exchange rate, from (35).

This result is frequently stated in New Orthodox policy documents (see, for example, IBRD 1983, 1988) but ignores the adjustment of the private sector (that is, sR) as well as the composition of fiscal income and expenditure – and thus by implication, that of the deficit itself.

In fact, differentiation of (34) yields:

$$\frac{dF}{dD} = \frac{1}{e}\left\{1 - s\frac{dR}{dD}\right\} \tag{36}$$

From (5), with a price level (p_2) independent of the demand level (Q_2) – either set as a mark-up on unit costs or reflecting world prices – because foreign exchange is freely available, then for a given margin (r_2) on costs:

$$\frac{dR}{dD} = \frac{dQ_2}{dD} \cdot \frac{p_s r_2}{1 + r_2} \tag{37}$$

From (37) it is already clear that the derivative is positive, but to show this formally, we must rearrange the domestic demand equation (30) for industrial output; substituting (27) and (28). The 'odd' term at the end reflects the 'netting out' of the budgetary impact on food demand:

$$p_2Q_2 = (1-a)w(l_1Q_1 + l_2Q_2) + (1-s)R + p_2I_p + D - agG \quad (38)$$

Differentiating (38) and substituting into (37) finally gives us a result for the net impact of the budget deficit (D) on domestic profits (R); which is clearly positive:

$$\frac{dR}{dD} = \frac{(1-ag)(1+r_2)}{p_2(1+sr)} \quad (39)$$

We can thus conclude that:

$$\frac{dF}{dD} = \frac{1}{e}\left\{1 - \frac{s(1-ag)(1+r_2)}{p_2(1+sr_2)}\right\} < \frac{1}{e} \quad (40)$$

for the simple reason that the budget deficit increases savings from greater profits, so that the total burden of the budget deficit is *not* borne by the balance of payments.[31] Note, however, that the larger the proportion of current expenditure in the budget (g), the less this effect will be, due to the direct impact on exports.

4.6 MONEY AND BANKING

The last step in my argument is the introduction of banks and monetary categories into the model. I shall do this in a stylized, but hopefully realistic form, linking the monetary variables to 'real' variables as I did in the fiscal analysis. The objective of the exercise is to develop the accumulation balance in its full financial form, which requires the introduction of a separate banking sector. We assume that households hold only cash balances (as workers do not save and capitalists 'do their saving' in their enterprises before distributing dividends) and do not receive bank credits, but deposit-holding and credit-taking by households could be included in our model without great difficulty. We include small unincorporated enterprises in our basic model definition of 'enterprise' here, although the model could be expanded to include them as a different category (FitzGerald, 1990b).

We start by expanding the accumulation balance (36) further to its full form as defined in the United Nations System of National Accounts (UN, 1968) and discussed in Chapter 2. To build up the flow of funds, annual changes in the financial balances are defined for each of the four sectors: government, enterprises, households and banks. First, the government sector balances its budget deficit (D) by an increase (C_g) in its net bank borrowing, and by net new borrowing from abroad (F_g).

$$D = (G + p_2 I_g) - T = C_g + eF_g \tag{41}$$

Second, changes in the financial balance sheet of the enterprise sector are made up of changes in deposits in the banks (N) and their own fixed investments ($p_2 I_p$). These are the uses of its funds. The sources of funds for this sector are 'retained' or 'reinvested' profits (sR) and net new credit from the banks (C_p). Funds from abroad for the private sector enter through the banking system, which includes the Central Bank. The accumulation balance for the enterprise sector is thus:

$$N + p_2 I_p = sR + C_p \tag{42}$$

Third, households do not accumulate fixed capital as such but they do require cash balances to cover consumption expenditure. The increased cash balance (H) needed by households is a proportion (u) of the *increase* in wages plus distributed profit income (that is, profits not saved by firms) because we are assuming a single period only in this model, after tax (T).

$$H = u\Delta\{W + (1 - s)R - T\} \tag{43}$$

This means that we must also modify the definition of the overall accumulation balance of the economy (35) in order to allow for the macroeconomic savings implicit in the demand for transactions cash balances by households:

$$sR + eF + u\Delta(W + (1 - s)R - T) = D + p_2 I_p \tag{44}$$

Finally, we have the banking sector itself, which includes the Central Bank. The uses of funds (that is, increased assets) are made up of increased bank loans to the enterprise sector (C_p) and to the government (C_g). The sources of funds are increased liabilities in the form of deposits (N), foreign borrowing for the private sector (F_p) and monetary emission (H).

$$C_g + C_p = N + eF_p + H \tag{45}$$

This gives us total foreign borrowing by the economy as:

$$F = F_g + F_p \tag{46}$$

These four flow-of-funds balances are summarized in Table 4.1. By definition, they add up to the accumulation balance (36) for the economy as a whole, as domestic financial transactions between those four sectors must cancel out once the sectors are aggregated.

Table 4.1 Sectoral accumulation balances

Sector	*Flow of funds*			*Equation number*
	Sources		*Uses*	
Government	$C_g + eF_g$	=	D	(41)
Enterprises	$sR + C_p$	=	$N + p_2 I_p$	(42)
Households	$u\Delta[W + (1-s)R - T]$	=	H	(43)
Banks	$N + eF_p + H$	=	$C_g + C_p$	(45)
Economy	$sR + eF + u[\Delta W + (1-s)R - T]$	=	$D + p_2 I_p$	(44)

The effect of monetary variations in the model can be explored by looking at ways in which the Central Bank can finance the annual fiscal deficit (D). Assuming that the government can decide on the level of domestic credit it obtained (C_g), then this creates *ex ante* 'gap' in the flow of funds (45) for the banks (including the Central Bank itself) as foreign borrowing by the government (eF_g) is exogenously constrained or set according to debt service targets. From the banks' point of view (and all too often that of the IMF and the IBRD) any increase in credit to the government (C_g) must be balanced by an opposite variation in credit to the private sector (C_p), which would restrain aggregate demand but reduce production and investment or else an increase in high-powered money (H) supply, private borrowing abroad (F_p) or attract more deposits (N) with higher interest rates (IMF, 1987).

The definition of changes in money (M) covers increases in cash balances (H) and bank deposits (N):

$$M = H + N \tag{47}$$

Remember the equality of the supply of and the demand for money must hold *ex post* in accounting terms. By substituting (45) into (47), we obtain for the supply side:

$$M_s = C_g + C_p + eF_p \tag{48}$$

while on the demand side, by substituting (44), (41), (42) and (43) into (47), we have a rather heterodox 'demand for money' expression, based not on aggregate output (as in monetarist theory) but rather on sectoral liquidity requirements:

$$M_d = u\Delta[W + (1 - s)R - T] + (sR + C_p - p_2 I_p) \tag{49}$$

That (48) is equal to (49) follows by definition from the national accounting identities in Table 4.1. The key question is, of course, what macroeconomic changes take place as the *ex ante* gap in bank funding is converted to an *ex post* monetary balance?

The way in which monetary equilibrium is achieved depends upon the policy followed by the monetary authorities. Here we shall look at three possibilities: (i) a 'passive' policy, which expands government credit (C_g) without varying private credit (C_p) or foreign borrowing (F_p); (ii) where private credit is cut to compensate increased government borrowing; and (iii) where foreign borrowing is used to finance the gap. In the first case, the effect of changes in the fiscal deficit on changes in the money supply (M) is simply found by substituting (41) into (48) and differentiating:

$$\frac{\partial M_s}{\partial D} = \frac{\partial C_g}{\partial D} = 1$$

I have already analysed the impact on savings (through price adjustment and increased profits) of the excess demand generated by the budget deficit when the foreign exchange constraint binds, which it will in this first case. On the assumption that firms do not demand more credit (C_p) and that planned investment expenditure is maintained, then the effect can be traced through the change in profits (R) and wages (W). From (44):

$$\partial(sR - p_2 I_p) + u.\partial[w + (1 - s)R - T] = \partial D \tag{50}$$

As in this first case C_p and F_g are fixed, then from (42):

$$\partial N = \partial(sR - p_2 I_p)$$

and thus:

$$\partial N + \partial H = \partial D \tag{51}$$

so that, from (47), $M_s = M_d$ at all times.

In case (ii), where firms do demand more credit (C_p) to cover working capital needs (due to price rises, for instance) then we would observe a compensating effect on bank deposits (N) from (42), due to profits being previously determined. Although this would not change the result for broad money (M), its internal composition *would* change towards a greater share of bank deposits.

Finally, (iii) is the same as (ii) from the firms' point of view, and is, in fact, equivalent to the government borrowing situation discussed in the previous section. However, the unconstrained access to foreign exchange would allow output and profits to rise as in (39), so that demand for deposits (N) and cash (H) would rise to match the increased supply consequent on the monetarization of the foreign loans.

In other words, the monetary equilibrium is established as part of the macroeconomic process of adjustment to the deficit: there is no need to establish a specifically *monetary* causality. Of course, there will be a correlation between changes in the broad money supply (M) and prices (p_2) but this is *not* due to any causal relationship running from the former to the latter. Rather, it is the result of the fact that changes in the fiscal deficit (D) affect both the supply of and the demand for money in the same way.

In the case of fluctuation in external account (particularly E) arising from a fiscal deficit where external credit can be increased, the same sort of argument applies, because the balance-of-payments effect is already defined in (40). Thus the result would not be directly monetary as such, but rather the result of adjustment in the real economy. Once again, it is easy to show that there will *apparently* be a monetary effect on the balance of payments, as H and B will be correlated; but this only arises because *both* arise from changes within the economy. In other words, increased money supply must be caused by some real-side change, which itself has its *own* effects on aggregate demand in the economy.

In this sense, we can argue that in this sort of semi-industrialized economy money is essentially 'neutral' in the aggregate. However, such passivity could be held to depend on the assumption made so far that bank loans to government (C_g) are expanded on request and added to existing total credit. An active (or more precisely 'tight') credit policy would, of course, imply that any increase in C_g (that is, of finance for D) can be met by cutting business credit (C_p) with no increase in monetary supply (M) at all. The alternative, that of cutting credit to government (C_g), would require simultaneous policy decisions on taxation and expenditure; and are thus essentially questions of fiscal, and not monetary, policy. The effect of cutting business credit (C_p) depends upon the reaction of the enterprise sector itself, and thus upon its own reaction to forced changes in its financial structure. The simplistic monetarist assumption is usually that a reduction in bank credit to enterprises will reduce their investment (I_p). However, not only is this unlikely in the short run because investment decisions are lagged, but also the macroeconomic consequences are ignored. On the one hand, any increase in government expenditure (however financed) will increase profits and thus internal company funds (sR), as we have seen; while, on the other hand, reduced company credit can be balanced by reducing company deposits in the banks. In both cases, the enterprise restores its financial balance without changes in its real output or investment.

However, this conclusion does imply a further consideration. Firstly, it is necessary to explore the possibility of further modelling the balance sheets (in terms of stocks) of firms. To the extent that firms have a 'desired' capital structure (in order to maintain liquidity, gearing, and so on) then changes in financial flows may force them to adjust real variables such as profit distribution – that is, $(1-s)R$ – or even prices. Secondly, these changes clearly affect the level and composition of demand for money (M) and thus the degree of financial intermediation, which could also be modelled.

I have not defined any role for the rate of interest in my analysis, not only because of the logic of the results discussed above, but also because of the evidence that interest rates do not substantially affect the aggregate rate of saving or investment in developing countries. My approach to the accumulation balance as the underpinning of the financial sector does not imply that interest rates have no effect on the economy, but rather holds that this effect is incidental to stabilization and possibly rather different from what the New Orthodoxy would believe.[32] Two such effects do seem to be important. Firstly, high real interest rates can have an impact upon production costs,[33] particularly in industry. This would require redefining my pricing (28) and profit (5) equations appropriately, and would have the general effect of increasing costs if rates were raised. However, the extra 'rental' income generated for depositors would, in my model at least, restore profit income automatically and raise prices through greater consumption demand. The net result, therefore, would be lower real wages and stagflation. It is important to observe, however, that this redistribution will improve the balance of payments (E) and increase savings (sR) so that, in this sense, it does stabilize the economy. My point, however, is that this does not occur directly through 'price'-equilibration on the savings fund market. Secondly, higher interest rates will undoubtedly cause a shift in portfolio composition in the sense of encouraging capitalists to shift funds out of 'hoarding', or the informal sector, into bank deposits. This is held to increase efficiency, although we would doubt that investment is really increased or channelled towards more productive uses by such a transfer. None the less, this would be reflected in my model by the balance *within* the demand for 'broad' money ($H + N$), which would leave my sectoral accumulation balances (as set out in Table 4.1) essentially unchanged. However, a model distinguishing between credit to households and corporations would generate interesting distributional results.

4.7 CONCLUSION

The object of this chapter has been to translate the general propositions of my approach to finance in semi-industrialized economies set out in Chapter 1 into specific analytical form. The application of my method, based as it is upon the specific structures of the sectors that make up the economy and underlie the accumulation balance, must inevitably be specific rather than general. The model presented here, therefore, should be seen as an illustration of the method as applied to a stylized economy; any particular country study would contain the structural characteristics derived from empirical observation of how that economy is organized.

None the less, it would seem that two conclusions of general application can be drawn from my analysis. Firstly, that monetary and financial analysis can be linked directly to major 'real side' variables within a determinate organizational structure. This allows us to examine both the validity of general monetarist propositions, and the distributional consequences of various stabilization policies. In principle, this provides the basis for a critique of the 'New Orthodoxy' based on the plausibility of its assumptions about private-sector behaviour. Secondly, that it is technically possible to design stabilization policies in particular and, by implication, financial policies in general, that are consistent with targets for production and income distribution as part of a strategy of structural transformation to achieve economic development. This, in turn, has implications both for the practice of short-run macroeconomic management and for the revival of development planning as a feasible practice of state intervention.

5 Employment and the Public Investment Criterion

5.1 THE PROBLEM

The determination of the shadow wage rate (SWR) is relevant not only to the practical problem of estimating the opportunity cost of labour in public investment projects, but also to the wider macroeconomic issues of rural–urban migration, choice of technique, and the balance of savings and consumption in the economy as a whole. Although the idea of regarding 'surplus' labour as a more-or-less free resource available to the state, for the finance of public works in particular, is to be found in the classics, it became a central point in modern development theory through the work of Lewis (1954) and Nurkse (1953) and was integrated to project appraisal methodology by Little and Mirrlees (1974).

In this chapter I extend the 'orthodox' analysis of the economic cost of generating employment in the modern sector of a semi-industrial economy beyond the internal migratory impact and the existence of urban 'underemployment', to include the effect of an overall constraint upon the supply of wagegoods (that is, food) in the model. This Kaleckian modification has the advantage that macroeconomic aspects of the relationship between the 'modern' and 'traditional' sectors in the economy can be made explicit. The problem arose in a policy context in the context of the planning of public investment in Peru during the 1970s,[1] where the state exercised widespread control over the modern sector of the economy and accounted for the bulk of modern investment, but the food supply was stagnant (due to the nature of peasant agriculture) and the import allocation for foodstuffs constrained. The problem of internal migration was also a serious one, with the reasonable suspicion that further employment in the modern sector would not reduce the already large urban petty service sector but rather exacerbate the rural exodus; expectations which were borne out by the experience of the subsequent decade. Public investment decisions geared to employment creation generated the need to establish the shadow wage rate for use in the Peruvian national planning system.

The key concept in the shadow wage rate discussion is the opportunity cost of labour absorbed by the modern sector (particularly on public investment projects) and this is expressed in terms of the effect on production in other sectors and the impact upon the consumption–savings balance in the economy as a whole. The original excursion into the field of the SWR by A. Lewis[2] supposes the existence of only two sectors in his formulation (urban–modern and rural–traditional) and a zero marginal product of labour in agriculture. Thus the absorption of labour into the modern sector does not reduce wagegoods supply, and as the equilibrium modern sector wage is assumed to be equal to average rural income (that is, the supply price), the shadow wage (that is, opportunity cost of labour to the economy as a whole) is thus zero.

Little and Mirrlees[3] introduce a positive marginal product in agriculture and an institutionally determined modern sector wage to their model for determining the SWR, which has subsequently become the orthodox methodology in this field. However, they avoid the wagegoods supply problem (and incidentally the internal-terms-of-trade issue as well) by taking wagegoods (that is, food) to be 'traded' so that domestic prices are exogenously determined by world market prices, and the effect of labour shifts on output and consumption are entirely reflected in the balance of payments. Harris and Todaro[4] develop the idea of an equilibrium relationship between urban unemployment, modern employment, and rural income. Although their conception of urban unemployment and migration based on the probability of obtaining modern employment seems inappropriate to many developing economies (as John Weeks[5] has pointed out), the idea can be reformulated (as I do below) to allow for low-income urban activity while retaining the valuable analytical concept of an internal migratory equilibrium. David Newbery[6] includes some aspects of wagegoods supply response, but in the narrower context of a two-sector model, and without the import constraint discussed here. The oversimplified Todaro scheme is, however, maintained in many policy models such as Squire (1981) or Cole and Sanders (1985), despite the evidence (Williamson, 1988) that job allocation is not a lottery, that migrants do not respond to discounted expected earnings, and that the 'informal' labour market has distinct behaviour. The main objective of this chapter, therefore, is the examination of the analytics of a labour market segment in three sectors within an overall constraint on wagegoods supply and the effects of changes in employment on accumulation and growth.

The accepted definition of the SWR (W) has two parts. Firstly, there is the net loss in current output (x) as a consequence of the modern sector withdrawing labour from other 'traditional' sectors for, say, employment on a public investment project. Secondly, to this 'static' effect is added the increase in workers' consumption (z) multiplied by the net cost of this (λ) to the economy as a whole, in so far as savings are reduced and thus future consumption forgone – the 'dynamic' effect.

$$Wx + \lambda z$$

The chaper proceeds by exploring a simple algebraic model of the three-sector labour market discussed above, examining the effect upon output (x) and consumption (z) of a small expansion in modern employment. The result of imposing a constraint upon imports of wagegoods is examined, and some general conclusions drawn. Then some illustrative parameter values are imputed to the model in order to indicate the orders of magnitude involved. Finally, the nature of the 'savings cost' in employment is discussed. Although the overall viewpoint is that of Latin America,[7] the systemic characteristics such as structural inelasticity of wagegoods supply, a large urban service sector, chronic balance-of-payments difficulties, and extreme concentration of income are common to semi-industrial economies.

5.2 A MODEL OF LABOUR ALLOCATION

We divide the economy into three sectors: 'modern', 'petty' (urban tertiary), and 'peasant'.[8] The *modern* sector is concerned with exports (including agribusiness), basic industry, large-scale manufacturing, government, certain services (for example, banking), and so on – all organized along 'corporate' lines, with high capital allocation per worker. The *petty* sector is made up of small family firms, services, and petty traders, organized on 'household' lines, and trading with the modern sector. The *peasant* sector is concerned with production of food (that is, wagegoods). A 'dual' economy exists in the sense that there are sharp differences in productivity and income between the 'modern' and the two 'traditional' sectors, and this duality is repeated through primary, secondary, and tertiary production; but they are very much interdependent. The petty sector subsists on the basis of the demand generated by the employees of the modern sector, while the peasant sector supplies the food requirements of urban areas. The modern sector draws its new labour from one of the two traditional sectors, as well as selling modern goods (particularly manufactures) to them.

I start with a definition of the work force of the modern (L_1), petty (L_2), and peasant sectors (L_3) standardized as proportions of the total work force:

$$L_1 + L_2 + L_3 = 1 \tag{1}$$

Given the nominal wage rate (w) in the modern sector, determined by institutional factors such as legislation and trades union pressure (that is, independently of the variables in this model), and modern employment (L_1), set by technology, output and installed capacity (and thus also exogenous), we have the modern wage bill (wL_1). As a first step in the explicit linking of the sectors we shall assume that the modern sector workers spend a certain proportion (β) of this wage bill on services, commercial distribution, and other output of the petty sector. This expenditure is divided among the petty work force, whose marginal economic product is assumed to be negligible. By this we mean that the petty sector is organized in a competitive manner such that an extra street trader does not increase total sales but receives the average income in such activities. we can thus define an average income per petty worker (u):

$$u = \beta w L_1 / L_2 \tag{2}$$

There is no shortage of candidates for employment in the modern sector, due to the income differential ($w > u$) and for analytical purposes it is assumed that peasants migrate in from rural areas to join the petty sector so long as average income there is higher than in their own sector (a), until the equilibrium:

$$u = a \tag{3}$$

is established.[9] The market-clearing mechanism is thus the declining value of the average share in urban service income as the number of participants (L_2) increase. This allows the establishment of the equilibrium work force allocation (as modern employment (L_1) is exogenously determined) from (2) and (3):

$$a = \beta w L_1 / L_2 \tag{4}$$

and substituting into (1) gives

$$L_3 = 1 - L_1\left(1 + \frac{\beta w}{a}\right) \tag{5}$$

and thus

$$L_2 = \frac{\beta w}{a} L_1 \tag{6}$$

The total wagegoods supply in the economy is peasant output (A) plus imports of food (M). To specify the supply relationship between modern and peasant sectors, it is assumed that a certain proportion (α) of the rural product is exchanged for modern-sector products (for example, manufactures) required by the peasants. This transfer might take the form of taxation, of course, although increasingly specific taxes on peasants (for example, land duties, marketing boards) inherited from colonial administrations have mostly been dismantled. This 'marketed surplus' (A) will form the basis of the food supply to the urban work force ($L_1 + L_2$). When imports (M) are included, the equilibrium in the food market is:

$$\alpha A + M = (1 - \beta)wL_1 + uL_2 = wL_1 \tag{7}$$

In the case where the real wage is fixed ($\bar{w}$) as a policy objective, and imports of food are allowed freely (that is, food is a 'traded good') then we find

$$M = L_1 - \alpha A \tag{8}$$

remembering also that

$$a = \frac{A}{L_3} \tag{9}$$

so that

$$L_3 = 1 - L_1(1 + \beta L_3/A) \tag{10}$$

and

$$L_2 = \beta \bar{w} L_1 . L_3/A \tag{11}$$

This I shall call the 'neo-orthodox' model, as it contains the essence of the Little–Mirrlees approach combined with a modified Todaro-style explanation of migratory equilibrium. There is still no constraint on wagegoods supply.

We can now turn to the consequence of a constraint upon the availability of wagegoods. In effect, imports of food are assumed to be constrained as, say, a proportion of total imports ($M = \bar{M}$). This would seem to be a realistic depiction of policy-making where the allocation of foreign exchange (particularly between wagegoods and capital goods imports) is treated as an independent decision prior to and not as a result of project choices. We now balance the supply and demand for food in urban areas by allowing for a *variable* real wage ($\bar{w}$) as the adjustment mechanism:

$$\alpha A + \bar{M} = \bar{w}L_1(1-\beta) + \bar{u}L_2$$
$$= wL_1$$

$$\bar{w} = \frac{\alpha A + \bar{M}}{L_1} \qquad (12)$$

Substituting (12) into (5), we get

$$L_3 = 1 - L_1\left\{1 + \frac{\beta(\alpha A + \bar{M})}{aL_1}\right\}$$
$$= \frac{1 - L_1}{1 + \beta(\alpha + \bar{M}/A)} \qquad (13)$$

This I shall call the 'structuralist' model, being the 'neo-orthodox' model with the wagegoods supply constraint added. It implies the effective abandonment of the 'traded' nature of wagegoods, and thus introduces the internal terms of trade as a dependent variable expressed as food prices in relation to the modern-sector wage rate.

5.3 THE OPPORTUNITY COST OF EMPLOYMENT

Having set up the model, we can now examine the effect upon production in the 'traditional' sectors of absorbing an extra unit of labour into the modern sector. Changes in the petty work force (L_2) do not affect aggregate output, so that the production effect will be confined to agricultural output (A). This ignores the 'cost of urbanization' implicit in the migratory effect, but this could easily be included.

We are required to solve:

$$\frac{dA}{dL_1} = \frac{da}{dL_3} \cdot \frac{dA_3}{dL_1} \tag{14}$$

Defining the marginal product in peasant agriculture:

$$m = \frac{dA}{dL_3} \tag{15}$$

and remembering that

$$a = \frac{A}{L_3} \tag{9}$$

we can easily resolve (14) for the neo-orthodox case by differentiating (5):

$$\frac{dL_3}{dL_1}\left\{1 + \frac{L_2}{L_3}\left(1 - \frac{m}{a}\right)\right\} = \left\{1 + \frac{\beta\bar{w}}{a}\right\}$$

$$\frac{dL_3}{dL_1} = -\left\{1 + \frac{L_2}{L_1}\right\} / \left\{1 + \frac{L_2}{L_3}\left(1 - \frac{m}{a}\right)\right\} \tag{16}$$

For realistic parameter values (for example, $L_3 > L_1$),

$$\frac{dL_3}{dL_1} = -1$$

that is, the creation of one modern job attracts more than one peasant to the towns, as the petty urban work force is increased by the expanded demand for services ($dL_2/dL_1 > 0$).

It is interesting to note that in the case where there are no scale effects in peasant output (that is, $m = a$), then:

$$\frac{dL_3}{dL_1} = -\left(1 + \frac{L_2}{L_1}\right)$$

In other words, for a given real wage rate, petty urban employment will expand in proportion to modern employment, a result similar to that obtained by Todaro (1969) and repeated in Cole and Sanders (1985), but with a different – and in my view more plausible – explanation for migration: the search for informal sector earnings rather than the expectation of modern sector employment. Moreover, in the case where no petty urban sector exists ($L_2 = 0$), the neo-orthodox solution naturally reduces to:

$$\frac{dL_3}{dL_1} = -1$$

which is the original Lewis/Little and Mirrlees 'orthodox' result.

Turning now to the structuralist model, the real wage rate ($\bar{w}$) has become a dependent variable, while the import component ($\bar{M}$) of supply is fixed. We must now solve (14) by differentiating (13) to yield:

$$\frac{dL_3}{dL_1} = -\left\{\frac{1-L_1}{L_3} - \beta\frac{\bar{M}}{A}\frac{m}{a}\right\}^{-1}$$

$$= -\left\{1 + \frac{L_2}{L_3} - \frac{L_2}{L_1}\frac{\bar{u}}{\bar{w}}\frac{\bar{M}}{A}\frac{m}{a}\right\}^{-1} \qquad (17)$$

Generally, we would expect that the contents of the brackets would be greater than unity, because from (7) and (11) we have $\alpha\beta > 0$ and $\bar{u}/\bar{w} < 1$ so that:

$$-1 < \frac{dL_3}{dL_1} < 0$$

and thus:

$$\frac{dL_2}{dL_1} < 0$$

In other words, when food supply is constrained expanding modern employment by one job will draw in *less than one peasant*, and thus *reduce* the urban petty work force – because the effect of greater employment is to reduce the real wage. The crucial economic assumptions here are that this change will not affect the supply of labour to the modern sector, nor the propensity of modern labour to purchase petty output (β), nor the peasant propensity to supply food to urban areas (α). These simplifications seem reasonable in the Latin-American context, particularly the first and last.[10] An absolute reduction in the real wage might take place through the inflated wagegood prices, but in a *growing* economy all that is required for this result is that the real wage should grow more slowly than would otherwise have been the case.

The relevant solution needed can now be found in the calculation of the SWR. In particular, the loss in production (x) and the workers' consumption increment (z). I do not consider the problem of 'shadow-pricing' output and consumption itself, which may be necessary where domestic relative commodity prices are very different from their counterparts on the world market. In the neo-orthodox case (subscript n), we have:

$$x_n = m\left(1+\frac{L_2}{L_1}\right)/\left\{1+\frac{L_2}{L_3}\left(1-\frac{m}{a}\right)\right\} = m.\phi \tag{18}$$

and as the real wage is fixed,

$$z_n = \frac{dM}{dL_1} + \frac{dA}{dL_1} = \bar{w} - x_n = \bar{w} - m\phi \tag{19}$$

In the structuralist case (subscript s), we have:

$$x_s = m\left\{1+\frac{L_2}{L_3} - \frac{L_2}{L_1}\frac{u}{w}\frac{\bar{M}}{A}\frac{m}{a}\right\}^{-1} = m\theta \tag{20}$$

and as imports are fixed:

$$z_s = \frac{dA}{dL_1} = -m\theta \tag{21}$$

To determine the SWR, however, a cost (λ) must be assigned to the increment in workers' consumption, taking into account any consequent loss in savings and thus future consumption. Although this will be discussed further below, the orthodox approach will be used here. In terms of the relative valuation of savings and consumption, the increase in workers' consumption means a savings loss, which in real terms might be expressed as an increase in food imports leading to a decrease in capital goods imports. The 'savings cost' parameter (λ) will vary between zero, when aggregate savings are considered adequate, to unity, when savings are very highly valued and all extra consumption is an absolute cost (Little and Mirrlees, 1974).

The definitional equation given above can now be substituted into the shadow wage rate (W):

$$W = x + \lambda z \tag{22}$$

for the two cases, to give:

$$\begin{aligned} W_n &= m\phi + (\bar{w} - m\phi)\lambda \\ &= m\phi(1 - \lambda) + \bar{w}\lambda \end{aligned} \tag{23}$$

$$W_s = m\theta(1 - \lambda) \tag{24}$$

On the reasonable assumption that there are still more peasants than modern workers ($L_3 > L_1$) in the semi-industrialized economy, although, of course, urban population may well be greater than rural ($L_2 + L_3 > L_1$), we have:

$$\phi > 1 > \theta$$

and also by definition, if savings and consumption are to be justified at all,

$$1 \geq \lambda \geq 0$$

and therefore:

$$W_n > m > W_s$$

In general, then, it would appear that in the 'structuralist' case the SWR is not only less than that for the 'neo-orthodox' case but also very small indeed, being less than the marginal product in food agriculture. This is because, under reasonable assumptions, the creation of one job in the modern sector (L_1) reduces employment in agriculture by less than one man, and hence the shadow wage is *less* than the marginal product in rural areas. A series of public investment decisions (for example, choice of technique and the viability of labour-intensive projects) taken on the basis of the former rather than the latter calculation might, therefore, lead to unfortunate consequences for employment and income distribution.

5.4 AN ILLUSTRATIVE SOLUTION

In this section, some illustrative data for the Peruvian case are imputed to the model in order to indicate the orders of magnitude involved. Before doing so, however, some conceptual difficulties in measurement should be mentioned. Although all the parameters and variables have an empirical meaning (unlike, say, concepts such as 'perceived probability of employment' or 'disutility of work') it still remains true that the estimation process itself will be dependent upon the specific form of the model. In particular, the assumption of homogeneity within each sector will be reflected in the average values derived from the data. Certain aspects of the model might be tested over time, however, particularly the relationship between the modern wage bill and petty-urban workers on the one hand, and the equilibrium between petty-urban and peasant income on the other. Finally, of course, there is the well-known elusiveness of the marginal product of labour in peasant agriculture.

As an example of the possible orders of magnitude involved, the Peruvian data[11] are typical of many semi-industrial economies. In approximate figures (defining the 'modern' sector as enterprises of more than ten employees, and 'urban' as towns of over 20 000 population: 'peasants' being the remainder), the set of variate values for 1972 is:

$$L_1 = 0.29; \quad L_2 = 0.24; \quad L_3 = 0.47;$$

$$\frac{u}{w} = 0.62; \quad \frac{m}{a} = 0.35; \quad \frac{M}{A} = 0.28;$$

This data set yields, for the net migratory effect in the 'neo-orthodox model':

$$\frac{dL_3}{dL_1} = -1.19; \quad \frac{dL_2}{dL_1} = +0.19$$

while in the 'structuralist model', the results are:

$$\frac{dL_3}{dL_1} = -0.68; \quad \frac{dL_2}{dL_1} = -0.32$$

There is thus a significant difference between the two models as far as employment policy is concerned, as well as in estimating the SWR. We already have, from the data set:

$$\frac{m}{w} = \frac{m}{a} \cdot \frac{u}{w} = 0.22$$

Finally, the effect of the 'savings cost' parameter is quite different in the two models. In the structuralist case, differentiating (24), we have unambiguously:

$$dW_s/d\lambda < 0$$

while for the neo-orthodox case (23):

$$\frac{dW_n}{d\lambda} = -m\phi + \bar{W}$$

and thus the directionality depends upon parameter values.

If, in the absence of other information (without prejudice to the argument in the next section), the relative valuation ratio between consumption and savings is set as:

$$\lambda = ½$$

then the complete result for the shadow wage rate expressed as a ratio (w) of the nominal wage rate, is in the 'neo-orthodox' case:

$$w_n = \frac{W_n}{w} = 0.69$$

These results might well be compared with what would be the original 'orthodox' formulation for the shadow wage rate (W_3), which turns out to be quite similar to the 'modified-orthodox' solution in this case:

$$w_o = \frac{W_o}{w} + \frac{m + (w - m)\lambda}{w} = 0.61$$

In the 'structuralist' case:

$$w_s = \frac{W_s}{w} = 0.08$$

the substantial difference between shadow wage rate in the two models is now clear, and is repeated over the range of parameter values for the 'savings coefficient' (λ).

5.5 THE EFFECT OF WAGE-CONSUMPTION INCREMENTS

We turn next to a brief discussion of the concept of 'savings cost' (λ) consequent upon the wage-consumption increment (z) included in the orthodox analysis. The effect that an investment increment might have on future consumption (upon which see the exploration by Newbery[12] in the context of a dual growth model, and also Chapter 6 below) will not be discussed here, but rather whether it is justifiable to assume that the workers' increment in consumption does, in fact, lead to an equal decrease in capital formation.

In the Little–Mirrlees model the effect is quite clear because the modern and public sectors are coterminous, there is a constraint on taxation, and any decrease in government current account surplus arising from the greater wage bill can be assumed to bring about a reduction in investment. In my 'modified orthodox' formulation, the same effect occurs through the increase in food imports and decrease in capital goods imports. In the constrained model, however, the impact of increased consumption is on domestic wagegoods supply and it is not clear that this would affect savings at all. The main analytical difficulty seems to be the orthodox supposition that a higher real wage bill will necessarily reduce savings. In terms of the public sector, the capital account as a whole (see Chapter 2) is made up of taxation (T), current (G) and capital (I_g) expenditure on the one hand, and domestic (D) and foreign (F_g) borrowing on the other:

$$T - (G + I_g) \equiv D + F_g$$

There seems no *general* reason to assume that public expenditure (G) and investment (I_g) are the only variates (that is, $dI_g = -dG$), which is what the orthodox model implies. It would seem just as reasonable to take, say, capital expenditure plans as given and allow changes in the public wage bill to affect other items of current expenditure (and thus a 'budgetary neutral transfer'), or possibly more realistically to increase borrowing requirements (D, F_g).[13] This, in turn, might affect private investment in other sectors if domestic finance were reduced or involve future resource transfers on foreign debt (see Chapter 3). Above all, it is difficult to believe that *in practice* high public wage rates are necessarily the cause of low state capital formation.

Logically, at an aggregate level, an increased wage bill might just as well lead to a reduction in middle-class 'salary' consumption out of profits as reduced savings. There is no evidence, indeed, that income concentration (that is, a high profit share in national income) is associated with high savings rates.[14] On the contrary, it can be argued that in so far as narrow domestic markets are a constraint on industrial expansion, and that it is market opportunities rather than finance (which can be obtained by reducing the high level of capitalist consumption) that determine the level of investment, an increase of the wage bill would *raise* investment and thus savings.[15] This is not a problem of Keynesian effective demand, but rather a matter of the *composition* of demand, a view widespread among structuralist economists as a result of the evident saturation of narrow domestic markets for the 'sophisticated' goods required by the middle class in the import-substitution process,[16] even though higher modern sector wage rates would exacerbate internal migration. In other words, savings behaviour cannot be reduced to assuming that a fixed proportion of all profits (including public enterprise surpluses) is reinvested, nor can all goods be taken as traded, thus excluding the problem of domestic demand. Thus the model of savings determination which underpins the orthodox approach to the SWR is clearly not valid for semi-industrialized economies. The high valuation of savings 'lost' by raising wages (λ) in the orthodox model further reinforces the bias against labour-intensity implied by the orthodox formulation of labour supply. Not only is this analytically incorrect, but it also has the unfortunate consequence of appearing to justify stabilization programmes based on wage repression (see Chapter 4) on the grounds that these will eventually create more employment.

5.6 THE PUBLIC INVESTMENT CRITERION AND THE ROLE OF THE STATE

In practice, the public investment programme in any developing economy forms the cutting edge of the planning process as well as a means of creating infrastructure and generating employment. Although policy instruments such as tariffs and investment licensing are also important, they depend upon certain reactions from private investors, and cannot be relied upon in the same way as the direct administration of public enterprise and government agencies. In principle, there are two ways of allocating the overall public sector investment budget to individual projects: *either* to set the output requirements centrally according to a predetermined bill of goods and then select the set of project variants that will achieve this at minimum cost, *or* to evaluate all possible project variants on the basis of their net contribution to economic output, selecting those with the greatest value at the margin. For a number of reasons, normally connected with the apparent failure of centralized planning in developing economies,[17] but equally attributable to the natural failure to implement it seriously in dependent capitalist economies,[18] the alternative model of planning by projects has become the favoured approach of the international 'aid' agencies and most of their client governments.

This model (Little and Mirrlees, 1974) decomposes the planning solution in that it allows decisions to be made project by project, which then add up to the best possible investment allocation. Decomposition in this sense is not quite the same as that implied by separability in the mathematical theory of decentralized planning, where the optimal prices set for use in project appraisal by the decentralized agencies are the dual solution of a programming exercise of which the centralized quantity planning solution is the primal.[19] It cannot be so because, in a typical developing economy, both the structure of production and the market price system are severely distorted. That is to say, they do not correspond to a Pareto optimum even with the existing distribution of income, which in turn is often highly undesirable. The methodological response to the first, structural, difficulty is to see public investment planning as a 'second best' approximation[20] to a local optimum. In other words, the object is to do the best that is possible to improve the existing production structure while controlling only public-sector projects. The response to the second, market, difficulty is to establish a series of shadow prices (corresponding to the opportunity cost of resources) which, when applied to inputs and outputs, ensure that a project with a positive net present value would make a positive contribution to aggregate economic value in the second-best sense. In addition (and this also applies to mature economies where market prices are conventionally taken as indicators of value) major 'externalities' of a project, such as the downstream effects of a large hydroelectric barrage, are usually taken into account.[21]

A central problem, therefore, is to establish an objective value for inputs and outputs which will allow projects to be evaluated at the margin: *empirically* in the sense of being calculated by the analyst from the economic evidence; and *independently* of government policy in that or other sectors.

In the approach recommended by the World Bank, United Nations, UK Overseas Development Administration, and the OECD,[22] the basis for decomposition, and the independent valuation of commodity inputs and outputs that makes it possible, is derived from the fact that the economies in question are price takers in the world economy: the border prices for imports and exports are exogenously set,[23] and even where they might vary with the volume of trade, the respective elasticity (and thus marginal revenue or cost) is given. Any input or output of a project which is currently imported or exported (not necessarily by the project), or will be if the project exists,[24] is classified as 'traded' and the opportunity cost of traded goods is expressed in terms of foreign exchange.[25] In effect, if all commodities in public projects were traded, then there would be only *one* commodity – foreign exchange – as all others could be converted to it at a fixed rate. In consequence, the project criterion would simply be to maximize net supply of this one commodity and an optimal production pattern could be achieved *without reference to the pattern of demand*. Whatever the 'bill of goods' required for consumption and investment, this would be the optimal supply pattern, the justification being the familiar one of comparative advantage, modified to take into account long-run costs over the project life. In effect, the maximum output of foreign exchange would guarantee the maximum supply of commodities, and decomposition could be achieved independently of the distorted domestic price patterns.

In the case of non-traded commodities such as water or electric power, their value as inputs (that is, opportunity cost) can be established by reference to the inputs required to produce an extra unit of a commodity, which can be reduced through the use of input–output techniques to a combination of traded goods, domestic labour and profits. Each of these can be valued in the new orthodoxy and although it is not our task to examine these methods here, it is worth pointing out (because I shall return to this point later on in the book) that in each case a precise definition of the role of the state is required to make them operational. Specifically, the 'planning discount rate' and the 'shadow wage rate' require a particular interpretation of state organization. To summarize the argument, the setting of the planning discount rate is supposed to result from the capital allocation process itself: the rate that will just allow enough projects through (that is, give then a positive present value) to balance the public investment budget. Clearly, then, the budgeting process must be organized in such a way as to produce this rate; if not, the rate will simply not exist. In practice, this difficulty is circumvented – rather than overcome – by using a conventional value combined with some form of administrative rationing.[26] In the case of the shadow wage rate, although the immediate opportunity cost of labour (for example, marginal productivity in peasant agriculture) may be a measurable parameter, the effect of greater employment (and thus wage bill) on accumulation depends once more upon the financial organization of the state.[27]

The neo-orthodox method[28] also includes provision for the use of 'income weights' to adjust the present value of a project according to the income effect upon different social groups – and specifically to bias project choice towards the poor. Underlying the obvious difficulties in giving consistent administrative effect to estimates of marginal utility of income is the fact that redistributive weighting must, in order to be taken seriously, form part of a wider process of social and economic reform.[29] This also requires a certain form of state intervention in the economy.

However, many goods and services in industrializing countries are 'non-traded' – either by their nature or by policy decision. The former group includes such commodities as electric power and water, and services such as road transport; there is normally no international trade in these, so there is no border price to use as a basis of valuation. The latter group includes those commodities that can be internationally traded but are not traded by the country in question as a result of government prohibition. This applies mainly to absolute protection against imports (a tariff does not prevent imports as an option) as part of a development strategy, for goods such as steel and foodstuffs. Here again the value of extra output is not the foreign exchange earned or saved, but its use-value to the domestic user. As the entire application of shadow pricing methods assumes that market prices are not a reliable guide to value, and consumer preferences not to be taken as the determinant of the production pattern, we cannot use these. Moreover, in the case of the output of public sector projects, the price will be related to production costs (modified by political and fiscal considerations) rather than an equilibrium market price, which it is usually the very purpose of public ownership to avoid.

In a limited number of cases, the marginal product of an extra unit of the non-traded good can be identified, as in the case of water supply to irrigate an import-substituting crop. But for this to be possible the output must be an intermediate good (that is, not a consumer good such as the household water supply) and destined for a single 'traded' use – the multiple uses of steel would prevent such identification. (It is in any case equivalent to redefining the project to include the final output and make the project output traded.) Thus for the majority of cases of non-traded output no marginal method of valuation is possible, and we seem to have come to a dead end. Even Lal (1974), in his otherwise excellent comparative survey, can only suggest that '...if the demand and supply for non-traded goods is always kept in balance...the Marginal Social Value of a non-traded good will equal its Marginal Social Cost' (pp. 11–12). This not only ignores the existence of shortages and monopoly profits in the private non-traded sector, but would also automatically prevent *any* investment in public non-traded output. Both IBRD (1975) and Little and Mirrlees (1974) suggest multiplying the market price by some ratio to reflect the relative value of users' and public income increments to find the Marginal Social Benefits. But the public non-traded output price is itself essentially arbitrary, and in any case not normally an equilibrium price – and if it were set at anything like cost, *any* investment could be justified.

The resolution of this problem cannot be found in the pursuit of a marginal valuation of non-traded output. Such a search is a category mistake: Gilbert Ryle's example[30] being (perhaps inevitably) that of a visitor to Oxford who, after seeing the colleges, schools, Bodleian Library and so on, enquires as to the whereabouts of the *University* – the mistake being to suppose that this last belongs to the same category as the others. Clearly, the output of non-traded goods must be set centrally, since it cannot be decided project by project. As domestic supply is the only source for the economy, production must be planned in relation to the input requirements of the other branches of the economy and the needs of the population. Once these output patterns are set, then the project variant that involves the minimum resource cost, in terms of traded and other inputs estimated in the way I have described, can be chosen without difficulty.

The setting of this output pattern involves a further theoretical problem, however, which finally leads us back squarely to the role of the state. The simplest way of setting the pattern is to anticipate market requirements in the normal way, and thus establish non-traded output as a response to the needs of the private sector and the consumer. The difficulty here is that the new orthodoxy specifically posits that this market is an inadequate measure of economic efficiency or social need, which is why, after all, shadow prices must be applied. In consequence, the input requirements of inefficient private enterprise and consumer demand distorted by income maldistribution ought not to be taken as a guide. Only if the public sector can also control *final* output can optimal decisions be made as to the supply of non-traded intermediate inputs, and only if the government has specific social development programmes can non-traded consumer goods and services be optimally programmed. These are, of course, necessary rather than sufficient conditions for consistency in the new orthodox method, and they have important implications for the role of the state in the economy.

Having outlined the requirement for state control of production implied by acceptance of the neo-orthodox method, we must attempt to ascertain the role of the state in the dependent capitalist economy that this requirement in its turn implies. This means, of course, an analysis of the political structure as well as purely administrative or legal arrangements. In fact, every government operates some form of investment licensing for the private sector, but this does not mean that the state plans or controls accumulation in the economy; whether it does or not depends upon the political structure, and particularly upon the relationship between the state and domestic capital. I cannot do justice to the complexity of the subject here,[31] but some form of typology is necessary if I am to complete my argument. I shall thus characterize, in a crude fashion, two types of state intervention in the economy – *support* and *control*.

The first case, and by far the more common one, is that of an economy where the state acts so as to support accumulation in the private sector, and thus the domestic bourgeoisie, probably in alliance with foreign enterprise. This support takes a number of forms, apart from the maintenance of a certain social structure: the provision of physical infrastructure such as roads; the supply of cheap industrial inputs such as power and steel; the extension of investment finance from development banks; and finally the grant of tariff protection and tax concessions to private enterprise. This process involves the transfer of surplus raised from taxation and foreign borrowing to the private sector, and the concentration of investment funds on its behalf; in terms of projects, it involves the choice of those that most increase capitalist profit and the adjustment of their output to the demands of the market. In consequence, we would hardly expect comprehensive planning of output, albeit in the modern sector, to be adopted even though the public sector might be at large. The control of the accumulation process by private capital (which might be predominantly foreign, of course) means that the state cannot undertake autonomous accumulation, and thus its intervention in the economy cannot work towards a restructuring of the system.

The second case, in contrast, occurs when the role of the state becomes more independent – by substitution for the domestic bourgeoisie – and an autonomous basis of accumulation is established in state capitalism. Surplus mobilization is centred on the state and the object of investment is not private profit but the economic development of the economy as a whole. The extent of redistribution depends on the exact combination of class forces controlling the state, but, given the élitist nature of state capitalism, it is unlikely that the poorer strata would benefit. In this case, central planning of the public sector, which itself will extend to cover most of the modern portion of the economy, will not only be present but also necessary to the articulation of the system. This combination of central planning and an economic development objective will then be consistent with the use of the new orthodox method in general and the resolution of the 'non-traded output' problem in particular. It is not that state control in the above sense is more desirable than state support for effective implementation of the method. The point is that, in the absence of direct state control of production, the new orthodox method ceases to be internally consistent.

It might still be asked whether the control measures open to any government – investment licences, credit facilities and tax concessions – might not be enough to ensure the adoption of the desired investment and output patterns in the private sector. But this contention reflects the illusion that the state is somehow 'above and beyond' the society in which it operates, while in fact it can only crystallize the dominant class formations,[32] and any independence gained comes about by direct participation in the relations of production – that is, by the direct administration of the dynamic elements of the economy. Even then, although domestic capital may be subsumed in its function to the state, the influence of transnational capital may inhibit such autonomy. In the case of the support state, then, we may argue that the traditional methodology of project appraisal,[33] which suggests that modified financial criteria should be used and public enterprise (confined to an infrastructural role) respond to the requirements of the market, is the more appropriate. Once it is admitted – albeit tacitly – that the expansion of private profit is the object of public investment, then the objections to the use of market criteria fall away.

This is not to say, from an objective point of view, that this is a desirable state of affairs, but rather that the methodology should correspond to reality. The 'distorted' markets and 'maldistribution' of income that the neo-orthodox methodology attempts to overcome are in fact highly beneficial to the domestic bourgeoisie – which includes not only the capitalist but also the senior bureaucrat – and they can only apply a decision criterion that sustains this. A relatively autonomous state apparatus can implement a wider 'efficiency' criterion involving shadow prices and central planning, but the redistributive aim is unlikely to carry much weight within the logic of state capitalism.

5.7 CONCLUDING REMARKS

In this chapter I have made an attempt to adjust the 'neo-orthodox' model of employment and the shadow wage rate used in evaluating public investment projects to the structural characteristics of the semi-industrialized economy, although my considerations probably apply more widely. My argument has involved the introduction of a petty urban service sector into the labour allocation model; the imposition of a constraint on wagegoods imports; and a critique of the simple 'savings cost' concept. Apart from adding realism, the first modification would tend to raise the SWR somewhat above that found in the neo-orthodox model, while the second would tend to reduce it substantially below, as would the third. By introducing illustrative data for Peru, the effect of the suggested changes can be seen to be substantial, and as far as the degree of reality is concerned, the import constraint and the urban service sector certainly correspond to semi-industrial experience, if not to the 'poor primary producer' basis for much of the original SWR analysis. The effective impact of expanding modern employment might even be seen as redistributing income within the modern working class (itself an élite compared with 'traditional' workers) rather than affecting resource allocation elsewhere in the economy. Over time, of course, the real wage rate would rise through the dynamic balance between the growth of modern wages and employment on the one hand and food production, import capacity, and population on the other. Finally, I have suggested that no system of shadow prices espoused by international aid agencies as an 'objective' criterion for public investment planning is itself derived from a particular view of the state in the dependent capitalist economy. The main conclusion of this chapter, however, is that the 'orthodox' method of calculating the shadow wage rate results in an excessively high estimate and thus might lead to an unwarranted bias among aid donors against the use of labour-intensive methods in public investment projects.

6 Financing Growth in the Mixed Economy

6.1 GROWTH AND INCOME DISTRIBUTION

Kalecki's interpretation of the 'problem of financing development' as the adjustment of planned aggregate output to the available supply of necessities (which we would now call basic needs), and the application of a progressive tax in order to reduce total consumption, has had a widespread influence on development economics.[1] Having explored the first, short-run version in Chapter 3, in this chapter I shall analyse the second version of Kalecki's model, which he cast in a dynamic format to find the maximum rate of planned growth in a mixed developing economy consistent with a stable income distribution.[2]

The object of the exercise is to set out and develop Kalecki's model formally, drawing where necessary on other parts of his work; because here he is uncharacteristically vague about certain aspects of the analysis, particularly savings behaviour, price formation, food supply, labour productivity and real wages. Unfortunately, this means that the main result is often reproduced almost mechanically without reflecting the full potential of Kalecki's analysis.[3] In particular, we shall be concerned with the relationship between planned investment and growth decisions in the industrial sector on the one hand, and the response of peasant food supply, foreign trade and labour productivity on the other. In other words, three dimensions of the relationship between state and civil society.

In this chapter I shall set out this second version of *Financing Development* in terms of three production departments used by Kalecki in the first version, with price formation rules and accumulation behaviour derived from his work on industrial market economies on the one hand, and planning considerations from his work on socialist economics on the other. I shall employ an analytics similar to Kalecki's own, and shall ignore the stability conditions because in this case they add little to the argument as this is a *planned* economy. All page references are to Kalecki (1972a).

Kalecki's approach is 'based to a considerable extent on a distinction between two types of consumer goods: necessities and non-essentials'

(p. 145). The chief items in necessities[4] are staple foods, although 'the list of necessities will widen with the long-run cost of living'. Two assumptions are made: there is to be no inflation in necessities; and consumer demand is to be restrained by 'direct taxes on higher-income groups or indirect taxes on non-essentials'. Using Kalecki's own notation, for a medium-term development plan with a certain aggregate income growth projection (r) and a stable income distribution, there will exist a determinate rate of growth (c_n) in demand for necessities dependent on the income elasticity of demand (e) less than unity (that is, Engel's Law) and population growth (q); yielding the only formally-stated equation in his paper:

$$c_n = q + e(r - q)$$

The growth rate of total consumption (c) is different, for part of income must be devoted to investment, and is thus a function of total income growth (r). Kalecki does not derive the equation but it is clearly the familiar relationship where growth depends on the savings propensity (s) and the capital–output ratio (k) such that:

$$s = rk$$

> It is clear that of the three growth rates in question c_n, c, r . . . [the model] determines two if one is given. Now in underdeveloped mixed economies it is c_n, the rate of increase of supply of necessities, that can be considered as given. The increase in production of necessities, especially of staple food, is limited by institutional factors, such as feudal land ownership and domination of peasants by merchants and money-lenders. As a result $c*_n$, the average rate of increase in the supply of necessities over the planning period, is kept down to rather a low level [pp. 150–1]. [This] determines the rate of growth of national income r which is warranted without infringing our basic postulates. Next is determined the rate of growth of total consumption c which makes a sufficient allowance for investment required for the expansion of the national income at a rate r. In order to restrain the increase in total consumption to the rate c appropriate taxation of higher income groups and non-essentials must be devised. *This seems to me the gist of the problem of financing economic development in a mixed economy.* (p. 152: my italics).

The required rate of taxation ($z*$) to finance supplementary state investment is described informally by Kalecki. In his notation, it will depend upon the 'voluntary' rate of savings (s_o) such that (extending his notation) the total savings rate ($s*$) which corresponds to the warranted growth rate ($r*$) is:

$$s* = s_o + z*$$

and thus:

$$\begin{aligned} z* &= s* - s_o \\ &= \frac{r*}{k} - s_o \\ &= \frac{1}{k_e}\{c*_n - q(1-e)\} - s_o \end{aligned}$$

From this point on Kalecki employs graphical exposition to explore the effect of higher rates of growth (inflation and deteriorating income distribution) and imports or credits (greater supplies and stable growth). Necessities supply growth is taken as given, despite the statement that 'the key to "financing" a more rapid growth is the removal of obstacles to the expansion of agriculture, such as feudal land-ownership and domination of peasants by money-lenders and merchants' (p. 152).

Thus, although the aggregate relationships and the overall logic of the argument are clear, the functioning of the model – particularly if it departs from the warranted growth rate ($r*$) – is not explicitly specified. Indeed the capital goods sector, the internal terms of trade, the real wage and savings behaviour are not even mentioned. However, the first version in Kalecki (1976) does contain a more complete formulation of the production structure (it is, after all, balance in product markets that lies at the heart of the Kaleckian approach) and by using this in combination with his standard approach for income distribution in the industrial sector of capitalist economies, we can arrive at a more complete specification of this seminal model.

6.2 KALECKI'S MODEL FORMALIZED

The first version[5] of *Financing Development* proposes a production structure based on three Departments, derived from the 'expanded reproduction schemes of Marx': investment goods (Department I) and consumer goods (Department II), divided between 'necessities' (Department IIa) and 'non-essentials' (Department IIb). The first and third are produced by capitalists with wage labour under the usual Kaleckian 'degree of monopoly' conditions, which could also be seen as government price controls with regulated profit margins. Necessities are in inelastic supply from the peasantry, as we have already seen, with an exogenous rate of growth. Formal exposition, however, requires a full statement of the behaviour of the industrial sector itself whose elucidation in turn requires some modification of Kalecki's own results in order to achieve consistency with the central thrust of his argument. According to Kalecki's analysis, output in developing countries is constrained by available capacity, unlike the situation in advanced capitalist economies, where the constraint is effective demand. Using our own notation, output (Q) in the two industrial branches (I and IIb respectively) will be determined by the capital stock (K) for given capital–output ratios (k_1, k_3):

$$k_1 Q_1 = K_1 \tag{1}$$

$$k_3 Q_3 = K_3 \tag{2}$$

The required output of the capital goods (Q_1) will be determined by the respective growth rates (α_1, α_3) of the two industrial sectors, as yet to be determined:

$$Q_1 = \alpha_1 Q_1 k_1 + \alpha_3 Q_3 k_3 \tag{3}$$

at a given technology with economies of scale constant for the plan period. Rearrangement of (3) yields an output balance (θ) within industry for any two growth rates such that, from the 'investment side':

$$\theta = \frac{Q_1}{Q_2} = \frac{\alpha_3 k_3}{1 - \alpha_1 k_1} \tag{4}$$

but, in fact, for a 'steady state' we can assume that sectoral growth rates are equal:

$$\alpha_1 = \alpha_3 = \alpha* \tag{5}$$

so that the industrial balance (θ) is, in fact, stable during the plan period for any particular industrial growth rate ($\alpha*$). The composition of investment can also be derived from (3).

The familiar Kaleckian model of the industrial sector has prices (p_1, p_3) based on unit labour costs with a fixed mark-up derived from the degree of monopoly.[6] We shall assume a single mark-up (g) and wage rate (w) throughout the industrial sector, although labour productivities (r_2, r_3) remain different. This simplifies the algebra without altering the main results, and is justifiable if labour and capital are free to move between industrial sectors:

$$p_1 = (1+g)\frac{w}{r_1} \tag{6}$$

$$p_3 = (1+g)\frac{w}{r_3} \tag{7}$$

Total profits (R) in the industrial sector will thus be:

$$R = gw\left\{\frac{Q_1}{r_1} + \frac{Q_3}{r_3}\right\} \tag{8}$$

For a given savings propensity (s) by capitalists out of profits, then the macroeconomic accumulation balance (that is, the *ex post* equality of savings and investment) can be defined. Kalecki assumes that only capitalists save, while workers and peasants do not:

$$sR = p_1 Q_1 \tag{9}$$

so that substituting (7) and (8) into (9) and rearranging yields another relationship for the industrial output balance (θ) from the 'savings side':

$$\theta = \frac{Q_1}{Q_3} = \frac{sg}{1+g(1-s)} \tag{10}$$

Note that the industrial output balance will shift towards the capital goods sector with a higher degree of monopoly (g), and with a higher ratio of productivity in the capital goods sector to that in the consumer goods sector (r_1/r_3). If the savings rate (s) is given, then (10) and (4) will define the steady-state industrial growth rate ($\alpha*$). However it should be remembered that Kalecki argues that the savings propensity

(s) can be adjusted by appropriate variations in tax pressure. In consequence, the accumulation balance (10) can be brought into line with the input–output relationship (4) to produce a solution for the required savings propensity (and thus tax rate) for any planned industrial growth rate ($\alpha*$). Rearranging (10) for an optimal industrial balance (θ) derived from (4) we have the savings rate ($s*$) required, with appropriate taxation if necessary, to warrant a determinate growth rate:

$$s* = \frac{1 + \frac{1}{g}}{1 + \theta\frac{r_3}{r_1}} ; \quad z* = s * - s_o \tag{11}$$

The limitation on the industrial growth rate that is imposed by food supply is simple to grasp in principle but tricky to define precisely because of Kalecki's uncharacteristic vagueness as to just who is consuming necessities (and from what income) and what is to be understood by price stability. If it is assumed that what he means is that the real wage ($\bar{w}$) should not decline, and if labour productivity (r_1, r_3) is given during the plan period, the real wage bill will rise proportionately to production and employment, to yield a stable labour share in total industrial income. As it is the number of workers who consume the necessities, employment (and industrial output) will only be able to grow at the food supply growth rate (α_2) which is assumed to be exogenous and thus the income elasticity of the demand for food will not come into play.

However, Kalecki clearly means real wages to rise (and thus Engel's Law to apply), implicitly rejecting the 'Lewis' model by having industrial output rise faster than employment. This I shall reflect in rising labour productivity at a specific rate (15), assumed common to all industry.[7] This yields an industrial employment (L) growth rate ($\alpha * - \beta$) and complementary real wage growth, also equal to β because labour productivity growth in (6) leads to an improvement in the ratio of wages to industrial prices. So for a given demand elasticity (e) and price stability, we have the required relationship as:

$$L = \frac{Q_1}{r_1} + \frac{Q_3}{r_3}$$

$$\frac{\dot{Q}_1}{Q_1} \geq e\frac{\dot{\bar{w}}}{\bar{w}} + \frac{\dot{L}}{L}$$

so that

$$\alpha * \leq \alpha_2 + \beta(1 - e) \tag{12}$$

I have now formally stated Kalecki's main result with the required degree of rigour, showing how it is necessary to bring the degree of monopoly (g), productivity growth (β) and savings behaviour explicitly into his model. Setting (12) as an equality for exogenous food supply growth (α_1) yields warranted industrial growth ($\alpha*$), the correct composition of industrial output (θ) is then found from (4), and finally the required tax rate ($z*$) from (11).

6.3 FOOD SUPPLY AND THE INTERNAL TERMS OF TRADE

The slow-growing food supply from the peasantry is central to Kalecki's model; yet he does not analyse this assumption in any more depth, which is curious in view of his wide development experience and Polish background. He assumes that only land reform will raise output growth 'if the problem of the inadequate increase of agricultural production were solved by means of an agrarian reform' (p. 153) but does not suggest how prices (that is, the internal terms of trade) might affect the food supply *both before and after the land reform*. Nor does he distinguish between total food output and the marketed surplus net of peasants' own consumption, despite the even greater sensitivity of the latter to relative price. In order to maintain this position, Kalecki sometimes assumes that all price increases are absorbed by merchants and moneylenders, thus swelling profits and leaving farmgate prices unaltered. This might be consistent with inflexible market supply, but it is hardly realistic, especially in the longer run. It also allows Kalecki to avoid the issue of what the peasants do with their income, and thus the terms of trade as such.

Here I assume that peasants sell their marketed output (Q_2) of food ('necessities' for industrial workers – in other words, Department IIb) at a market price (p_1) which they do not control. With the income thus acquired, they purchase producer goods (Q_1) at the mark-up price (p_1) determined by industry. Food market clearing thus determines the terms of trade (T):

$$T = p_2/p_1 \tag{13}$$

An improvement in the internal terms of trade will increase real peasant incomes, even if they do not receive all this increment. In developing countries, the marginal propensity of small farmers to save is high;[8] while that of both rural and urban workers is very low. Let us suppose that marketed supply (Q_2) depends on the capital stock (K_1) in agriculture. The coefficient (f) is not exactly a capital–output ratio, therefore, but rather a 'capital–sales' ratio:

$$Q_2 = fK_2 \tag{14}$$

and increases in this stock are based on accumulation (I_2) of a given proportion (s_1) of gross peasant income (p_2Q_2). In this case:

$$I_2 = s_1 p_2 Q_2 \tag{15}$$

Note that, strictly, the aggregate demand for capital goods in (3) should now be revised, but this should not affect the results. We now have food supply growth (α_2) as an *endogenous* variable, depending crucially on the internal terms of trade:

$$\begin{aligned}\alpha_2 &= \dot{Q}_2/Q_2 \\ &= \frac{fI_2}{Q_2 p_1} \\ &= fs_1T \end{aligned} \tag{16}$$

In other words, the better the internal terms of trade (T) the higher the growth of food supply, and thus, in the last instance, the real wage.

We must modify the previous model to allow for this interaction, and formulate the internal terms of trade clearly; so as to be able to redefine the warranted rate of growth. To do this, I define food price formation through the market clearing process for necessities (which are only consumed by industrial workers) at a given demand elasticity (a):

$$p_2Q_2 = w^aL \tag{17}$$

so that:

$$p_2 = W^a \frac{L}{Q_2} \tag{18}$$

Now, substitution of (18) and (6) into (13) yields, for a given food supply level in the previous period ($Q_{2,0}$), the terms of trade as a function of food supply growth:

$$T = w^{a-1}\frac{L}{Q_{2,0}(1+\alpha_2)}\frac{r_1}{Q_1(1+g)} \tag{19}$$

The joint solution of (19) and (16) determines the levels of food supply growth (α_2) and the internal terms of trade (T) for a particular set of parameter values (w, r_1, f, s') and industrial employment (L). In particular, there will exist equilibrium values of the terms of trade ($T*$) and marketed food supply growth (α_2*). This latter is, in fact, a maximum, and limits real wage growth: lower values of T restrict volume supplied, and higher values restrict demand. However, Kalecki's explicit concern is not for the dynamic stability of food markets, but rather for income distribution in the industrial sector. To model his objective of real wage stability requires a definition of the appropriate composite price index for workers, including both necessities and non-essentials (p); this is required for Engel's Law to have any meaning at all:

$$p = p_2{}^a p_3{}^{1-a} \tag{20}$$

so that the real wage ($\bar{w}$) becomes a function of the internal terms of trade, from (6), (7), (13):

$$\begin{aligned} \bar{w} &= \frac{w}{p} \\ &= \frac{r_3}{1+g}T^{-a}\left\{\frac{r_1}{r_3}\right\}^a \end{aligned} \tag{21}$$

Real wage stability is only guaranteed by terms of trade stability, therefore, for given parameter values (g, r_1, r_2, a). This in turn will require dynamic stability in the food market (16, 19) to produce the corresponding terms of trade ($T*$) and food supply growth rate (α_2*):

$$\alpha_2* = fs_1T*(\bar{w}) \tag{22}$$

maximal industrial growth ($\hat{\alpha}*$) can then be found from:

$$\hat{\alpha}* = \alpha_2 * (\bar{w}) + (1 - a)\beta \qquad (23)$$

Result (23) reproduces more rigorously Kalecki's original formulation based on the Engels elasticity but more rigorously defined in terms of the real wage ($\bar{w}$). However, to achieve this the 'plan' value of the internal terms of trade (T) must be higher throughout the plan period, and thus from (21) either the real wage ($\bar{w}$) must be cut at the outset of the plan or the profit margin (g) must be reduced. The former step would hardly be consistent with the spirit of Kalecki's political approach, although it is common practice.[9] The latter course would involve appropriate price controls (on manufactures, not foods) *and* an upward adjustment of the tax rate (z) on capitalist consumption. Only if neither of these courses is possible does there exist a single warranted rate of industrial growth derived from (23).

Of course, growth is usually accelerated without these precautions, the internal terms of trade improve (on the parallel market at least, if food prices are officially held down) and real wages deteriorate. If the internal terms of trade are effectively contained through state procurement and rationing, in an attempt to sustain real wages, then food supply growth (α_2) will decline and so will the real wage.[10] Such is also the experience of many socialist economies, even though capitalist consumption (that is, the proportion of Q_3 not consumed by workers) is replaced by government expenditure on administration or defence.[11]

These results seem to be very much in the Kaleckian tradition, and make his model not only much more realistic, but also more consistent internally. Above all, the central constraint becomes income distribution and thus social relations. Wuyts (1988) argues that this sort of model-building does not adequately reflect the social dimensions of the state–peasant relationship which underlies the internal terms of trade in a semi-industrial economy. It is certainly true that my model has a limited scope in that it does not include, for instance, peasant labour supplies to state farms, or rural taxation. None the less, in my reply (FitzGerald, 1988) I have already pointed out that a historical account of the 'agrarian question' was not Kalecki's objective. On the contrary, the institutional structure is taken as read in his 'stylized facts' and the implications worked out logically. Moreover, an account of institutional development can only be carried out in an historically specific context – as I will attempt to do in Chapters 7 and 8 below.

Figure 6.1 Dynamics of marketed food supply and demand

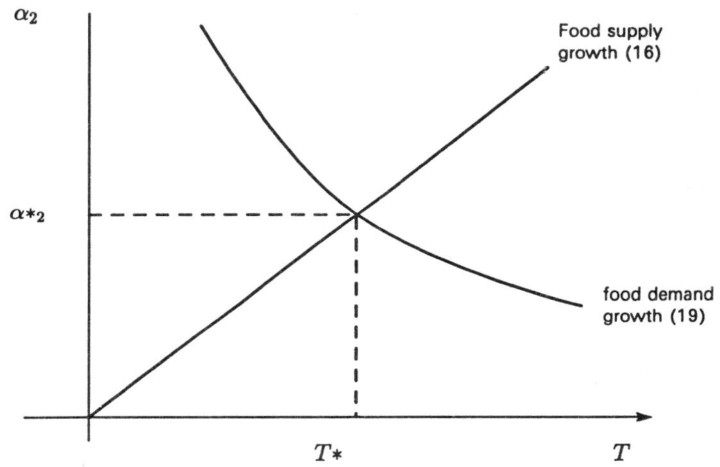

6.4 FOREIGN TRADE AS BALANCE AND CONSTRAINT

Kalecki brings foreign trade into his model by introducing the possibility of increasing the supply of necessities, and lifting the underlying constraint on equitable growth, by importing food. This is his only way of increasing their supply in the short run and permits a higher industrial growth rate without depressing real wages. He does not clarify the productive character of the export sector, but by implication it is some sort of 'enclave' (frequent reference is made to oil-exporters) and equivalent in effect to foreign grants.

To the extent that those exports (X) are additional resources, importing more necessities (ΔQ_2) for the work-force will not be sufficient to permit higher industrial output, as Kalecki points out (p. 155), because new capital goods (ΔQ_1) will also be required in order to raise industrial supply and maintain the overall equilibrium, the proportion being governed by the ratio (ϕ) already established between Q_1 and Q_2:

$$\phi = Q_2/Q_1 = \frac{\dot{Q}_2}{\dot{Q}_1} e^{-(1-a)\beta t} \tag{24}$$

where the sectoral balance steadily shifts away from food imports towards capital goods during the plan period.

Obviously, more export output (ΔX) or an improvement in the external terms of trade (ΔE) determine how much extra supplies can be obtained, and thus the rate of industrial growth attainable during the plan period, where:

$$\begin{aligned} \Delta(X.E) &= \Delta Q_1 + \Delta Q_2 \\ &= \Delta Q_1(1+\phi) \end{aligned}$$

so that the extra industrial growth ($\Delta\alpha*$) obtained will be (for small changes) inversely related to the Engel elasticity (a) because:

$$\Delta\alpha* = \frac{\Delta(XE)}{(1+\phi)\dot{Q}_1} \tag{25}$$

In the 'first version' of *Financing Development*, Kalecki defines the export sector a little more clearly (though not really satisfactorily) by assigning, to Department I in particular, an export branch (not itself of capital goods) to finance imports of capital goods. In a sense, then, exports replace to a considerable extent the capital goods sector (Q_1) itself.[12] Let us take the simplest case, where capital goods are all imported, plus a certain proportion (m) of inputs to manufactured consumer goods production (Q_3), both at a fixed world price (p_4). Department I (Q_1) is redefined as a primary export sector facing a given world price (p_3) at a unitary exchange rate. Assuming that the economy expands up to the trade balance, and the exchange rate is standardized at unity:

$$Q_1 p_3 = (I + mQ_3)p_4 \tag{26}$$

$$E = p_3/p_4 \tag{27}$$

The required production proportionality (θ) for the warranted rate of growth from the 'savings side' reflected in (10) will not be changed.

Instead of the domestic 'investment demand' schedule (3), leaving aside peasant demand (I_2) to simplify the algebra, we have:

$$I = \alpha_1 k_1 Q_1 + \alpha_3 k_3 Q_3 \tag{28}$$

so that substituting (28) into (26) yields a new determination of the value of the industrial balance (θ) which now reflects the 'export orientation' of the economy:[13]

$$\begin{aligned} \theta &= \frac{Q_1}{Q_2} \\ &= \frac{m + \alpha_3 k_3}{E - \alpha_1 k_1} \end{aligned} \tag{29}$$

Combined with the simultaneous domestic ('savings') determination of the industrial balance from (10), this establishes a maximum rate of steady industrial growth ($\alpha*$) consistent with a stable income distribution ($\bar{w}, g$), during the plan period:

$$\alpha* = \frac{E\theta - m}{\theta k_1 + k_3} \tag{30}$$

Of course, if the stability of income distribution is abandoned as a central element of the plan, more can be invested in the export sector (θ can be raised and $\alpha*$ with it) for (26) no longer binds. However, Kalecki clearly feels that 'in general it will be increasingly difficult to balance imports by a rise in exports because of certain limitations of either supplies of export goods or of foreign markets' (p. 55), while import substitution (that is, reducing m) is limited by technological constraints. This is realistic in the medium term, even if superable in the long run with appropriate restructuring. This would make both E and m functions of output such that:

$$\partial E/\partial Q_1 < 0; \quad \partial m/\partial Q_3 < 0$$

$$\partial^2 E/\partial {Q_1}^2 < 0; \quad \partial^2 m/\partial {Q_3}^2 > 0$$

The relevant elasticities would presumably be less than unity, so that maximum value for industrial growth ($\alpha*$) will be found beyond which further stress on exports (and thus lower $\bar{w}$) will, in fact, reduce the industrial growth rate. The optimal (that is, maximum attainable) growth point will thereby be given.

An alternative to raising exports is, of course, foreign loans; but Kalecki was perceptively pessimistic about their availability, political cost, and repayment schedules for developing countries. Analytically, of course, 'optimal borrowing' could be simply introduced to this model, relating interest rates charged to the export growth required to service them; and thus affecting the industrial balance (θ) of investment.[14]

6.5 EMPLOYMENT AND PRODUCTIVITY

The second version of *Financing Department* is far from clear on how employment and labour productivity combine; indeed, population and per capita income are used as indicators, unlike elsewhere in Kalecki's work. In the first version, however, wages, employment and industrial output are mentioned; especially the effect of increases in productivity in the two industrial sectors. This lowers industrial prices (in relative terms at least) and slows down the transfer of labour from the agricultural to the industrial sector; real wages rise, as do peasant incomes, because of the higher pressure for agricultural products and lower prices for industrial commodities (p. 50).

> But the situation is not so favourable as it would appear from this description, because there would be no shift of population from the countryside to the town, which is one of the main causes of the increase in the standard of living in the course of economic development. Disguised unemployment would not be reduced, and the country would be split into two sectors: primitive agriculture and modern industry. The other extreme is the case where productivity does not increase at all and the increase in industrial production is achieved merely through a shift of population from the rural to the urban districts. In such a case, disguised unemployment would be diminishing radically, but at the same time considerable inflationary pressures are likely to develop, because it may be difficult to expand agriculture so as to satisfy the rapidly rising urban demand. The optimum pattern usually falls between these two extremes; the increase in industrial production should be based on the rise both in productivity and in unemployment.

Fortunately, in Kalecki's work on the planned economy, similar problems are handled with more analytical detail. Industrial development is considered to consist of two stages: in the first there is surplus labour (not just the peasantry, but also housewives and so on) and output growth takes place with stable productivity and real wages, absorbing a maximum amount of labour.[15] Using Kalecki's notation, the steady rate of growth (α) is mainly determined through the investment coefficient (i), adjusted by the capital–output coefficient (k); but it is also affected by the rate of depreciation (d) and a variable (u) which reflects the utilization[16] of existing capacity 'due to improvements in the organization of labour, more economical use of raw materials, elimination of faulty products, etc.' (p. 11):

$$\alpha = \frac{i}{k} - d + u \tag{31}$$

and employment growth is strictly proportional to the increase in the (net) capital stock less productivity growth (β). Only when employment rises to absorb all the available work force, does a second relation come into play; where labour productivity growth (β) and the natural expansion of the labour force (n) limit the overall growth rate:

$$\alpha \leq n + \beta \tag{32}$$

In either case, employment will grow at a rate (e) determined by:

$$e = \alpha - \beta \tag{33}$$

There exists, however, a maximum growth rate ($\alpha * = n + \beta$), beyond which further increases in the rate of accumulation (i) will have no effect in a labour-scarce economy. Technical progress such as (β) is *incorporated* through the process of investment in new plant: 'overall labour productivity increases annually *pari passu* with labour productivity in new plants as they are brought progressively into operation . . . in the case of uniform growth' (p. 22) because 'old' plant with the lowest productivity is continually being scrapped at a determinate rate (d). For existing plant, increased efficiency is achieved through better utilization of labour (u). There can be some effect of accumulation on technical progress as such, in a process of capital restructuring which Kalecki calls a 'period of recasting', when the existing stock of equipment receives heavy investment in order to increase its capital-intensity. However, he does not see this as being very relevant[17] for labour-surplus economies, because 'the idea of raising the capital–output ratio, given a reserve of labour, would probably yield no benefits at all even in the long run unless the rate of increase of labour productivity resulting from technical progress, is very small' (p. 88). There is no suggestion of substantial substitutability between labour and equipment.

Kalecki assumes that labour is freely available for industry, and that the transfer does not affect food supply (Q_2); but the evident existence of a large urban 'informal' sector does not concern him.[18] He evidently expected – as did all his contemporaries – industrial employment to grow much faster than the labour force as a whole; but the postwar experience (in sharp contrast to previous decades) indicates that productivity and output growth were such as to maintain a more or less stable proportion between the two. Within the Kaleckian sectoral structure I have developed above, informal urban labour (L_4) can be included[19] as a fourth sector. Total labour force (L) is defined as:

$$L = L_1 + L_2 + L_3 + L_4 \tag{34}$$

L grows at a natural rate, L_1 and L_3 are determined by industrial output and productivity growth as described before, while peasant 'employment' (L_2) is, in fact, the residual after migratory flows towards the other three urban sectors. Informal-sector income (U) can be taken as a determinate proportion (γ) of the urban wage bill:

$$U = \gamma w(L_1 + L_3) \tag{35}$$

Migration will take place so long as peasant incomes are less than those obtainable in the urban informal sector:

$$\frac{p_2 Q_2}{L_2} \leq \frac{U}{L_4} \tag{36}$$

reaching (or at least tending towards) a balance, although this will be steadily shifting due to the differential rates of growth in the production sectors. Taking (36) as an equality and substituting in (35), (6) and (16), yields a determinate balance (π) between rural and urban informal labour in terms of industrial employment and the internal terms of trade, both already determined above:

$$\pi = \frac{L_4}{L_2} = \frac{\gamma r_1}{(1+g)T} \cdot \frac{L_1 + L_3}{Q_2} \qquad (37)$$

This may be combined with (34) to produce a determinate solution for L_2 and L_4. By inspection of (37) it is clear that α will rise during the plan period because $\alpha_1 < \alpha'$; but also that if T or g rise, then π will fall, easing the migratory pressure, because of the decline in the wage share of aggregate income in favour of the peasantry or profits respectively. Again, this would modify Kalecki's results considerably, but still remain within the spirit of his approach.

No explicit microeconomic relationship running from real wages to labour productivity is posited in Kalecki's writing; the link is in the other direction and through the product market, with increased labour productivity in wagegoods production raising real wages through decreased (relative) prices. He maintained this position even for planned socialist economies with full employment, despite strongly supporting workers' councils as a complement to central planning in Poland.[20] Kalecki's solution to the problem of determining the appropriate balance between accumulation and distribution is to introduce a 'government decision curve' based on the perceived social trade-off between increments in the accumulation rate (that is, reductions in the real wage) and the increased growth obtained thereby: the slope of this curve is 'the higher [it is] the stronger are the objections against reducing consumption in the short run' (p. 30). This is a political decision (that is, not merely a social rate of time discount) and between the lines can be read a hint of resistance by workers (real or feared) to any reduction in current living standards. The result, particularly in the labour surplus economy, is to create another constraint on planned growth which intersects, so to speak, with (31). The prior conditions established in *Financing Development* on income distribution in terms of real wage stability can, in fact, be seen as a simplified (to be more precise, a 'kinked') version of the government decision curve.

Kalecki obviously intends this decision curve to be a heuristic device, and not subject to empirical measurement, but it is essentially macroeconomic. However, the experience of both socialist and capitalist economies is that labour intensity does respond positively to real wages: in other words, there exists a *microeconomic* relationship between productivity and wages which reflect the 'labour decision curve'. Equipment per worker may be raised and potential productivity (β) increased in the sense of what machines can produce with a given labour force, but if workers are not willing to use the new machines effectively (that is, to modify their work practices, raise intensity, and so on unless wages are raised), they are not efficiently utilized (u). This is not only true of an industrial economy where the positive branch correlation between value-added per worker and wages is well known, but also for a developing economy; with the additional factor that when workers have other income-earning opportunities within the household unit, much of the benefit of industrial employment may come from the holding of the job as such (that is, social security, stability, housing, and so on) rather than from productivity-unrelated wage levels. Of Kalecki's two coefficients for productivity growth (β, u), only the former is embodied in the new machinery and is related to the rate of accumulation; the latter is explicitly based on improved organization, and is related to real wages. Such an approach would not only be realistic and potentially measurable, but would also be more consistent with the microeconomic foundations (for example, the degree of monopoly, which derives not only from market conditions but also from labour relations) of Kalecki's macroeconomics.

To illustrate this, I can simplify my model to one industrial sector, for I have already determined the intersectoral balances (θ) in terms of industrial growth, and established a specific 'incentive' mechanism (that is, T) for agriculture. For a given level of output (Q) at any one point in time; prices (p) and nominal wages (w) set for the plan period; and technical labour–output ratio (r) determined by investment decisions (that is, incorporated technology) in the *previous* plan period; then we have profits (R):

$$R = Q\left\{p - \frac{w}{r}\right\} \tag{38}$$

The accumulation balance requires that for a savings rate (s) and planned investment (I):

$$pI = sR \tag{39}$$

so that the accumulation rate (i) is a function of the real wage ($\bar{w} = w/p$):

$$i = \frac{I}{Q} = s\left(1 - \frac{\bar{w}}{r}\right) \tag{40}$$

This real wage level can be taken as given for the plan period, being adjusted from one plan to another. According to Kalecki's formulation in (31), the achieved growth rate (α) in a labour-surplus economy will depend on the capital–output ratio (k) and the depreciation rate (d) and the utilization factor (u). However, we have argued that the rate of improvement in utilization (u) is itself a function of the real wage set for the plan period, presumably reflecting declining marginal returns to wage increases ($0 < \beta < 1$):

$$u = b\bar{w}^{\beta} \tag{41}$$

Thus

$$\alpha = \left(1 - \frac{\bar{w}}{r}\right)\frac{s}{k} - d + bw^{\beta} \tag{42}$$

The maximum growth rate attainable will be determined, therefore, by

$$\frac{\partial \alpha}{\partial w} = -\frac{s}{kr} + \beta u = 0 \tag{43}$$

which obtains (because $\partial^2 \alpha / \partial \bar{w}^2 < 0$) for a specific real wage rate ($\bar{w}*$) which is, in fact, 'optimal' for the plan period:

$$\bar{w}* = \left[\frac{krb}{s}\right]^{1/1-\beta} \tag{44}$$

From Figure 6.2 it can be seen that, generally, attempts to achieve a higher than optimum growth rate (based perhaps on Kalecki's original formulation) will result in *both* a lower wage rate and a lower growth rate than those which would otherwise be attainable. Specifically, the result indicates that higher rates of saving or of embodied technical progress will imply that maximum growth requires higher real wages as well. Moreover, if the level of investment (I) is constrained by foreign exchange shortages, stimulating industrial output through productivity-linked real wage increases, based on an improved domestic supply of wagegoods, may well be more effective than borrowing abroad. It is an empirical issue, of course, whether for the planned semi-industrial economy this optimal real wage rate lies above or below that determined by planners – applying Kalecki's decision curve or his income distribution criterion – but experience seems to indicate that the former is generally the case.

Figure 6.2 **Real wages and industrial growth**

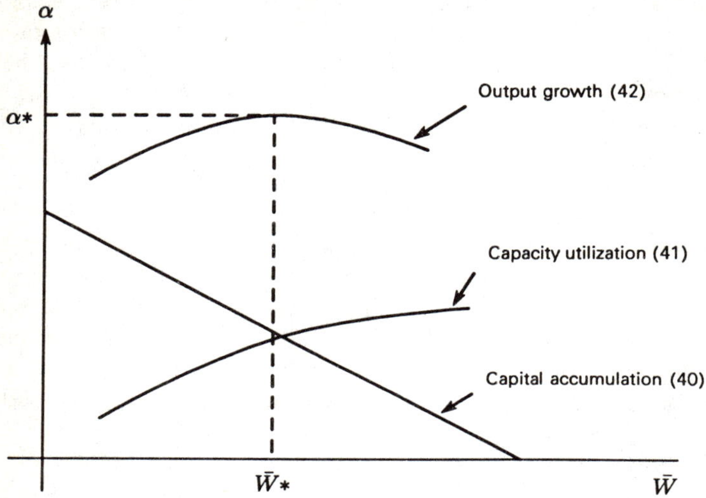

7 Planning for Sectoral Balance at the Periphery

7.1 THE PERIPHERAL PLANNED ECONOMY

Historically, attempts to construct socialism in practice have taken place in poor economies at an early stage of industrial development, rather than in the metropolitan capitalist societies as had originally been expected. In consequence, the relation between a 'peasant' food-producing sector (the basis for wagegoods supply) and a 'state' industrial sector (the basis for accumulation) is a central theme in classical debates on socialist planning, and the problem of decentralization of decisions becomes central to the determination of the balance between consumption and investment.[1] However, attempts to construct socialism in the post-war decades have taken place in countries which are not only underdeveloped, but also rely on foreign trade as the central element in their growth strategy, exports being a major component of the primary sector and providing foreign exchange for the import of production inputs and equipment. None the less, foreign trade has been seen largely as a problem of covering marginal production shortfalls in the larger economies or of comparative advantage within a planned common market for the smaller ones. The problem of the balance between investment and consumption (and thus of 'growth' versus 'welfare') is not only, therefore, one of balance between a 'traditional' food sector and 'modern' state industry, but also one of the balance between production for export and for domestic use.

This chapter aims to contribute to an understanding of macro-economic practice for semi-industrial planned economies where in varying degrees these characteristics of internal dualism and external dependency are common, such as Cuba, Nicaragua, Algeria, Mozambique, Angola, Tanzania, Vietnam and Ethiopia.[2] Analytically, the chapter explores some implications of Kalecki's work and draws on more recent discussions of basic needs and stabilization policies by characterizing the sectoral balances of the 'peripheral planned economy' (PPE) in terms of consumption, income distribution and investible surplus and identifying the issue of 'accumulation bias' expressed as an over-emphasis on exports. We shall assume a popularly elected government, that state control of large enterprises and wholesale trade exists, and that political conditions obtain for the planning objective of raising the living standards of the poor.

7.2 THE STRUCTURE OF THE PERIPHERAL PLANNED ECONOMY

In the classical formulation of the structure of an industrializing economy,[3] there are two output sectors – producer goods and consumer goods – concerned with the provision of the means of production and the means of reproduction of the labour force respectively. The balance between the output of these two sectors, in a closed economy, determines the real levels of consumption and investment, whatever the nominal level of wages and profits may be. It is useful, in practice, to distinguish within the category of consumer goods between wagegoods proper (which would nowadays be called 'basic needs') and non-essential consumption goods. In a planned economy, the latter category not only defines the differential living standards of technicians and administrators, but is also a response to the aspirations of workers and the basis of commercial exchange with small producers, particularly peasants. We have, then, three 'Departments': producer goods (I); basic consumption goods (IIa), also referred to as wagegoods or 'basic needs'; and non-basic consumption goods (IIb).

In the traditional analysis of the early stages of socialist economic planning, the model contains only Departments I and IIa; these are 'industry' and 'agriculture', producing, as it were, Ricardo's iron and corn. They are understood to be based on two forms of production – state ownership and collectivized peasant enterprise respectively. In other words, the divisions of the economy in terms of 'departments', correspond both to the sectoral classification based on technology on the one hand, and to the organizational classification based on types of firm on the other. In this way, the problem of balance can be reduced to that of the 'dual economy': the relative proportions of industry and agriculture, the levels of investment and consumption, and the extent of direct state control all coinciding.

In a peripheral planned economy, the situation is much more complex. There is usually only an infant heavy industrial sector;

Department I is mainly limited to construction, electric power and possibly some minor tools and productive inputs. *It is the foreign trade sector which, through exports of primary products at exogenous international prices, provides these producer goods and thus constitutes the 'heavy industry' of such 'incomplete' semi-industrialized economies.* In many (if not most) cases this primary export sector is, in fact, agriculture. Production is organized in large units, using relatively modern technology for production and processing. This sector is generally under direct state control, either through public ownership, or at least under very close regulation by marketing boards, nationalized banks, input supplies and so on. In other words, although prices are exogenous, output levels (subject to the vagaries of the weather) are subject to the plan. The same is true, if not more so, for mining. In export agriculture or mining, moreover, the technology (especially that embodied in equipment) is largely imported. Thus the dynamic it provides for the economy as a whole is similar to that of the 'classical' model in terms of providing (albeit indirectly) production inputs, but it does not necessarily have any technological impact or capacity to concentrate surplus.

What manufacturing capacity proper there is (that is, excluding energy, construction and export processing) may well be of a non-essential nature, particularly in the early stages of transition from dependent capitalism, having served a narrow market based on a skewed income distribution. However, this capacity is generally shifted towards 'superior' consumption goods (furniture, electrical goods, motor bicycles and so on) in order to provide incentives for higher worker productivity, a privileged standard of living for administrators and technicians, and for exchange with the peasantry. This could also include a range of services, such as holiday centres, restaurants, cinemas and so on. In this 'Department IIb' (for which 'non-essential consumption' is clearly an inadequate title) there generally exists central control over prices and output and an organization in large, state-owned units. In other words, *IIb is the most 'plannable' of the three Departments*, though its service sector will necessarily be more decentralized in view of the diversity of its output.

Department IIa, the 'basic needs' sector, is a complex one containing several disparate elements organized in different ways. We may distinguish three: food, clothing and basic services. Food supply is essentially a question of small-scale agrarian production by peasants or co-operatives. Some production may be on large state farms, but the general experience has been that central planning of agriculture is ineffective and market incentives to petty producers is the most effective way of guaranteeing the food supply. Similarly, small shops will be involved in its distribution, even though the state acts as wholesaler. For clothing and shoes, large state-owned units will control production of cloth and leather; but production and distribution may be decentralized and very much influenced by local market conditions. Finally, basic services include primary health and education, housing and transport. These can be provided by central or local government; but in many cases they are organized by local 'popular' groups (trade unions and so on) and thus constitute a special kind of 'petty commodity production'.

In sum, unlike the classical model (with its two Departments corresponding to two sectors and two forms of production), *the PPE can be better described as three Departments.* These embody the conventional output sectors, with industry occurring in all three Departments and agriculture in two. The most important distinction, however, is that Department I has plannable output but exogenous prices (the external terms of trade), while Department IIa has plannable prices (internal terms of trade) but production outside state control; only Department IIb is really plannable in terms of both output and price.

The proper commercial articulation of these three Departments with one another and the world economy is probably more important than the setting of production levels; indeed, the relations of exchange may be as important as the relations of production in such an economy. The essence of the problem is that planners of the PPE can only obtain capital goods and wagegoods by trading with two sectors outside their own direct control; in other words, whatever the formal institutional situation, the PPE is largely market-oriented. The formation of prices outside the economy affects the valuation of outputs from Department I and inputs to Department IIb. The external terms of trade determine the relationship between exportable output and the real volume of imports of current productive inputs and investment goods. The real volume of imports determine, for given 'technical' import coefficients, the level of output attainable in the 'modern' sector – Departments I and IIb, for these use far more foreign exchange than the more 'traditional' or service-orientated basic needs sector. This 'incompleteness' of domestic industry and its inability to substitute for imported inputs, is the meaning of 'dependency' in the context of the PPE, rather than foreign ownership of productive assets or exploitative external markets.

Given a planned level of investment (and thus import of capital goods), the allocation of imported inputs (that is, foreign exchange) between Departments I and IIb will determine their levels of production. In practice, however, the output level of Department I may well be difficult to alter in the short run, and in any case its generation of foreign exchange presumably has priority in import-allocation. Thus the level of output of Department IIb (non-basic consumption) will vary in the short run in response to changes in the balance-of-payments situation, particularly the external terms of trade. Two important points follow from this: firstly, that foreign exchange supply rather than labour availability will be the main constraint on 'modern' output in both the short and long run (since capital goods are imported); secondly, that the criterion for determining output in Department I as a whole cannot be microeconomic efficiency, but rather the desired output level in the modern sector.

The supply of basic needs depends in part on the activities of government and popular organizations, and thus on 'non-economic' criteria. But much of the supply of food and of artisan clothing, shoes and services, depends upon market incentives to small producers. Indeed, in recent years there has been a tendency to argue for a shift towards basic needs production by small producers (either individually or in co-operatives), not to create employment for social welfare purposes as in the case of capitalist economies, but because this appears to be more efficient in terms of utilization of the whole labour force.[4] The internal terms of trade, the ratio between the prices for Departments IIb and IIa, must be such as to allow small producers (particularly peasants) to purchase simple inputs and non-basic consumer goods. However, while the prices of Department IIb are administered by the government, and reflect a mark-up on wage and (essentially imported) raw materials, those of Department IIa are 'market' prices which reflect peasant supply response and the proportion of monetized income spent on basic needs.

Underlying the determination of the internal terms of trade is the question of how much manufacturing output (or government services) the planners provide to peasants in exchange for their food supplies.[5] The crucial planning decision is one thus not just between investment and popular (that is, peasants' and workers') consumption, the allocation between industrial goods for wage-earners and for peasants. There is limited scope for depressing peasant incomes by manipulating the internal terms of trade (thereby saving foreign exchange and allowing higher investment) without cutting real wages too by debilitating basic needs supply – a lesson that was clearly set out by N. Bukharin but that has to be relearned with depressing regularity by socialist planners.

Income distribution as a whole is underpinned by the average consumption requirements of peasants and workers. The average real wage will depend on the number of workers and levels of output in the modern sector, on the one hand; and upon the total supply of (basic and non-basic) wagegoods on the other. The crucial economic variable is the internal terms of trade, more particularly the industrial pricing policy which itself reflects the accumulation strategy. Whatever the nominal wage is, the real wage will depend upon the peasant supply response function (assumed to be given for a determinate institutional structure) and the allocation of Department IIb output to that sector. The latter, in turn, depends on its foreign exchange allocation; that is, the difference between Department I exports and investment allocations.

Peasant incomes are in part secured by their own food supplies (and thus more 'cushioned' than wages in the modern state sector) and in part determined by the manufactures supplied in exchange for marketed food. The higher the planned real wage, the higher must be peasant productivity and thus the greater the supply of rural inputs and consumer goods. In other words, real peasant incomes and real wages should be complementary; any argument for a 'trade-off' is either an attempt to disguise the nature of the surplus generation process or must be based on the false assumption that the food supply can be kept independent of the supply price. Forcing the internal terms of trade downwards is eventually a means of reducing real wages and saving foreign exchange; it cannot be seen as a matter of 'urban bias' between workers and peasants, as we have seen in Chapter 6.

I have assumed so far that the only two consumer groups are peasants and workers. In practice, of course, the bureaucracy (widely interpreted to include army and technocracy) will also be a major consumer, especially of Department IIb goods. In fact, any shift of manufactures away from the peasantry (and thus a decline in workers' consumption), may not lead to more investment with the foreign exchange saved, but rather to higher bureaucratic living standards. Any realistic model of the PPE should include this group, which presumably expands in relation to the modern sector in general, and accumulation in particular.

Typically, the labour process and workers' standard of living are inherited from underdeveloped capitalism. Firstly, intensive work schedules were enforced by means of institutionalized violence and economic pressures such as unemployment, seasonal labour, differential access to social services, and lack of individual means of production, particularly land. In other words, a process of absolute exploitation and primitive accumulation ensured an ample and cheap labour supply and made low technology, extensive production forms profitable, especially in the primary export sector (Department I) which is the centre of accumulation. Secondly, low wages and unequal internal terms of trade in Department II permitted a minimization of the real wage, while social services were provided only to salaried workers at the level required to maintain urban stability. Thirdly, the expansion of production for the domestic market (particularly Department IIb) was limited by the lack of domestic demand, even though the process of urbanization and the expansion of the wage labour force permitted a certain degree of industrialization of wagegoods, such as textiles and beverages.

The 'revolution' (or more usually, a successful struggle for national independence) necessarily upsets this framework. Firstly, in the absence of the former methods of coercion, work intensity naturally declines, leading to falling production or to intense labour shortages. Wage pressure rises with new labour legislation and free trade unions. Labour discipline as a whole will also be reduced, until new methods of social organization are introduced. When social services such as health, education, housing, and food rationing are extended to the whole population, including those in the non-wage sector, the economic incentive for proletarianization is reduced (all the more so if the land reform distributes land to rural labourers and artisan co-operatives are supported). Secondly, the effective demand for wagegoods, and generally for the output of Department IIa, is increased by the social pressure that the poor (and also the party organizations) place upon the state to improve living standards rapidly. Moreover, the socially acceptable quality and contents of the wagegoods basket itself are extended by political change and the spread of urban standards to the countryside, effectively transferring goods and services from Department IIb to IIa. Thus the socially necessary labour time for production increases more-or-less immediately, while at the same time the social cost of labour reproduction rises, against a background of stagnant or declining production. This in turn puts a severe strain on the economy and creates inflationary pressure with serious political consequences.

The recovery of labour productivity begins with the restoration of previous levels of labour intensity, because higher levels of technology require a longer period of accumulation. How to achieve this recovery has led to debates about the relative value of moral and material incentives to the labour force.[6] Moral incentives (that is, more effort for a given wage) are sometimes regarded as a precursor of Communism, as a demonstration of an ability to overcome production relations based on the sale of labour power. This is logically connected with the ability to distribute wagegoods according to need. However, except at certain moments of national cohesion (emergencies, aggression and so on) when voluntary labour may also be forthcoming, the experience in socialist economies has been that the more elementary socialist principle of 'to each according to the amount of work' is more effective for sustained productivity where wages are essentially based on piecework. This does not have to lead to individualistic attitudes among workers: union negotiation of work norms and piece-rates imply collective control of the labour process, while the increasing technical division of labour in turn requires the definition of productivity in terms of teams or even sections of the enterprise. Material incentives can take the form of wage increases or specific items (televisions, holidays and so on), but in any case these incentives must be supported at the macroplanning level by an increased supply of goods and services which are not part of the basic needs (Department IIa) package.

In consequence, Department IIb should play a key role in stimulating productivity in every sector of the planned economy; and not just that of enterprise workers, but also of professionals and petty producers. It is not by nature a 'non-necessary' sector in the Kaleckian sense, nor is its expansion merely a desirable improvement in the standard of living; rather, it is an essential component of the reproduction of the new economic system. In this sense, increased consumption is needed for growth, although not necessarily as a proportion of the total social product, because the incentive payments may not represent the entire value of the increased output. Curiously, although material incentives are an integral part of what might be termed 'socialist microeconomics' consumption is not reflected in the corresponding theory of aggregate economic balances.[7] In the longer run, productivity should increase with the increased use of technology (machines, inputs, and labour skills), although the real wage bill as a whole can only increase if the output of Department II increases as well. However, in the medium term, considerable increases can be achieved by the reorganization of the labour process itself, better care of machinery, reduction of wastage and so on. To be able to mobilize this creative force effectively, widespread worker education is necessary, as is effective participation in the management of the enterprise. Participation does not, therefore, become merely a matter of access to the surplus (that is, wage incentives based upon the profitability of the firm) but rather one of social control over the labour process itself as part of the process of emancipation.

The aspirations of workers for an early increase in real wages as a result of the revolution itself are usually confronted with limited wagegoods production capacity, declining productivity, and pressure for improved terms of trade by the peasantry. Improvements in community living standards, particularly if based on voluntary labour which receives its social reward directly, may be regarded as a right rather than an incentive. At the same time, the consumption claims of technicians, administrators, and professionals (many inherited from the past) must also be met; as must those remaining claims of capitalists in the initial stage of the transition if they are to achieve simple reproduction – that is, to stay in the country. Finally, if an increased supply of wagegoods is to be obtained from peasants and artisans (that is in turn, if they are to increase their work intensity under prevailing low levels of technology), then they too must receive increased amounts of incentive goods in return.

In sum, there are two contradictory characteristics of labour and distribution for the planned peripheral country. The first is the tension between the political requirement to overcome the grinding poverty of the majority of the population through expanded supply of basic goods and services (Department IIa) on the basis of need, on the one hand, and the economic necessity of real wage differentiation (Department IIb) in order to recover labour productivity and secure sufficient labour supply, on the other. This may require the assignment of an increased proportion of the social product to consumption (Department II rather than Department I) and thus reduce the rate of accumulation or bring about a foreign trade crisis. The second characteristic is the competition between the different forms of production for the available labour supply, where the widespread existence of petty mercantile production may become an increasingly attractive alternative for wage labourers, particularly when extensive land distribution has taken place or proletarianization has been a relatively recent historical phenomenon. This, in turn, may lead the state to constrain or even suppress these petty forms of production in order to secure control over the labour force, as both an economic and a political strategy.

In order to integrate an economic structure by the articulation of the forms of production, insertion in the international division of labour, and the conditions of reproduction of the labour force, a price structure is necessary that is also consistent with the desired pattern of appropriation of the surplus. Unfortunately, we do not possess an appropriate theoretical framework to analyse this process.[8] Early progress is typically made towards fulfilling basic consumption requirements (distribution of Department IIa output) on the basis of need. Similarly, decisions on accumulation and foreign trade (distribution of Department I output) are made on the basis of a plan rather than on criteria of profitability. Even the 'incentive' consumer goods (Department IIb) are distributed according to the contribution of the recipient to production, and not merely according to ability to pay. Thus distribution becomes largely socialized, despite the fact that prices must be used as a detailed rationing device because of the shortage of goods relative to social requirements. Of course, it has always been clear that the existence of multiple forms of production in an underdeveloped economy requires that there be mercantile exchange between them (Preobrazhensky, 1965). This is obviously true in relation to peasant and artisan production, which may represent a significant part of output. Insertion of a large part of the primary sector into the international division of labour also implies mercantile exchange for industrial inputs and capital equipment.

In foreign trade, the small economy confronts a virtually elastic demand schedule and a price vector which is essentially exogenous, while supply is endogenous to the plan. These prices represent the valuation of the labour time incorporated in the export products used to pay for the imports in question. In turn, the price offered to petty producers by the state will depend upon the volume demanded from them in order to fulfil the plan, because supply is price elastic. The price represents the labour value of the industrial goods that the state offers these small producers in exchange for their products (or labour time). These two exchanges are essentially 'unequal' because of the different ways in which prices are formed and imposed. As we have seen, foreign trade involves a transfer abroad of the surplus centralized by the state, even through this may be compensated by foreign aid. Similarly, the internal terms of trade imply a transfer of value from small producers to the state, even though this too may be compensated by specific transfers in the form of social services or infrastructure. Even when the institutional exploitation of the peasantry characteristic of the pre-revolutionary past is overcome, there will still exist unequal exchange because prices in the state enterprise sector include margins to cover accumulation requirements, while petty producer prices are based on the cost of reproducing the family unit. Small producers, in other words, value their labour power at the margin or below the existing wage level in the enterprise sector, and thus well below the latter's prices (Caballero, 1984).

In the planned (state enterprise) sector, prices should reflect an 'economic calculus' based on the costs of production and the required surplus margin to be distributed between social expenditure in the firm or its locality, direct investments, and contributions to the central accumulation fund. This is clearly necessary in order to impose criteria of economic efficiency on the enterprises and to allow them some degree of administrative flexibility. However, in view of the importance of the petty production sector in determining the relative prices of domestic output in relation to wagegoods supply (and thus real wages) on the one hand, and the external sector in setting input and output prices on the other, a planned rate of accumulation and certain provisions for surplus distribution will more or less fix producer prices in the planned sector as well.

These three factors sustain the operation of the law of value within the planned economy, due not to the logic of the accumulation of private capital, but rather to that of the (conflictive) reproduction of international economy, the petty producers, and the state sector.[9] In particular, the importance of internationally traded goods in the economy means that, for their efficient use, they should be priced according to their foreign exchange value within the production system (see Chapter 5). This correspondence need not include short-term fluctuations (especially in the case of primary products) but to set prices at any other level would lead to wasteful use of foreign exchange under the rules of the economic calculus. None the less, production decisions can be based on criteria other than comparative cost; for example, on national food security. It is still necessary, however, to know how much this will cost in foreign exchange losses, precisely because this represents the social surplus. In other words, the problem is one of consciously modifying the international operation of the law of value rather than ignoring it.

Once the production and distribution plan is determined, price (including indirect taxes as a form of price) will serve to distribute the monetary surplus among production units and between them and the central fund. For any given investment programme, there then exists a corresponding price structure that guarantees both the reproduction of individual enterprises and a centralized financial surplus equivalent to the planned level of investment or other state activities. Alternatively, the state banks can be used as the mechanism for redistributing the surplus. These requirements for price setting, along with the considerations mentioned above, close the system of price formation.

This relatively complex interlocking system of prices implies that any set of administered prices that does not correspond to this structure will lead to such distortions as inflation, black markets, shortages, and unrealizable money balances. Even so, the existence of non-state production forms will make it very difficult to control the monetary incomes of firms and individuals. It is thus necessary to have some sort of 'sink' in the system with flexible prices to clear excess demand in the economy; this is a particular function of Department IIb markets, where high clearing prices in state stores may be seen as a form of taxation.

In empirical terms, the economic surplus is usually defined as the difference between the total material product (net of replacement of the means of production used up therein) and the consumption socially necessary to reproduce the labour force. Within my stylized framework, this surplus manifests itself in two forms peculiar to the economic structure. Firstly, the workers and producers from Department II produce more than enough to maintain themselves (and their families), and to sustain those in other Departments that produce the inputs they need or the goods they receive in exchange. This surplus maintains the army, public administration, and the Department I workers who produce for accumulation. Any attempt to increase this surplus by pressuring the internal terms of trade (providing fewer industrial products to the peasantry, for example) tends to result in a reduction in petty-commodity production, and thus a fall in real wages. Moreover, this form of the surplus cannot be simply materialized as in the classical closed-economy case, where it allows more labour to be sustained in the capital-goods sector. Nor, for that matter, will the centralization of monetary balances in the central accumulation fund automatically provide the investment goods required, although it may serve to reduce inflation by helping to adjust domestic consumption demand down toward the output of Department II.

The surplus that can be accumulated is essentially that acquired through foreign trade: the excess of exports from Department I (or credits, of course) over the imports (M') needed for the simple reproduction of all the sectors is available to import capital goods and the inputs to the limited domestic production of, for instance, cement.

This is equivalent, of course, to the previous definition of the accumulable surplus in macroeconomic terms – the difference between total net product (I + II $-M'$) and socially necessary consumption (IIa) - except that one form is not translatable into the other because consumption goods and services are not generally traded. To the extent that Department II output requires imported inputs, the reduction of this output will release foreign exchange to import consumer goods, but the effect will be disproportionate (depending on the import coefficient) and lead to severe distortions in the economy. Thus the only way to increase accumulation is to increase exports, which means investment in Department I.

As the foreign trade sector is centralized by the state and the other forms of production are paid in local currency, these cannot accumulate at will and the accumulable surplus is, in fact, in the hands of the state – a particular form of 'primitive socialist accumulation'. The extent of this surplus is a complex matter. On the one hand, it will depend upon the structure of Department I itself: its previous capitalization, the extent of the natural resources, the intensity of the labour process, the import content of real wages (which depends on productivity in Department II), and the import content (direct and indirect) of the inputs it requires. On the other hand, it depends upon the international terms of trade for the commodity basket exported and imported, and the extent of the differential rent for the country in question. Non-essential consumption (that is, Department IIb) is often identified as a potential source of surplus, in the sense that capitalist consumption can be drastically reduced without affecting the workers' standard of living (Mandel, 1962). This may be true at an early stage in the transition, but to the extent that the nature of Department IIb is transformed into one of incentive to the productivity previously obtained by coercion, the saving may not be as large as expected. Moreover, much of the luxury consumption was in the form of housing, personal services and so on, which cannot be converted directly into foreign exchange.

7.3 ACCUMULATION AND PLANNING

We have seen how the current balance of output and income distribution is determined in the PPE, with basic needs supply underpinning the level of popular consumption (particularly at the early stages of development) and the balance of payments determining the surplus available for accumulation (though the two are interconnected). The planned rate of investment will determine the required surplus and imports of capital goods, and thus establish a new consumption equilibrium through the disposition of imported inputs for Department IIb. However, investment must be allocated between different production sectors, and this will alter future equilibria, in terms of both relative output levels and labour productivity. The achievement of the correct balance between consumption and investment is the task of the plan. However, a major problem in any real socialist economy is 'accumulation bias':[10] the tendency for the state managers to subordinate popular consumption to investment and, by implication, to 'generate more accumulation than the population as a whole would have wished if given a choice' (Nuti, 1979, p. 248). This is not necessarily just due to the managers' own class interests, but might arise from their more 'strategic' viewpoints, although even these latter could be attributed to inappropriate ideological concepts of the nature of economic development in general, and industrialization in particular. None the less, attempts to lower the rate of consumption seem eventually to meet with considerable social resistance and result in economic crisis. In other words, the restrictions imposed by the underdeveloped production structure on the one hand, and the lack of complete plan control over the labour process (that is, productivity) on the other, will severely limit the accumulation plan that can be feasibly implemented.

Departments I and IIb, providing exports, energy and construction on the one hand, and non-basic consumption on the other, are the basis for industrialization and the main destinations for imported capital goods. The allocation between the two Departments depends upon future growth plans, because investment in the export sector permits a higher rate of accumulation in the future. The allocation to non-basic consumption affects not only future possibilities for expanding the wagegoods basket, but also the supply response from peasant food producers. It is not difficult to show that, for stable external terms of trade, the two Departments should expand at more or less the same rate. If they do not, there will either be an excess supply of foreign exchange to no purpose (if Department I expands more rapidly than Department IIb) or a chronic deficit will develop (if the reverse is true). It can also be shown that for each planned growth rate, there is a definite opening balance of both output *and* investment in the two Departments, which the development plan should start (after an appropriate adjustment period) and then maintain through the plan period.[11] The natural tendency of planners, or of state managers as a whole, is to push for high rates of modern sector accumulation and growth, and thus an 'accumulation bias' expressed as an emphasis on Department I rather than Department II. This will be transmitted as a lower stimulus to Department IIb, a lower rate of growth of Department IIa (because the internal terms of trade deteriorate), and thus a lower rate of growth of consumption overall. The aggregate growth rate of the economy will apparently be slowed down by Department IIb, particularly if this is dominated by small-scale agriculture. Attempts to overcome this problem by forced collectivization have generally proved unsuccessful, while mechanization of the sector via state farms will reduce the capital resources available for the 'modern' sector, the real problem being in the relations of exchange rather than the relations of production.

The 'choice of technique', or the relative degree of capital intensity in different branches, is a key determinant of any development model, affecting as it does the distribution of income and the growth rate in the long run (Dobb, 1970). The logic of my analysis so far would indicate several things. As high a degree of economic autonomy (that is, minimum imports) as possible would be sought in basic needs production (Department IIa) so as to guarantee minimum standards of living for the population independently of external fluctuations. The maintenance of petty production (albeit in co-operative form) in this sector would seem to imply, in combination with the autonomy criterion, a relatively low level of mechanization and thus high absorption of the labour force. In contrast, the need to raise real wages and maintain international competitiveness in Department I would involve a relatively high level of technology (and thus import-dependence), and a correspondingly low rate of labour absorption.

The transition process itself, however, creates new accumulation possibilities. Firstly, the expansion and standardization of consumption, as a result of redistribution of income, should permit the expansion of basic industries in Department IIa to mass produce consumer goods (textiles, footwear and so on), inputs for the social services (books, medicines and so on), and basic production as part of Department I (cement, fertilizers and so on). This planned expansion of the internal wagegoods and input supply (which the previous model was unable to create because of narrow markets and enterprise competition) should allow the necessary standardization and economies of scale to be reached more easily, and costs to be kept down to international levels. Secondly, the economy can benefit from a certain advantage of its reduced size in the sense that it can import the latest technologies embodied in capital goods without setting up a heavy industry of its own, making a virtue out of a necessity. Thirdly, it is possible to specialize in the technology pertaining to a selected few of its own activities, such as agricultural inputs or natural resource processing – initially to develop the economy itself, but later as export activities in their own right.[12] Fourthly, it should not be forgotten that the training of the labour force itself is the best form of investment, allowing the best possible use of existing resources as well as the effective absorption of imported technologies.

In this broad sense, industrialization is the essence of economic development in an economy where basic needs provision is the strategic priority. This does not mean priority for 'industry' over 'agriculture' as if the former leads necessarily to faster productivity growth or more rapid proletarianization of the work-force than does the latter.[13] However, the central part played by the external terms of trade in the accumulation balance means that as the terms of trade deteriorate it may be necessary to invest even more in the export sector and sacrifice consumption growth in order to maintain necessary accumulation. Uncertainty as to future price fluctuations may vitiate planning: in general this means that 'investment' in foreign exchange reserves may be desirable. In particular, the structure of the PPE is such that export goods can be converted into wagegoods through imports but not the other way around, so that faced by an unanticipated deterioration in the external terms of trade, the investment programme can only be maintained by disproportionate cuts in consumption. An unanticipated improvement can simply be converted into imported consumption goods, to maintain the desired balance. Thus there are strong arguments, in the presence of uncertainty, for planning a higher rate of export growth than otherwise, but in order to create working capital (that is, reserves) rather than fixed assets.

The real living standards of the population, especially in the early stages of planned development, depend upon basic needs provision – the rate of growth of Department IIa relative to that of the population. This depends upon increasing productivity in social services; but also upon productivity in the peasant sector which in turn, once the fundamental land reform and so on have been carried out, depends on the internal terms of trade: the supply of material inputs and consumer goods that permit higher farm output and make it worthwhile from the farmers' point of view. As development proceeds, the wagegoods basket will contain a steadily higher proportion of the 'superior'

Department IIb goods, and social services may well become more 'technical' (hospitals, universities and so on) too. This will make the trade-off between investment and consumption more and more direct. In the early stages, however, the foreign exchange constraint should not bind so tightly on basic needs, so that necessary consumption can be raised without detriment to investment. However, this is only possible if reliance is placed on mobilizing the labour force itself, instituting peasant co-operatives and self-help housing schemes, for example; it cannot be done through the capital-intensive state sector. This may require political developments if basic needs are to depend upon development of production relations rather than productive forces, so to speak, because it would effectively place control of the reproduction of the labour force in the hands of that labour force, rather than under direct control of the state.

Changes in income distribution over time would presumably follow from three separate trends. The first is the expansion of basic needs supply, which will underpin the overall level of popular consumption which will rely in part upon adequate Department IIb supplies. The second is the absorption of labour into the modern sector. In the simplest cases where modern sector output grows at a steady rate without increasing capital intensity, the availability of industrial wagegoods per employee (either directly, or indirectly in exchange for peasant food) will, in fact, be stable, so the real wage will not rise. In other words, the wage share in personal incomes will rise and the income distribution (in the sense of the relation between peasant and proletarian incomes) will improve, as peasants become proletarianized at a constant real wage. If capital-intensity in the modern sector rises, then wages can rise with increasing labour productivity in Department IIb; but this will mean less absorption of peasants into the proletariat, and thus a worse distribution. In other words, rapid accumulation will lead to greater differentiation. Thirdly, there is the question of the incomes of the administrative and technical class. This is essentially a matter of Department IIb output, and if incomes per head are to rise, the class's productivity must rise (which is difficult) unless their share of social product is to increase, because presumably their number will increase in proportion to the expansion of modern sector production, including Department IIb output itself. Thus there is some reason to believe that rapid accumulation will lead to greater differentiation here, too. In sum, it would seem to be reasonable to suppose that with rapid capital accumulation in the PPE, after an initial expansion of basic needs based on land reform and mass mobilization, there will be a natural process of deterioration in relative income distribution, even though the per capita income of no single class is actually falling.

So far, we have considered distribution between three social classes: we have also noted the negative response of food producers to poor prices – that is, to inadequate supply of Department IIb goods. I have argued that the rate of accumulation can be raised by squeezing real wages directly and indirectly, although this will not release a large amount of resources (foreign exchange) unless very big cuts are made. The source of accumulation is essentially rent, followed by wage-workers, not the peasantry – because the main constraint on accumulation is foreign exchange, not the availability of industrial workers or the food to sustain them. None the less, I have assumed that increased investment will increase production and, as the mechanization of the modern sector proceeds, raise labour productivity. The experience of socialist planning in practice appears to have been, however, that unless such mechanization is accompanied by appropriate material incentives (essentially a supply of Department IIb goods), then labour productivity will not rise. In other words, the potentially greater output from new investments has not been realized, and may even have been counter-productive. This seems to suggest that there is in some sense a 'supply curve of effort' in the modern sector labour process, not entirely distinct from the reaction of peasant farmers to the internal terms of trade.

I have also assumed, as Kalecki does, that there exists a 'government decision curve' representing the trade-off between consumption and growth, through the accumulation balance, where increases in the rate of growth can be obtained by cuts in real wages. The point on that curve 'chosen' by the government is seen as an essentially political decision, and although planners and workers might disagree on the point chosen, it can be implemented, albeit with undesirable consequences for democracy or external debt. However, if it is true that the growth in 'achievable' labour productivity is positively related to real wage growth, it may not be possible to choose any point on the decision curve – which essentially traces a negative relation between 'potential' productivity growth and real wage growth. On the contrary, the two curves may cross, so to speak, to provide a natural equilibrium within a given institutional situation. If this is the case, the result of an attempt to 'force' output growth at a high rate and planning for low wage growth will, in fact, produce a lower output growth rate than could have been produced by adopting a more realistic plan with equilibrium growth rates. This consideration reinforces the Kaleckian argument that 'the socialist planner should not be willing to raise the share of accumulation in national income if this leads to higher income but not to higher permanently maintainable consumption, the positive impact of growth on consumption levels being more than offset by the negative impact of higher rates of accumulation'.[14]

These arguments have clear implications for the analysis of the conduct of economic planning in the PPE. Planning, understood in the widest sense as the social organization of the economy according to the needs of the community rather than those of the property-owner, is severely limited by the fact that neither foreign prices (and thus the true 'output' of Department I) nor all basic needs provision (and thus the true output of Department IIa) are under state control. Central aspects of economic strategy must therefore be the management of commercial relationships with the world economy (covering price stability and credits, as well as the external terms of trade as such) and with the small-producer sector (covering community welfare and infrastructure support as well as the internal terms of trade), rather than the planning of production in the state sector itself. Avoidance of 'accumulation bias'[15] will involve less emphasis on the large export projects beloved of planners and more on popular consumption; this in turn requires more attention to Department II (superior consumer goods, and inputs for small producers) and a reconsideration of the development of production relations in Department III. Indeed, it requires a reconsideration of the role of small producers in planned economies, a redefinition of basic needs services as essentially productive, and industrial investment as the basis of the wagegoods basket.

As a whole, *this means a shift of planning objectives* (and thus of models) *away from investment and growth, towards the planning of consumption and financial stabilization.* The former aim should be seen not only as an objective, but also as a means of achieving higher productivity in a democratic society where, by the nature of things, peasants and workers cannot exercise direct control over the national economy and thus must still 'negotiate' with state managers through the production process. The latter aim means that more attention must be paid to 'market forces' to make sure that the volume and composition of demand is kept in line with the availability of foreign exchange and wagegoods in any one year. This may well involve the use of the financial system in a much more active way than is usual in planned economies: requiring both a strict monetary policy and the use of state banks as planning agents at the local level, especially with small producers. Both those foci of attention are a necessary addition to, not a substitute for, the need for long-range planning of the necessary economic and social infrastructure.

7.4 SOME CONCLUDING REMARKS

The general line of argument in this chapter has been that the structure of the peripheral planned economy where a popularly-elected government attempts to give priority to basic needs provision is fundamentally distinct from the 'classical' socialist economy upon which the planning literature has been based. Essentially, this derives from the fact that the constraint on growth is foreign exchange and not the supply of labour or wagegoods as such. In consequence, the possibilities for accumulation depend on international rent, and depression of popular consumption does not, in fact, contribute much to the rate of growth. The Kaleckian critique of the 'accumulation bias' of socialist planners, when applied to the PPE, becomes one of not only the undesirability of excessive export-orientation, but also the limitations imposed by the 'productivity response' of workers and peasants.

Little theory appears to have been developed for this sort of economy despite Kalecki's insights in the context of practical experience in the 'socialist Third World'. Crucial points such as the importance of the socialization of the relations of exchange and the forms of insertion into international markets have hardly been touched upon. None the less, the problems of sectoral balance in the peripheral planned economies do seem to have been a major cause of crisis in such countries, and thus warrant further debate if more just societies are to be constructed in the Third World.

8 State Accumulation and the Market

8.1 SYSTEMIC IMBALANCES IN THE PERIPHERAL PLANNED ECONOMY

Those countries of the Third World which embarked upon 'non-capitalist' development strategies in the post-war decades appear to have encountered a number of systemic economic problems that might be expected to have been overcome by central planning.[1] Among these problems are the recurrence of food shortages and parallel markets, budget deficits and underfinanced state investment, balance-of-payments difficulties and underutilized manufacturing capacity, and even declining real wages and conflicts with the peasantry.

These imbalances might be attributed to the very real exogenous difficulties faced by any underdeveloped country, such as hostile world trade conditions and inappropriate production structures inherited from previous regimes; and indeed their governments often justify poor plan results by reference to these factors. Alternatively, it might be suggested, as multilateral financial institutions are prone to do, that such disequilibria are the result of ill-conceived (or 'ideological') expansion of the state sector and public expenditure. The former explanation, however, denies any specificity to economic organization, and thus gives little scope for rational improvement of development strategy. The latter, in suggesting that these problems can be simply resolved by relying upon market forces to organize an efficient economy, ignores the reasons for the transformation itself.

The purpose of this chapter is to contribute to the analysis of macroeconomic and intersectoral disequilibria in these 'peripheral planned economies' in the light of current debates on apparently similar phenomena in the more industrialized economies of Eastern Europe. It is my contention that effective planning in semi-industrial economies relying on primary exports and a large peasant/artisan sector requires explicit recognition of heterogeneous forms of production, the proper role of foreign trade, and pressure for basic needs satisfaction.

Those Third World nations which explicitly adopted a non-capitalist development strategy generally inherited an underdeveloped economy based upon a primary export sector providing foreign exchange with which to purchase producer goods, while a large proportion of the population was still engaged in small-scale production activities organized around the household. None the less, the new regime was immediately faced with greatly increased economic responsibilities, to be carried out largely by the state.[2] Investment had to be raised so as to industrialize the economy appropriately and overcome underdevelopment in the long run; much of the population needed (and demanded) considerable improvements in nutrition, education, health and housing to bring them up to minimal levels of basic needs satisfaction in the medium term; while military and security capacity was strengthened in order to defend national sovereignty and the new social order.

Such an inevitable expansion of activities has usually required vastly more resources than those already at the disposal of the state, such as tax income or public enterprise profits, even allowing for external assistance. In consequence, some way of mobilizing resources from the domestic economy had to be worked out, by design or by default. What is more, the state became responsible for redistributing income between classes and sectors in the economy as a whole, and thus constructing a 'social mode of surplus appropriation' because the immediate economic interests of enterprises and households cannot be expected to coincide with those of the economy as a whole.[3] Our analytical problem arises from the fact that such a 'mode of appropriation' appears in practice to have such a disequilibrating effect upon the economy that the original strategic social objective itself becomes even more difficult to attain.

In Chapters 6 and 7, I attempted to deal with some of the more technical issues involved in the analysis of this problematic by adapting the Kaleckian framework for industrialized socialist economies and developing mixed economies to the case of the planned peripheral economy where the export sector effectively takes the place of the classical 'Department I', and 'Department II' can be seen as basic needs provision. These technical exercises indicate very clearly the material constraints faced by 'forced growth' concentrated upon the state sector, and the disequilibrating effects on income distribution and non-state output of attempts to reach plan targets outside those limits. However, they do not indicate why such imbalances should recur so frequently. What is more, such exercises tend to imply that the problem is one of 'policy error' that could be rectified with relative ease –

requiring only a greater command of economics and more political foresight on behalf of planners.

It is necessary, therefore, to explore those areas of the institutional aspects of the planned developing economy which might lead to disequilibrating state accumulation. In this chapter, I shall proceed as follows. Firstly, I shall examine the theoretical debate on the institutional origins of the disequilibria in decentralized socialist economies, particularly the theories of Kalecki and Kornai on the relationship between plans and market forces. Secondly, I shall attempt to define the essential differences between accumulation in industrial and less-developed socialist economies so as to modify the Kalecki–Kornai model appropriately. This enables a third step to be taken: of identifying the origins of excess state accumulation in such economies, and its limitations, particularly the reaction of various economic groups to the extent and manner of resource mobilization. Finally, the consequences for economic management of undertaking the reforms necessary to overcome this systematic distortion are discussed.

8.2 MACROECONOMIC IMBALANCE IN INDUSTRIALIZED PLANNED ECONOMIES

The combination of excessively high levels of accumulation, chronic shortages of producer and consumer goods, low labour productivity and enterprise inefficiency is hardly a new subject of debate in planned economies. Indeed, it is central to the discussions of 'reform' which have been flourishing for over two decades. However, in the light of the difficulties encountered in introducing market forces into a planned economy, a number of different interpretations of the origins of macroeconomic imbalance have emerged in recent years.

One approach is to conceive of the problem in terms of the aggregate balance between investment and consumption, which is taken to be subject to central strategic policy decisions. Kalecki[4] gives the classic analysis of the consequences of over-accumulation for both industrial and non-industrial planned economics; in terms of inflation, deteriorating income distribution, balance-of-payments deficits and production inefficiency. However, he sees the decision on the rate of accumulation as being very centralized: the cabinet (or the central committee) chooses a point on what he calls the 'government decision curve' which represents a trade-off between present and future consumption by the population. The implicit solution to an incorrect choice is more clear-sightedness in the cabinet, or perhaps a change in its composition. In fact, Kalecki proposes that the countervailing power of workers' councils be exercised at a sectoral level within vertically-integrated production combines.[5] In the last resort, this becomes an essentially political problem of democratic choice in economic policymaking: the effective participation of citizens in the construction of central plans.

This approach is not dissimilar in essence from that of those authors[6] who would argue that the macroeconomic problems are basically Keynesian in nature, in the sense of being the result of excess demand generated by high budget expenditures in an economy already operating at full capacity. Here, the implicit solution is less ambitious growth targets. However, it is not clear why such problems should be so endemic to planned economies and so difficult to solve because, in Eastern Europe, the degree of social hegemony is such as to permit quite radical changes in expenditure patterns when required. In any case, socialist financial practice is marked by extreme monetary caution and strict control over consumer demand aggregates.

Another approach is to see the problem of 'accumulation bias' as not so much one of policy error, but rather as one of vested interests.[7] It is suggested that state managers (that is, senior bureaucrats, enterprise directors, engineers and so on) have a joint interest in high rates of state accumulation and the suppression of small enterprise because their own advancement depends upon managing larger production complexes, new technologies and so on. Their own income levels do not derive from production efficiency, nor do their consumption levels reflect those of the population as a whole, but rather rely upon their privileged access to goods and services to which their position in the state apparatus entitles them. This situation not only leads to what might be called 'class conflict' between state managers and workers (and, by implication, with peasants and artisans, too), with severe political consequences, but also to state enterprise inefficiency because of extreme bureaucratization under the central planning system. Decentralizing reform measures introduced from above in order to increase efficiency and raise consumption meet overwhelming resistance from state managers.

'Feasible socialism'[8] from this point of view would involve, therefore, a considerable degree of reform in enterprise organization, particularly the expansion of small enterprise to create competition, and the extension of consumer choice to make enterprises responsive to demand. The social phenomenon identified is a very real one, but the motivations attributed to state managers do not seem to be so very different from those of administrators in capitalist economies, so there must be some further systemic institutional root to the problem, other than vested interest.

The most suitable starting point for such an analysis is probably the model of socialist state enterprise proposed by J. Kornai,[9] which is in essence a development of the Kaleckian approach to oligopolistic behaviour. Kalecki had argued that 'market socialism'[10] of the type propounded by Oscar Lange, Otto Sik and Branco Horvat, was based upon an illusory optimism about enterprise behaviour in markets, for 'the concept of free competition in the classic form in which it is treated in the political economy textbooks never existed in capitalist economies'.[11] In an industrialized socialist economy, full decentralization (even without private property) would lead to price collusion between firms, and leave no means of adequately adjusting to infrastructural bottlenecks. Kalecki stresses that whereas the capitalist economy is demand-constrained (ensuring productivity by bankruptcy and unemployment), the socialist economy is supply-constrained and, as it can be planned, is potentially a superior institutional system. Kornai takes this as his point of departure to build up a picture of oligopolistic state enterprise behaviour under conditions of shortage, where firms are no longer price responsive.

This situation of endemic shortage is not due, in Kornai's view, to Keynesian excess demand, but rather to the 'soft' budget constraint on state firms. In essence, his concept contains three central propositions: firstly, that enterprises can undertake new investment and expand production without limits of profitability or own saving, because their access to funds (from banks or budgets) is unconstrained economically, and limited only by bureaucratic delay. *Ex ante* planning is the main allocation system, but *ex post* adjustments are always needed due to uncertainty, which justifies the soft budget but does not release the corresponding goods. Secondly, that enterprises cannot go bankrupt even if they suffer financial losses or have productivity levels far below domestic or international standards, reflecting the social primacy of gross output and employment criteria over those of efficiency or financial return. Thirdly, that prices are based on average costs for the branch in question. The soft budget constraint is quite compatible with overall budgetary equilibrium because *ex post* savings are brought up to *ex ante* investment through the centralization of profits. Monetary policy is passive in such a system, adjusting automatically to transactions demand.

The heart of Kornai's contribution, however, is enterprise behaviour and its effect upon other sectors of the economy, particularly households. The demand for producer goods (that is, the output of 'Department I' in the classical scheme) does not depend upon income or price, but rather upon the autonomous expansion programmes of firms themselves, supported by their respective ministries. Households, in contrast, have a 'hard budget' based on salary income, but must suffer from the continuous 'suction' of consumer goods and services (that is, Department II output) from distribution channels by enterprises and government entities for 'on site' consumption by their own work-forces and, in the last resort, for special commissariats and so on. Thus there is a double conflict over resources: between Departments I and II for inputs, on the one hand, and between enterprises and households for Department II output, on the other. Similarly, it is the pressure to import producer goods by enterprises (and not exchange rate distortions or consumer demand) and the ease of selling exportable goods on the home market, which lead to balance-of-payments difficulties.

This form of behaviour is not accidental; it arises from the logic of the planned economy itself. The distribution of a great part of consumer goods and services according to need – socially or administratively determined – rather than market demand (that is, ability to pay) creates a continuous expansion of planned output growth; while the strategic commitment to full employment lowers the efficiency of labour and creates skill shortages. The 'paternalism' of the state towards its enterprises in terms of finance and subsidies allows investment demand to rise unchecked (particularly in Department I itself) because the objective of state enterprise is to produce, not to make profits. The input shortages permit Department II producers to neglect quality control and technical progress, thus reducing living standards. Production in a planned economy is thus not co-ordinated through the 'law of value' with its demand constraints, unemployment and bankruptcies as disciplinary instruments that make the market 'work'. Planning provides the output targets and fixes prices *ex ante*, but cannot enforce productivity norms *ex post*; unless they are adopted voluntarily.

The labour market in socialist economies has characteristic features, according to Kornai. Whereas in the capitalist economy, employment is constrained by aggregate demand in a Keynesian fashion (and indeed, wage control and job flexibility are explicitly maintained via unemployment), full employment is a fundamental feature of the socialist economy and is indeed a constitutional right. The result is what Kornai calls 'internal labour slack' within enterprises because of lowered worker discipline, reinforced by the tendency for firms to hoard labour. This concept is similar to that of 'internal labour markets' identified within the stable work-force of large capitalist firms. This slack is effectively only available for individual mobilization in the 'second economy' (that is, the informal sector), which also makes use of materials obtained from the enterprise. He argues that this labour shortage arises not from the achievement of a high stage of economic development, but rather from the institutional characteristics of the system itself.

Wage scales are set centrally so as to preserve macroeconomic balances; and although labour can move between firms and branches, it does so more in response to job conditions than to wage differentials as such, although wagedrift is observed for skilled workers. Capital-intensive investments are made, not in order to save on expensive labour, but rather in order to economize on employment and improve conditions for the existing enterprise work-force, not least the managers and engineers. The institutional conditions are such, therefore, that the labour market (as in the case of goods markets) cannot be analysed in neoclassical terms, even if 'distortions' are invoked to explain inability to clear via price. Firms are not responsive to input prices and workers enter the labour market through institutional channels; so even if wage controls and job security conditions were to be relaxed, the Marshallian equilibrium would not be achieved.

Unfortunately, Kornai does not deal with the influence of foreign trade upon enterprise efficiency, nor with the interaction of the state sector with small producers; which is surprising in the current Eastern European context. None the less, his model does provide a convincing microeconomic view of enterprise organization in the planned economy, as a complement to Kalecki's macroeconomics.

8.3 THE ORGANIZATION OF PRODUCTION AND EXCHANGE IN PERIPHERAL PLANNING

I cannot proceed to transpose the Kalecki–Kornai framework directly to my peripheral planned economy without first defining the institutional structure within which production and exchange take place, and the resource constraints involved. To do this clearly implies an enormous degree of generalization, so the following paragraphs should be regarded as 'stylized facts' rather than as a universally valid description.[12]

The central feature of such economies (which is clearly derived from their pre-revolutionary history as subordinate sources of cheap raw materials for industrialized countries) is the combination of very diverse enterprise forms and production systems within a heterogeneous social structure. The economy is integrated into the world market primarily as an exporter of raw materials, in exchange for which a substantial part of the producer goods necessary for the economy to function are obtained. This implies that production decisions respond to a considerable extent to world-market demand at international prices. There also exists a very extensive petty-commodity production sector, comprised of both peasants and artisans, that plays a large part in the supply of consumer goods and services. The state sector as such is confined to 'modern' corporate enterprises and governmental entities, and directly controls foreign trade, banking, wholesale commerce, factory industry and the like. The degree of foreign trade dependency and the 'mixed' nature of ownership reflects the size of the economy and its degree of industrialization, rather than political choice.

In terms of the classical production departments, foreign trade plays a crucial role in supplying producer goods (that is, Department I), so that it is the export sector which provides much of the growth dynamic. Of course, the domestic construction sector accounts for up to half of fixed investment in developing countries,[13] while local supplies of energy, chemicals, agricultural machinery and so on may be quite advanced. What is more, lack of skilled labour is often a constraint on investment capacity – that is, the ability to translate mobilized resources into increased production. None the less, many spare parts and new machines necessary for the expansion of state enterprises are imported; and these must be purchased with processed raw materials, at terms of trade which are not under the planners' control. It is one of the objectives of industrialization strategy, of course, to overcome this technological dependency; but it remains a central characteristic of such economies for a long period.[14]

The consequence of Department I having this characteristic is that the expansion of the state enterprise sector in particular requires greater amounts of foreign exchange, and not just labour (plus the corresponding wagegoods) for heavy industry as in the classical socialist growth model. This expansion generates pressure to reallocate domestic resources away from consumption and into exports, or for state enterprises to direct imports to the rest of the economy towards their own requirements. The 'suction effect' identified by Kornai exists, therefore, but in rather a different form from his model; while the constraint on Department I expansion is more severe than in his model, because it is imposed exogenously by the balance of payments.

Consumer goods and services (Department II), in contrast, are increasingly supplied from domestic sources in the peripheral planned economy; both because the luxuries consumed in the early period are no longer imported, and because of the conscious effort to satisfy the basic needs of the population using local resources and labour as part of 'self-reliance'. The product composition of Department II is also transformed by the rapid expansion of social services, particularly in rural areas. The production of these basic needs also becomes increasingly socialized; due not only to state involvement in social services, but also to widespread 'popular mobilization' in housing, basic education, primary health care and so on. When combined with food rationing and subsidized public transport as means of direct poverty alleviation on the one hand, and limited supply of consumer durables on the other, those characteristics lead to the distribution of Department II output being based on citizen entitlement derived from 'need' (albeit mediated by the political process) rather than commercial criteria as such. This popular mobilization involves systems of self-financing to obtain necessary inputs or skills (for example, teachers) and not just labour-accumulation in public works; such financing implies in turn appropriate forms of local administration.

The expansion of Department II is thus not constrained by market demand; rather it is driven by the considerable social pressures from below exercised by the newly-enfranchised population and the strategic desire of the new state managers to overcome basic needs deficiencies as part of modernization, as well as obvious political and ethical considerations. To the extent that the population will mobilize itself on a community basis to provide extra labour power, then there will be less constraint on supply, but in practice increased government budgets, inputs of producer goods, wagegoods and imported equipment become necessary to complement labour accumulation; although 'self-provisioning' can be obtained by *exchange* with the state sector. This is particularly so where the expansion of labour-intensive primary services (for example, rural health clinics) generate institutionally supported demands upon secondary services (for example, regional hospitals) which are themselves capital-intensive. In contrast to Kornai's model of Eastern Europe therefore, consumption demand is less subject to central control; and while Department II does compete with Department I for resources, it is somewhat less disadvantaged in the contest.

In my example, state enterprises and government entities do seem to behave in a similar fashion to that described by Kornai, although again with significant differences. State enterprises do have 'soft budgets' in terms of local currency resources, derived from cost-plus pricing policies, subsidies on basic services, and virtually unlimited credit from state banks. They are not allowed to go bankrupt, however inefficient (although directors may, of course, be moved), nor can they lay off labour easily. On the contrary, labour is hoarded because not only are skilled workers in very short supply nationally and employment protection legislation enforced, but also because it is difficult to find labour at all when it is needed because of the other alternatives available in a mixed economy, particularly where agriculture is seasonal.

These factors make state enterprises in the Third World (both capitalist and non-capitalist) largely unresponsive to the prices of inputs and outputs, while the motivations for expansion and the soft budget to acquire local resources are as in Kornai's model. Labour is attracted by employment conditions as much as by wage levels (leading firms to introduce extensive welfare services) but its intensity of effort does not respond to bonus payments. The difference with Kornai's model lies in the hard *foreign* currency budget that enterprises face, as production cannot be maintained nor expansion take place without access to imports. Foreign exchange is strictly rationed by the central authorities and, although this may not be allocated on strict profitability criteria, it certainly will not be freely available to any enterprise. This, in turn, makes preferential access to foreign credits crucial to state enterprises because loans tend to be branch-specific and thus 'softer'.

Government institutions in industrialized socialist countries come under strict budgetary control, and are fully financed by turnover taxes. In my example, as we have seen, the social pressure for basic social services and military exigencies are quite independent of the natural expansionary proclivities of bureaucracy or of limits of a narrow tax base. Once quantitative targets are set, ministries feel entitled to spend any sum required in order to meet them, as long as it is in domestic currency. Thus the only effective control open to the financial authorities is to limit public sector wages (leading to an unmotivated civil service) and to restrict imports, leading to underutilized hospitals and so on. Local purchasing of goods and services by the government puts particular pressure on Department II markets, in contrast to state enterprises, which tend to squeeze Department I more.

The motivation for state expansion is also somewhat different in my example from that described by Kornai. He sees this as the result of the natural but unconstrained ambitions of state managers under soft budget constraints, combined with the growth ideology of national leadership, implicitly concerned in both cases to 'catch up with capitalism'. He contrasts this with demand-constrained oligopolistic capitalist firms, for whom unprofitable expansion would spell ruin. In the case of the Third World, both the motivations and the basis of comparison are different from Kornai's model. As far as state managers are concerned, the ideology of modernization is more concerned with 'overcoming backwardness': a combination of a moral reaction against absolute poverty and the nationalist assertion of economic sovereignty. This seems to require the construction of a strong state sector as a vehicle for rapid economic transformation: strong in terms of both resources and political support. Two further factors of a non-economic nature are probably relevant. Firstly, the military nature of many revolutionary movements and the subsequent need to rebuild national defence capacity lead by extension to a hierarchical perception of economic organization. The provisioning of the armed forces themselves, and the mobilization of sufficient, skilled manpower, also seem to require greater resource centralization in the state. Secondly, the rigid and outdated notions of both Marxist–Leninist theory and planning practice that have been transmitted from the industrialized socialist countries[15] give the impression that state ownership is both a necessary and sufficient condition for building socialism.

The comparison with capitalist enterprise is also different from the viewpoint of the Third World. Large private firms in developing countries (including transnational corporations) benefit from considerable state protection in the form of tariff barriers, price regulation, market shares, infrastructure provision and so on. They also benefit from preferential access to bank credit and natural resources. In this sense, corporations in capitalist developing countries may well have what amount to 'soft budgets' and not be truly constrained by demand or finance or efficiency. Private exporters must, of course, face international competition, but then the same may be said of state enterprises selling on world markets. The main difference between private and state enterprise (apart from the obvious subjection of the latter to greater ministerial control than the former) is the fact that private entrepreneurs can move their capital to more profitable branches (including speculation), indulge in luxury consumption, or shift their financial assets overseas. State managers cannot do this on any considerable scale, and can only accumulate by expanding production in their own branch or in closely related activities.

Petty commodity production, in both rural and urban areas, is a characteristic feature of poor economies: the relationship between the state sector and the peasantry, of course, has been a central feature of the debates on socialist transition since the NEP.[16] This was so then because practically the entire food supply (considered as equivalent to Department II) was in the hands of peasants. In my example, petty commodity production cannot simply be equated with peasant food producers, despite their evident importance. On the one hand, state enterprises supply a considerable proportion of the wagegoods basket itself (processed foodstuffs, textiles and so on) as well as the goods required for exchange with the peasants for the food they market. On the other hand, small farmers may well be supplying major export crops (and thus effectively forming part of Department I), while artisans provide essential goods and services (such as footwear). Small traders probably form an essential part of the retail distribution network. Finally, many social services, which are outside commodity production altogether, are organized by local community groups and are consumed directly by their producers. As these groups form part of the market economy themselves, this is a good reason for linking social services provision to collective forms of producing commodities. All these activities, moreover, require inputs supplied by the state, either in the form of imports and producer goods or in that of infrastructure such as water, roads or energy.

The nature of petty production is clearly *quantitatively* distinct from the situation in industrialized socialist countries. The proportion of the work-force engaged in such activities is much higher, and its contribution to output in a number of labour-intensive branches much greater. The state is materially constrained by its lack of administrative capacity and the dispersed nature of the production process from directly controlling much of the economy. This is not just a question of the relative efficiency of state farms and peasants; rather that there is no realistic alternative to peasant production. This situation, it should be noted, is independent of the frequent long-term desire on the part of socialist planners to absorb the whole 'informal' sector into the 'modern' sector in a Lewisian fashion over the long run, for even if this were desirable or feasible, it would require an extended period of massive accumulation to provide sufficient wage employment.

The nature of petty commodity production is also *qualitatively* different from the situation in industrialized socialist countries. The commodities produced and sold by peasants and artisans are generally unsophisticated consumer items or raw materials; almost the reverse obtains in advanced socialist economies where petty production is encouraged in areas such as specialized tailoring, quality restaurants, consumer durables repairs or private holiday housebuilding. Of course, in both cases there are 'grey' areas of transactions involving illegal activities and stolen goods, but it is essential to contrast the supplementary nature of petty production in developed socialism with its fundamental role in basic production in developing countries.

The petty production sector requires access to the resources controlled by the state: on the one hand, production inputs to its own production process (barbed wire, fertilizers, cement, cloth and so on); and on the other, consumer goods to maintain household consumption. The exchange relationship with the state involves both these categories: the former closely related to credit and extension programmes; the latter to official marketing channels. The internal terms of trade (reflecting the prices of inputs, outputs and consumer goods) are a major determinant of the petty producers' disposition to produce for the market and to sell through regulated channels. However, it is the *availability* of exchange-goods as much as their relative prices which will determine this disposition, and even the ability to produce at all. Shortages of inputs lead not only to parallel markets in produce, but also in the inputs themselves.

In Kornai's model, the soft-budgeted state enterprises crowd out (or 'siphon off', in his terminology) the hard-budgeted households. In my economies, state enterprises are soft-budgeted in local currency, but hard-budgeted in foreign exchange, so crowding out takes the form of reducing petty producers' access to productive inputs available on the domestic market by using their greater purchasing power and more favoured administrative position. State enterprises and government entities also drain off 'exchange' goods for their own use. This is combined with a policy inclination to hold down the official prices of consumer goods (particularly food) in order to sustain the real value of wages in the state sector, in response to demands by organized workers. In sum, the 'siphon effect' operates between the two enterprise forms, rather than between enterprises and households, as in Kornai's model.

What is more, while Kornai's households have hard budgets made up of centrally-planned wages (and no consumer credit), in my example households are as often as not engaged in small-scale production themselves, which allows them to increase their monetized demand at times of shortage quite independently of wage policies. Indeed, an optimal 'household strategy' may well involve having some members in the state sector (to obtain access to official services and rationed goods) and others in the petty commodity sector, in order to augment monetary income.[17] Although such 'multi-modal' households do face a hard-budget constraint (in the sense that they do not generally have access to endless credit, nor can they raise their own prices) they do appear to have much more autonomy as economic actors than their counterparts in Eastern Europe. This is derived from their ability to generate non-wage incomes and to gain access to non-state marketing channels, thus enabling households to 'compete' much more effectively with state enterprise than in Kornai's model. Indeed, the 'multi-modal' household can constitute a powerful mechanism for petty-capitalist accumulation in the rural economy, once family survival has been guaranteed.

8.4 THE ACCUMULATION PROBLEM

From the discussion so far, it should be clear that the planning of aggregate investment is highly constrained by the institutional framework of the economy. Both the level and composition of capital formation are bound by the intersectoral balances required in such a heterogeneous economy, and above all by the effects of resource mobilization on non-state sectors. In perspective planning theory[18] as applied to industrialized socialist countries, the long-term consumption levels set for the population permit production output targets to be derived for final and intermediate goods, required capacity expansion to be estimated, and the corresponding investment to be programmed – subject to short-term consumption requirements and trade balances. It is assumed in such theory that the state controls all these variables directly, but in my example this is not true. Quite apart from exogenous shocks (such as the weather), the state does not directly manage either the conditions of world trade or petty-commodity production; its relationship with those two sectors, which determines to a great extent what happens in the plan period, is essentially one of exchange rather than control. The state is confined, so to speak, between the internal and external terms of trade.

The composition of investment will depend in the first place upon the balance chosen between export production and supply for the domestic market, as these two generally involve different products or branches. Any long-run growth target will (for a given forecast of the external terms of trade) require a specific export level to finance sufficient imports, thus determining by iteration the correct sectoral balance.[19] Too low an assignment to exports leads to subsequent exchange crises, depressed growth and underutilized capacity; too high an assignment, to excessive consumption repression and declining labour productivity. The choice of export branches themselves will depend not only upon anticipated world price levels (forecast or directly negotiated) but also upon the capacity to penetrate overseas markets, implying in turn both geopolitical relationships and specific processing technologies. In contrast, investment for domestic supply can rely upon planned domestic consumption requirements, which in the case of poor countries is undoubtedly simpler to ascertain, being essentially a question of basic needs satisfaction, rather than the variegated and mutating consumer demand of Europe. The expansion of producer-goods supply in existing branches can then be derived from the export and consumer-goods programmes, although the creation of new branches, particularly in capital goods, will require strategic technology decisions.[20]

The supply plans for export commodities, inputs, and consumer goods cannot have a mechanical 'input–output' relationship to one another. On the one hand, the essentially *exchange* relationship between petty producers and the state means that both inputs specific to small-scale technology and appropriate consumer goods should be programmed in proportion to expected deliveries to official marketing channels, which in turn implies specific investments or import allocations. On the other hand, the establishment of wage incentives for productivity in the state sector implies that (on the assumption that basic needs are covered by the base-wage and social provision) specific 'incentive' goods should be available in order to make such incentives meaningful. Again, specific investment or trade decisions will have to be made accordingly. Planners seem to overlook the fact that such consumption has a direct effect on production,[21] and that if those supply categories are neglected, labour productivity throughout the economy will decline, despite rising investment.

The choice of technique in investment projects and the nature of technology imported will also be conditioned by the balance between forms of production. It is not logical to adopt labour-intensive methods in the state sector in order to generate employment in a socialist economy where access to basic necessities is met socially, and in any case unemployment is no longer endemic to the economy. None the less, such entitlement must in practice be explicitly linked to the place of employment or community where people live, which will have an obvious effect on the supply of labour between sectors. Moreover, in sectors such as export processing, industrial import-substitution, communications, or banking, a reasonable international standard of technology is necessary in order to maintain competition. The petty production sector, however, can operate effectively at much lower levels of capital intensity even while undergoing the technological transformation necessary for its voluntary collectivization around common production facilities.

Thus balanced growth requires that specific accumulation targets be set for the petty production sector and the appropriate machinery, training and inputs be supplied: this technological diffusion is best carried out from the state sector itself, rather than in competition with it.[22] If the whole growth burden is born by state industry, not only will production suffer, but the capital investment requirements will drain off resources from the rest of the economy and place great pressure on the balance of payments. Mechanization is clearly necessary in order to raise and sustain the per capita productivity of the population, but this need not take place exclusively in manufacturing, nor in state enterprises. Indeed it may well be that in small economies without large domestic markets, higher education and research geared to the adaptation of international technology (particularly in the export sector) on the one hand, and the development of domestic technical capacity in branches such as construction, export inputs, food production, energy and transport on the other, would be a more viable nursery for infant industry. Progress in industrialization then affects the appropriate balance between forms of production, as greater division of labour permits further socialization.

Turning to the problem of resource mobilization to support the industrialization process (as well as that needed for economic and social infrastructure, defence and so on) we can identify two immediate sources characteristic of developing socialist economies: foreign exchange generated in the export sector (particularly to import machinery), and the use of surplus labour (particularly for construction). In the former case, the economic surplus available in the foreign trade sector is the difference between export receipts and costs, which can be expressed as direct or indirect imports, including the cost of wagegoods for the labour force. Export prices for raw materials are exogenous, and ultimately determined by the marginal production cost in competing capitalist export economies, which rely upon very low wages and limited social services. Socialist economies necessarily have higher costs of reproduction for their labour force so productivity must be higher in order to compete internationally, requiring modernization and further investment. Nonetheless, a good part of the surplus generated will in fact be rent, in the sense of taking advantage of a particular natural resource endowment or geographical location. The value to the economy of this rent depends upon the external terms of trade, and this is reduced by the process of unequal exchange in world trade. This is even true of trade with industrialized socialist countries which use 'world' (that is, capitalist market) prices as the basis for trade agreements.[23]

The economy as a whole, and the state enterprise sector in particular, has access to foreign assistance in the form of loans, donations and technical cooperation.[24] This forms an essential part of accumulation during the early stages of reconstruction, when both production and trade patterns have been distorted by social and institutional transformation; in any case commercial credits (beyond short-term trade liquidity) are not normally available to such countries. In the longer run, loans have to be repaid, implying the allocation of a considerable proportion of the producer goods (imported on lines of credit) to the export sector or to effective import-substitution, unless joint ventures are set up which are repayable in export commodities. However, such external assistance also strengthens the drive towards state enterprise autonomy. This arises in part from the fact that enterprises (or their sponsoring ministry) can in practice directly negotiate agreements with foreign firms and rely upon the central bank to service them subsequently, independently of the profitability of the plant itself. It also arises because the counterpart agencies tend to support state accumulation in particular branches as a client for their own exporters' technologies.

For my example economies with their large investment requirements, the relatively small and inefficient state enterprise sector cannot finance the entire domestic resource programme (or put up matching funds for import credits) out of its own profits. We have already argued that attempts to drive down the internal terms of trade in a Preobrazhensky fashion as a source of surplus (that is, generating large profits out of state sales to the peasantry) are counterproductive. Moreover, state intervention tends to produce what Saith (1985) calls 'selective commoditization', where particular commodities (such as coffee for export) are supported because surplus can be appropriated from them more easily, to the detriment of integral rural development.

Taxation has always been held to be the most stable method of financing state investment[25] but its limitations in my example are many. Direct (income) taxation could be levied on state enterprise or petty producers. The former has been useful for its administrative consequences (particularly if firms are encouraged to reinvest 'own funds' and grant profit bonuses to the work-force) and permits intersectoral profit transfers, but it clearly does not resolve the problem of financing the state. The latter, however, is difficult to collect, particularly because it relates, above all, to rent (in the sense of supernormal profits arising from land quality, location and so on) requiring data from land registers and accounts which, by definition, the sector does not normally generate. It is precisely the fact that the state cannot mobilize funds from petty producers which gives strength to my argument that local basic needs should be financed through territorial forms of collective production and finance. Indirect taxation, if it is not to be a concealed deterioration of the internal terms of trade or a disguised cut in real wages, must take the form of taxation on non-essentials. In socialist economic practice, this takes the form of state appropriation (through marketing companies) of the margin between production costs to the state enterprises and the market clearing price for such commodities or services.[26] This also corresponds to Kalecki's solution for the problem of financing development in mixed economies, not only to generate funds but also to prevent any deterioration in income distribution.[27] However, taxation does not generate foreign exchange; rather, it gives the state greater (and non-inflationary) command over domestic resources, particularly labour, wagegoods and construction materials. Macroeconomic balance is only maintained if these local resources are what state accumulation requires. Taxation may well be, therefore, a more appropriate source of finance for the government services and construction; while capital goods imports should be financed from export profits.

The non-state sector does have considerable accumulation potential on the basis of its own resources, which are not available for state appropriation because of the localized production process involved. Petty producers can mobilize surplus labour within the household or co-operative in order to carry out land improvements, construction, animal breeding and so on, as long as they are supplied with appropriate tools, and goods are available to buy with increased income. Denial of those facilities will reduce national investment without an equivalent investible surplus being released for state enterprises, while the labour surplus is not available on a continuous basis suitable for wage employment. This, in turn, is related to the state's own rural strategy and whether it is based on surplus extraction (by the terms of trade and selective commoditization) or on broadly-based basic needs provisioning and rural accumulation. The social differentiation that might arise from 'private' accumulation can be reduced by a combination of direct taxation, cooperative organization and restrictions on enterprise size. Such differentiation cannot be a sufficient reason, however, for suppressing this form of accumulation (particularly since it can rapidly alleviate shortages of wagegoods as well as raise the living standard of peasants and artisans themselves).

Community organization for local investment projects to satisfy basic needs requirements is a second form of non-state accumulation, which mobilizes underutilized labour without payment in dry seasons, weekends and so on, because the resulting facilities (latrines, schools, roads and so on) have use value for the social group concerned. Again, a certain amount of state input is needed in order to undertake such projects, but the labour mobilized would not be available otherwise, so the net gain for national accumulation is considerable. Moreover, as I have argued above, the state input for such accumulation (for example, cement) or services (for example, doctors) can be locally financed with resources (savings, taxation, or sales) not otherwise available to the state for national accumulation. Whereas in a capitalist economy there might be some sense in the radical critique of such self-help schemes[28] as a means of lowering the social costs of labour power and overexploiting the work force, it would appear that in a socialist society this could reflect a process in which households gain control over their own welfare as part of a wider process of emancipation.

At the macroeconomic level, even after an appropriate balance has been struck between foreign and domestic production on the one hand, and between enterprise forms on the other, the classic problem of the balance between aggregate consumption and aggregate investment remains to be resolved.[29] As we have seen, the planners' perception is usually such that there is perceived to exist a considerable range of feasible and administrable rates of state accumulation, with accompanying short-term austerity in return for long-term prosperity. The choice between the two is usually seen as an essentially *political* one,[30] but, in fact, there are severe structural constraints on high accumulation rates (although not on large investment *expenditures*) and that the minimum feasible consumption level may itself be relatively high.

The fact that non-state investment is 'crowded out' by being denied access to means of production or to markets (through planners' design or state enterprise 'suction'), does *not* mean that the labour surplus mobilized in such unofficial activities becomes available to the state, as we have seen. The national rate of accumulation would thus fall as state investment rose if this latter were based on diverting relevant producer goods (such as agricultural inputs, construction materials, and transport equipment) where the marginal productivity of the diverted resources is higher in the non-state sector. The level of aggregate consumption would also decline.[31]

The limits on investment capacity in any developing country (capitalist or socialist) impose a severe constraint on the rate of accumulation, even if supplies of imported plant and equipment are elastic. This occurs because of the limited state capacity to design, construct and put into operation a large number of substantial projects, particularly when these are 'green field' investments rather than the extension of existing plant. The problem becomes worse when major infrastructural investments must also be made in order to support the projects. In a soft-budget regime, therefore, there is a marked tendency to initiate more projects than can realistically be implemented during the plan period, leaving many of them uncompleted and creating inflationary pressures on supplies of construction materials and skilled manpower. State managers know from experience that once a project has been initiated, funds will always be available to continue it, and construction will eventually be completed. However, the net effect is to depress the rate of real (that is, completed) investment below what it could have been, while raising the rate of investment expenditure.

The essentially ethical commitment to meeting the basic needs of the population requires that a considerable part of current investment be assigned to supply those needs (that is, expansion of Department II), rather than to a 'growth' sector such as exports (that is, Department I).[32] The minimal commitment that consumption per capita should not actually *fall* already implies a considerable planning constraint in this respect. Kalecki's formulation of this problem[33] (in terms of a stable real wage) further limits the growth of the state sector as a whole because the supply of wagegoods to its own work-force must grow at a rate considerably *faster* than state employment in order to satisfy demand from rising incomes (see Chapter 6). If the basic needs commitment is broken, not only social discontent results, but also inflation (or black markets), which can only be overcome by reducing growth or importing wagegoods. The consumption constraint is, in practice, even more severe when combined with the foreign-exchange constraint than Kalecki states,[34] because state enterprise investments tend to be far more import-intensive than basic consumption projects, so that the fall in aggregate consumption required to balance increased investment is disproportionately large.

The level of aggregate consumption is not only constrained by egalitarian principles: practical management needs will also tend to raise it. In the first place, the efficiency principle of 'reward according to work' cannot be properly applied because of the initially low productivity of many groups, which would leave them below a socially-acceptable poverty line. In other words, a proportion of the population may well be entitled to a consumption level above their marginal productivity, which has to be subsidized by other social groups. Secondly, we have seen how 'incentive' or 'exchange' goods are necessary to maintain the intensity of effort. Indeed, state investment may even expand productive capacity without raising production if wagegoods supply is not raised sufficiently.

8.5 MACROECONOMIC POLICY IN THE MIXED ECONOMY

We can now turn to the problems of macroeconomic policy in such 'mixed' developing countries, where complete central planning is not feasible and the problems of financial control and pricing criteria must be addressed within the context of heterogenous behaviour by economic agents.

In the supply-constrained Kalecki–Kornai 'shortage economy', there is no lack of effective demand, and greater net expenditure will not lead to an increase in output. Money is passive in such an economy, even though budget deficits have been usually scrupulously avoided in industrialized socialist countries,[35] and inflation as such is not a major problem. However, in developing planned economies, fiscal deficits and inflation can become quite serious. Such deficits tend to result from the combination of extensive expenditure commitments and a narrow tax base arising from the attempt to accelerate development in a backward economy. This domestic deficit (over and above foreign finance for state imports) is financed by monetary emission because a capital market does not exist and bank savings from the non-state sector are unlikely to be sufficient. The general inflation associated with such deficits is none the less a result of excess demand (for example, state employees spending wages on food) and is not a monetary phenomenon as such, while the 'location' of such inflation in queues or flexibility in specified product prices depends on administrative decisions.

These budget deficits might be considered simply as 'forced savings' in the Kaldorian sense.[36] For a given *ex ante* level of domestic investment and foreign credit, increases in government 'dis-saving' are matched automatically by the savings of non-state entities and households *ex post*: either as 'voluntary' savings of unspendable cash balances if prices are fixed, or as involuntary reduction in private consumption if prices are allowed to rise. This latter may well appear to be an attractive equivalent to taxation, falling only upon the non-state sector if state enterprise wages and prices are adjusted accordingly. Both practical experience and relevant theory would tend to indicate otherwise. At first sight, the social (or even political) implications of inflation in terms of real income decline for wage-earners or other groups might seem to be the most critical of these consequences.[37] However, in a mixed economy, inflation will disarticulate markets for the various producers with consequences far more difficult to foresee or control. In the face of excess demand, petty producers are in a position to raise their own prices (possibly even more rapidly than state enterprises) so that the redistributive effect is forced back on wage-earners and the state itself. If the authorities attempt to fix prices, parallel markets will spring up immediately, leading to social conflict if they are repressed administratively.

It is true that the non-state sector will require a certain amount of monetary instruments (particularly cash) to carry on its own production and trade,[38] and that the government can run a small deficit in order to supply this liquidity, for which the petty producers pay seigniorage. Deficits of any size will have the effect of creating a progressively greater mass of cash in the hands of the non-state sector, with two destabilizing consequences. Firstly, this sector can more easily escape from credit control, accumulate speculative capital, bribe officials, and so forth. Secondly, as the national currency ceases to serve as a store of value, other instruments such as foreign currency or even commodities take its place. The involuntary creation of such a parallel economy implicitly redefines distributional priorities and can even affect political alliances.

The state sector also suffers the disarticulating consequences of inflation. Wage employment is relatively unattractive compared to speculative activities (particularly with state property) in the market sector; and there will be increased difficulty in obtaining labour. Financial control over state enterprises and budgetary institutions becomes almost impossible as accounting categories become increasingly meaningless, and soft budgeting reaches its logical extreme. Finally, the existence of large cash balances outside the banks in a situation of supply shortages and foreign exchange control increases the pressure on parallel currency markets and encourages smuggling, not only of consumer goods, but also of unobtainable spare parts by state enterprises themselves. Such phenomena are in any case intrinsic to planned economies because *ex hypothesi*, the allocation of foreign exchange according to strategic priorities differs from demand expressed in the market-place (for instance, tractors rather than colour televisions), even if at an aggregate level monetized demand and supply are in balance.

Inflationary state finance is thus not only an ineffective means of centralizing the surplus, but also disarticulates production itself, making macroeconomic management even more difficult than it is already. Reasonable price stability is a necessary condition for effective planning, possibly even more so than in a developing capitalist economy. Effective management of the economy thus implies not only aggregate demand balance, but also effective control over sectoral behaviour. My argument so far would imply that much depends upon overcoming the problem of the 'soft budgeting' of state enterprise and upon establishing adequate exchange relationships with the non-state sector. It can be assumed that the system of basic needs distribution becomes progressively 'demonetized', in the sense that distribution is according to need and organized on a community basis even though production may not be, so controls are essentially social in nature. General wage rates can only be set centrally because the aggregate wagefund must be matched with the planned supply of wagegoods in a shortage economy.

Given the extent of integration with the world economy, it may well be that the most effective way of implementing a 'hard budget' for state enterprises, concentrated as they are in the modern sector of the economy, is to express this in terms of foreign exchange. Such a procedure employs border prices for traded inputs and outputs (and applies indirect calculation of costs of supplying non-traded items such as electricity) and although developed for investment project evaluation in the public sector, is logically applicable to the whole state sector.[39] This would, in fact, be very much in line with the price reforms carried out in Eastern Europe, to ensure technological competitiveness with the West.[40] For a developing economy, it reflects the need for efficiency relative to other Third World exporters and the need to set relative prices for traded goods so as to reflect foreign-exchange scarcity. As most state enterprises cannot operate without imports, the linkage of access to foreign exchange to their own 'net balance' does provide a strong incentive for efficiency as export prices cannot be raised, and domestic goods can be constantly compared with import costs. The objection cannot be made that adoption of border prices for state enterprise accounting implies blind acceptance of the existing patterns of comparative advantage (rendering impossible the nurturing of infant industries) because major production or trade projects would still be subject to central evaluation on the basis of the strategic accumulation criteria discussed above.

A hard budget also implies the possibility of bankruptcy, closure or takeover if a firm is consistently unprofitable; a requirement which is related not only to the ultimate sanction for management and workforce, but also to the process of restructuring production as technologies and markets change. The latter is particularly important for peripheral economies, which must necessarily have flexible export systems in order to survive. On the domestic market, competition between firms (whether state enterprises, co-operatives or petty producers) is probably most relevant in cases of consumer supply (Department II); for producer goods, being able to match import prices (at reasonable levels of protection) seems a better criterion. However, in all three cases, the organization of labour transfer, spatial allocation of new plant to replace old, and income support during transitional unemployment are essential to reduce institutional resistance to plant closure, against which price policies alone will not be effective.[41]

Exchange relations with the petty production sector imply that state purchasing prices become a key planning variable. Targets may be set for food deliveries by peasant co-operatives, based on the physical consumption requirements of the rest of the population, but only if the correct supply price (taking into account input costs, prices of alternative output and so on) is set, and supported by credit, will such targets be met. In this sense, the position is the reverse of that for foreign trade, where prices are exogenous, but the volume can be planned. For major products, therefore, a constant process of *relative* official price adjustment has to be carried out because, given the supply concentration and the composition of market demand in a shortage economy, to deregulate such products would only create distorting 'suction' from the state sector itself.[42] Minor product markets can be deregulated more easily, but only if overall monetized demand in the economy is in equilibrium with such supply, for otherwise 'free' prices will rise disproportionately to regulated ones, distorting delivery patterns away from basic necessities.

At first sight, an alternative might appear to be simply to apply the same border price criteria as I have suggested for state enterprises, but there are good reasons for doubting this. Firstly, one of the long-term strategic objectives of socialist development is the voluntary collectivization of small-scale production in larger units with higher productivity, which implies technical specialization, building up co-operatives, social infrastructure, training and so on, all of which require considerable long-term financial stability and state supervision. Secondly, exogenous prices will not guarantee basic needs targets (for example, food delivery volumes) or support petty-producer incomes at low levels of technology, thus making income redistribution strategy much more difficult. Thirdly, households or small co-operatives do not have the capital resources or institutional strength (unlike state enterprise) to withstand short-term fluctuations in world prices.

There is no reason to expect the two price systems to be consistent with each other; and there may also be good reasons for having a distinct set of relative prices for consumers, especially necessities such as basic foods. It must be recognized that the conjunction involves a considerable tension between world prices (which the economy must respect due to its openness) related above all to accumulation, and domestic prices (to ensure supply from the small-scale sector) related above all to consumption. As Chapter 6 demonstrated, the 'correct' price set is highly dependent on the interaction between the internal and external terms of trade on the one hand, and the desired rate of growth on the other. Taking border prices as a standard would necessarily entail a 'cross-subsidy' system, but this is the logical consequence of adopting a domestic market system distinct from world market 'rules' and cannot be avoided, if only for reasons of income distribution. The question is, therefore, one of how to minimize the negative impact of relative prices on production efficiency. The planning authorities will be concerned with monitoring prices and costs in some detail, and with ensuring that subsidies support policy objectives in reality.[43]

An economy organized along these lines will inevitably rely to a considerable extent on the banking system for operational control of the economy, once a rational pricing system and hard budgeting is introduced. The tendency I have mentioned for socialist banking practice to take a passive position, financing any activity sanctioned in the plan, also requires reconsideration. This cannot be done by simply adopting the position taken by banks in a capitalist economy, where credits are granted on the basis of the borrowers' capacity to repay and underwritten by alienable assets as collateral. In a socialist economy, where state enterprises and co-operatives form part of a larger, planned system, loan criteria cannot be based on the profitability of the firm itself (which determines repayment capacity only in a capitalist economy) while property is not alienable to a bank at all. This appears to imply that banks would have to adopt an active 'planning' role (as management consultants, so to speak) in their relationship with firms, within a broader sectoral and macroeconomic framework set by the planning authorities themselves.

8.6 CONCLUSION

My attempt to apply the Kalecki–Kornai model of the industrialized socialist economy has revealed that once certain (considerable) modifications are made to allow for the existence of a large petty-production sector on the one hand, and a subordinate position in the world economy on the other, such a model does shed light on apparently intractable macroeconomic disequilibria. I have shown how the manifestations of the 'shortage economy' cannot be simply interpreted as inept government expenditure policies or excessive rates of accumulation; they are rooted in intrinsic institutional characteristics of the centrally-planned economy in general, and the dynamic of state enterprise in particular.

My analysis has emphasized the severe restrictions placed upon balanced state accumulation by basic needs requirements, non-state production forms and world markets. None the less, this cannot be taken to imply that state enterprises are necessarily pernicious, and that some sort of petty-production system under central monetary control would be a feasible alternative. The state sector alone has the capacity to transform economic structures, mobilize resources on a large scale, redistribute income, and negotiate with the world economy. It is thus inevitably the centre of any industrialization strategy: the problem is how to make such a model socially and economically efficient. My conclusions on macroeconomic policy and pricing systems suggest that a feasible planning system would be based more on the social management of the financial and commercial relations between the various institutional sectors of the economy than on direct production control by central planners.

Notes

Chapter 1

1. Chenery *et al.* (1986) p. 85.
2. See Chapter 2.
3. This has, of course, been true of policy studies from the time of the classical political economists, see Deane (1989).
4. See Sylos-Labini (1969), Asimakopulos (1988), Chamberlain (1990), and Davidson (1986), Kregel (1973) and Wood (1975), for instance.
5. See, for instance, Williamson (1985) and Stiglitz and Mathewson (1986).
6. IBRD (1983, 1988), IMF (1987), and Corbo *et al.* (1987).
7. See, for instance, Ellis (1988), and Eitman and Stonehill (1979).
8. Taylor (1983), and Edwards and van Wijnbergen (1989).
9. FitzGerald and Cooper (1989).
10. See Deane (1989).
11. The similarity is striking between the views of the 'founding fathers' of development economics and those of the classical political economists. O'Brien (1975) concludes his chapter on 'The Classical Theory of Growth and Development' by referring to 'development economists who really have something useful to say about economic development . . . [whose] . . . approach is wholly in the line of descent from classical economics' (p. 235). Although the former were undoubtedly familiar with the classics, there is no indication that they consciously imitated the latter; rather it was a question of similarity of circumstances and — in the case of those outside the Anglo-Saxon tradition of neoclassical economics (which Blackhouse (1985) limits to the period between 1890 and 1939) – of a continuity of intellectual tradition. O'Brien (1975) also makes an important point that is usually overlooked by the New Orthodoxy: the classical political economists – including Smith – supported a considerable degree of state intervention in infrastructure, education, health, transport, and not least in the regulation of banks.
12. This can clearly be seen in the reminiscences of the 'pioneers' of development economics collected in Meier and Seers (1984), which is somewhat ironic because the volume was commissioned by the World Bank as an anniversary celebration.
13. See Blackhouse (1985, ch. 27) on the relationship between the two schools, and Thirlwall (1987) for a discussion of Keynes' own views on economic development. Toye (1987) also stresses this source of inspiration for early development economics. On Keynes' microeconomics, see Deane (1989).
14. This tradition is not well researched, but authors such as Mandelbaum, Kaldor, Singer and Rosenstein-Rodan (and of course Kalecki) were influenced by Maniolescu and List as well as by Marx the economist.

15. See Rodriguez (1980) and Love (1981) on the ECLA school; and Meier and Seers (1984) and Blackhouse (1985) on Lewis. These 'peripheral' origins of development economics, in which the Indian tradition was also important, deserve much greater research.
16. See Kregel (1973) and Sawyer (1982). Kalecki and Sraffa (who profoundly influenced North–South trade theory) should logically be called 'pre-Keynesians'.
17. The theoretical concept of 'sound finance' was (and still is) the bankers' doctrine, based in turn on the classical idea of 'sound money'. What this meant in the inter-war period is set out in Sayers (1937); for its application to the Empire, see Plumtre (1947) and to Latin America, Joslin (1963). The overall approach in economic theory of that period to what was to become the Third World is explained in Blackhouse (1985, ch. 17).
18. See Lewis's contribution in Meier and Seers (1984). This very interesting reminiscence shows how Lewis has been misrepresented by the simplification of his 'dual economy' model, particularly by Fei and Ranis (1975).
19. Meier and Seers (1984, p. 134).
20. This comparison is made and developed further by Thirlwall (1978).
21. Baer and Kerstenetsky (1964) and Eshag and Thorp (1965) both survey this debate. It is unfortunate that subsequently the ECLA side became ensnared in the 'dependency debate' instead of developing its position analytically.
22. Shaw (1973) and McKinnon (1973) are the canonical texts.
23. IMF (1987) gives a summary of the theoretical position of the IMF on stabilization policy, while Garritsen de Vries (1987) explains the historical background to the IMF experience of balance-of-payments adjustment.
24. Davidson (1978), Weintraub (1978), Kaldor (1982) and Wood (1975) are good examples; Kregel (1973) gives an excellent survey of the post-Keynesian framework.
25. Dornbusch (1980) is the best modern critique of the Keynesian position on the open national economy, but as Davidson (1982) shows, the former can be successfully restated as a model of the world economy.
26. Steindl (1982) and Sylos-Labini (1969) provide the basis for such work, which has been mostly continued in a microeconomic context (for example, studies of multinational corporations) and still lacks a corresponding macroeconomic formulation.
27. Toye (1987) has an interesting discussion of the role of uncertainty in development economics, and makes reference to the neoclassical identification (Arrow, 1974) of uncertainty as a cause of market failure, because limited knowledge and uncertainty mean that the markets for investment, credits, technology and labour are imperfect and fail to clear through the price mechanism.
28. This does not mean that New-Orthodox protagonists are completely unaware of differences in economic structure between countries and markets. They themselves are often the best critics of their own theories. Nevertheless, the atomistic profit and utility maximizing behaviour and flexible, price-clearing markets always form the benchmark case in the analysis. This holds no less for the theoretical foundations of the IMF

approach to stabilization policy, despite its own claim that the programme design is 'eclectic' and not based 'on a particular view of the economy or on the convictions of a single school of economic thought' (IMF, 1987, p. 2). The IMF explicitly recognizes that markets are not always flexible in LDCs and that price signals may not always be effective. However, these are merely analysed as distortions; systematic differences in behaviour between economic actors and institutions are not integrated in the theoretical framework.

29. Sawyer (1985) gives an excellent synthesis of Kalecki's theoretical work on developed (that is, industrial capitalist) economies, and resolves a number of inconsistencies arising from his habit of rewriting his theories in successive versions. On the evolution of Kalecki's microtheory of distribution in particular, see Kreisler (1987). Unfortunately, similar treatments of his writing on socialist and developing economies are not available.
30. Feiwel (1975) reports Kalecki's post-war work for the UN, which, according to Sachs (1977), had a major influence on development economists at that time. Arndt (1985) suggests that he also made a significant contribution to Latin-American 'structuralist' economics.
31. See Feiwel (1975), Sawyer (1985) and Kreisler (1987).
32. Meier and Seers (1984). His papers on the subject are collected in Kalecki (1976).
33. Perhaps this is because:

    > The difference between highly developed and underdeveloped non-socialist economies can be formulated in a very simple way. In one case, existing resources have to be utilized and modern capitalism has learned the trick of doing it. In the other case, resources have to be built up and this requires far-reaching reforms amounting to revolutionary changes. This simple fact explains the difference in the economic and political situations in these two groups of countries and, in a sense, determines the present phase of history. (Kalecki, 1976, p. 27)

    Although it should be pointed out that his earlier work on the politics of the business cycle had been rather more pessimistic about 'the trick of doing it'.
34. Kalecki (1976). Robinson also argues here that Kalecki anticipated Keynes in the 'discovery' of the concept of effective demand. However, as Sawyer (1985) points out, the two approaches were quite different and that in any case the Stockholm school has a more legitimate claim.
35. Kreisler (1987).
36. See Chapters 5 and 6 respectively, where these sectors are modelled explicitly.
37. Kalecki (1976). I developed this concept further in my book on Peru (FitzGerald, 1979c).
38. For instance, Eshag (1983).
39. Kaldor (1975), see also Thirlwall (1986).
40. IBRD (1988), and IMF (1987).

41. I was adviser to the Ministry of Planning and the Ministry of Industry for various periods in the 1970s.
42. Lewis (1954) is the classic example, but this is also used by Fei and Ranis (1964) and even underpins modern industrial investment methodology (Little and Mirrlees, 1974).
43. See FitzGerald and Wuyts (1988) for a bibliography.
44. Davis and Charemza (1989) explain this debate very well.
45. An early version of this chapter was published in Spanish in *Revolución y Desarrollo* (1983, 1 (1)) as a contribution to the Nicaraguan policy debate of the time, which led to the shift towards a more 'pro-peasant' policy after 1984 – see also FitzGerald (1990a).

Chapter 2

1. Chenery *et al.* (1986).
2. The foundations are in Stone (1966, 1971); Bain (1977) gives a good survey of subsequent work on flow-of-funds analysis in industrial economies.
3. I am indebted to my colleague Rob Vos for his valuable contribution to this section.
4. For reviews of SAM-based and other CGE models with elaborated financial sectors and flow-of-funds structures, see Roe (1985) and Vos (1990).

Chapter 3

1. The first version of *Financing Development* was apparently originally delivered as a lecture in Mexico City in 1953 and published in Spanish, as Kalecki (1954). The second version, focusing on growth, was published much later, as Kalecki (1970a) although the date of writing might well be earlier. The two versions are republished as successive chapters in the posthumous Kalecki (1976) as 'The Problem of Financing Economic Development' and 'Problems of Financing Economic Development in a Mixed Economy', from which all the page references are taken unless otherwise indicated.
2. See, for example, Eshag (1983) whose Chapters 2 and 6 are explicitly based on Kalecki; Taylor (1983) is another example.
3. Stewart (1985) shows that the analysis of functional income distribution is essential to the macroeconomic framework for the 'basic needs' approach now espoused by the UN, many aid agencies and a growing number of Third World governments despite the exigencies of structural adjustment.
4. The second – and in my view less analytically satisfactory – of the two versions appears to be the one with which most economists are familiar. Both Eshag (1983) and Sawyer (1985), for instance, use only the second version which is discussed in more depth in Chapter 6 below.
5. Kalecki held the then conventional view (see, for example, Lewis, 1954) that higher peasant incomes would prevent the 'shift of population from

the countryside to the town, which is one of the main causes of the increase in the standard of living in the course of economic development. Disguised unemployment would not be reduced, and the country would be split into two sectors: primitive agriculture and modern industry' (p. 49).

6. This point is pursued further in Chapter 6 below.
7. The long-term burden of interest charges is foreseen, but 'problems of a more basic nature' (p. 56) are: political conditions on grants; distorted growth patterns from direct investment; and current balance of payments instability from capital flight. His notion of long-run bilateral trade agreements with the industrialized countries as a solution was included in the Brandt proposals some thirty years later.
8. On the empirical application of this Kaleckian principle to fiscal research in developing countries, see Toye (1978).
9. Kalecki regards selective credit controls as difficult to operate and recommends the indexing of financial assets as a remedy for speculative hyperinflation; but does not apparently foresee the consequences for industrial costs and thus (through the mark-up) for prices.
10. An appropriate term in view of this paper's appearance in a collection dedicated to Roy Harrod. According to Eshag (1983, p. 54) by 'mixed economy' Kalecki means a 'typical developing economy in which, although the bulk of production and of distributional activities are controlled by private enterprise, certain key production activities are undertaken by public enterprises, and in which the government plays an active role in promoting development through its investment, fiscal and monetary policies'. Presumably trade control, development finance, social services and infrastructure should be added to this list.
11. Chapter 6 contains a formal model of the second version of *Financing Development* which extends Kalecki's growth analytics to allow for the effect of the internal terms of trade on peasant accumulation, of foreign trade on income distribution, and of real wages on labour productivity.
12. Kalecki himself observes that necessities include much more than food; presumably the wagegoods basket could contain 'non-essentials', while the respective definitions would themselves change over time with rising incomes. Necessities are not exclusively produced by peasants either: government health services and manufactured beverages are two examples.
13. This implies a constant budget composition and thus a unitary income elasticity: this is not really consistent with Engel's Law, which Kalecki explicitly employs in his growth model (see Chapter 6 of this volume). The familiar Linear Expenditure System can easily be included in such models (for example, Taylor, 1983, p. 39). Using the notation of the Appendix:

$$p_1Q_1 = awL + \beta p_1$$

$$p_2Q_2 = (1-a)wL + (1-s)R - \beta p_1$$

However, the simpler formulation has been used here as it facilitates exposition without altering the conclusions.

14. The empirical evidence presented in ILO (1979) suggests that about a half of wage-earners' budgets is spent on food in developing countries. However, it should be remembered that in practice much of this food is manufactured, while even fresh products bear enormous transport and commercial margins: so the share of wage expenditure actually *received* by farmers may well be less than a fifth. This is not to deny that food is a necessity for the reproduction of the labour force, but rather that the economic linkage is not so strong as is often supposed.
15. Caballero (1984) provides an interesting model of price formation in peasant and capitalist sectors that could form the basis for an analysis of such supply functions.
16. Saith (1985) makes this point for the classic Soviet experience and a number of developing economies in transition. The 'backward sloping peasant supply curve' is often hypothesized but seldom borne out in practice, except in peculiar cases such as food marketing to pay colonial taxes, although even here it must be supposed that there is no rural trade in industrial goods (that is, $T=0$ in Equation 7).
17. Kalecki did not consider that the interest rate would affect aggregate savings; a view confirmed by the available empirical evidence for developing economies (Gupta, 1984). Any one firm's investment decisions would be limited by the cost of borrowing as interest rates rose against it in response to increasing risk of illiquidity.
18. Kalecki did not believe that a capitalist society could achieve rapid growth without internal reform (1971, ch. 12); although his discussion of the 'intermediate regime' (1972, ch. 15) implies that in those developing countries with weak bourgeoisies, strong state intervention could achieve industrialization in a 'mixed economy'.
19. This is not the same thing as asking where the additional surplus is *generated*; which would also involve consideration of worker productivity and the transfer of labour into manufacturing. For a discussion of Kalecki's views on this, see Chapter 6.
20. There is also a strong case for including construction, non-routine maintenance and technical education in Department I (see Chapter 7).
21. This is particularly true in cases where both exports and wagegoods come from the agricultural sector, not only where the same good (for example, rice in Thailand) is both consumed and exported, but also where output capacity (for example, land and labour) can be rapidly switched between export and consumption crops. A Kaleckian model for such a case is set out in Chapter 4.
22. This is because we have assumed that investment has no local labour input. The result will still hold so long as the employment created by one dollar of industrial inputs is greater than that created in the installation of one dollar of capital equipment, which is generally true. The long-run effects are another issue, of course, on which see Chapter 6.
23. Particularly because orthodox theory is surprisingly uninformative on the sources of financial savings, avoiding in particular discussion of profits and corporate deposits in the banking system (FitzGerald and Vos, 1989). It is usually assumed (Gupta, 1984) that bank credit is a real constraint on investment in the short run (as well as interest rates) and that money

supply determines the price level, without defining the transmission mechanism. Although Eshag (1983) claims to take an explicitly 'Kaleckian' approach to development finance, he only uses the second version of *Financing Development* and does not refer to Kalecki's monetary theory for industrial economies (synthesized in Sawyer, 1985, ch. 5).

24. Kalecki (1962) was originally given as a lecture at Cambridge in 1955, two years after the delivery of the first version of *Financing Development*. The only explicit reference to empirical experience in this paper is to 'such hyperinflation as occurred recently, developed in war or post-war periods' (p. 275), but it seems reasonable to suppose that Kalecki would have held the principle to be applicable to any situation where severely constrained supply and chronic budget deficits are combined.
25. See Sawyer (1985, ch. 11) on this topic. For his formal model of socialist planning, Kalecki introduces a 'government decision curve' with an implicit welfare criterion to balance investment against consumption. However, the relationship between wage rates and labour effort implicit in his practical policy recommendations would provide an alternative and more satisfactory closure. Chapter 8 contains a comparison of the Kalecki and Kornai models of 'accumulation bias' in planned economies.

Chapter 4

1. See FitzGerald and Vos (1989) for case studies of very different structures, which none the less can be formalized simply in models of this kind. Gibson (1985) presents a model with a 'real side' similar to that presented here.
2. As Kaldor (1975) points out, it was 'unfortunate that the very success of Keynes' ideas in explaining unemployment and depression – essentially a short-period analysis – diverted attention from the "foreign trade multiplier" which over longer periods is a far more important principle for explaining the growth and rhythm of industrial development'.
3. Examples of how the specific behaviour of the private sector determines macroeconomic stabilization are given in FitzGerald and Vos (1989): for example, the savings behaviour of small farmers in Thailand dampens, to a great extent, the cyclical effect of world rice prices, so that it is the peasantry rather than the monetary authorities who are responsible for macroeconomic stability.
4. See the discussion in Leff and Sato (1980), for example; as well as Chapter 2.
5. See Dornbusch (1980), and Kaldor (1975).
6. This approach is often identified with the Latin-American economists of the ECLA school surveyed in Rodriguez (1980), but can also be seen in post-Keynesian writings such as in Eshag (1983).
7. Taylor (1983) is the best exponent of what might be called 'analytical structuralism', but his financial analysis is far from complete.
8. Particularly the early (1954) version of *Financing Development*, reprinted in Kalecki (1976); upon which see Chapter 3.

9. This is most obviously true when food crops are exported; even where, say, cotton is grown for export and maize for local consumption, labour and capital resources can be moved from one to another, though land cannot. Moreover, yields from perennial tree crops can be varied at the margin by varying labour input and the application of herbicides and so on, even if new coffee bushes require several years to become productive.
10. This could, of course, be modelled by making food a non-traded sector, with demand forcing up its price and resources shifting away from the traded sector in the manner of Dornbusch (1980), but the effect would be the same and the analysis less clear. See, however, FitzGerald and Vos (1989, ch. 6) on how this can be done.
11. This sort of agriculture serves as the background for the analysis in Kalecki (1976), explored in detail in Chapter 3. For an interesting study of the food–export trade-off, see Braun and Joy (1968).
12. This is also the approach in Chapters 3 and 6, and implies a separate primary sector, which may be 'enclave' agriculture such as sugar or bananas under plantation enterprise organization.
13. Such linkages are extensively explored in Taylor (1983): they generate important planning insights, but would not affect our financial analysis substantially.
14. Such a system can easily be expanded to allow for different coefficients in various industrial branches (or indeed a whole input–output matrix), see Taylor (1983).
15. On the size and stability of the propensity to consume food, see ILO (1979). Note that this balance could be reduced to that of the 'traditional' structural model with fixed exports in the short term by setting $a = 0$, so that $E = Q_1$ and leave workers consuming manufactures only; but separating food agriculture from primary exports, as is done in Chapter 6 might be more realistic.
16. The absorption of migrant labour into an informal urban service sector, where demand is generated by wage expenditure, is modelled in Chapter 5.
17. The 'Kaleckian' approach to the macroeconomics of semi-industrialized economies requires an implicit reading of his discussion of developing economies in combination with his method of analysis for industrialized countries. Kalecki is not very explicit on the role of inflation as a mechanism of forced savings (rather, he looks at ways of avoiding it), but Kaldor (see Thirlwall, 1978, for an application to LDCs) sees it as the equivalent to Keynesian savings rising with nominal income, but after the capacity constraint has been reached.
18. This case could usefully be compared to the analysis of traded and nontraded sectors (in our case, Q_1 and Q_2 respectively) in Dornbusch (1980), which is also discussed in FitzGerald and Vos (1989) ch. 6, on Ecuador.
19. See Braun (1975), and for a wider discussion of the phenomenon in the framework of neo-Ricardian 'unequal exchange' theory, Evans (1984).
20. This view is often associated in the development economics literature with Griffin (1970) and Weisskopf (1972), but it can, in fact, be found (in a far more rigorous presentation) in a 1954 essay by Kalecki (1976). For recent empirical confirmation, see Gupta (1984).

21. See Thirlwall (1978).
22. Rodriguez (1980) gives the best intellectual history of the ECLA theory of structural underdevelopment; unfortunately it is only available in Spanish.
23. Roughly, the requirement is that $pQ_1 > p_3 mQ_2$; in other words, from (1) and (6) $aW > eF$, which seems reasonable. It might not be the case for very aid-dependent (high F) and industrialized (low a) economies, of course, but here we are explicitly dealing with the semi-industrialized case.
24. Hirschman (1968).
25. The differential for the primary sector is, in fact

$$\partial R_1/\partial w = l_1 Q_1$$

and for the secondary sector it is:

$$\partial R_2/\partial w = l_1 Q_1 - \frac{1}{s}(l_1 Q_1 + l_2 Q_2)$$

which is positive for reasonable parameter values.
26. Within reason, of course: presumably sectoral profits should remain positive, or above some minimum level.
27. Kalecki (1976).
28. Killick (1981).
29. Wolfson (1979) for instance, represents almost the last major work in the tradition founded by Hicks, Prest and Musgrave. The level of fiscal analysis in World Bank (1988), for instance, is very superficial.
30. This point is made by Reddaway (1963) in his critique of Nurkse (1953); albeit in the slightly different context of the effect of public works programmes using 'surplus' labour, where real wages are driven down by employment expansion in the presence of limited food supply. See Chapter 3 for a formal analysis of this particular fiscal impact. The equivalent concept in a developed economy is, of course, the Keynesian 'balanced budget multiplier'; although such a concept cannot be applied to an output-constrained economy such as that described in my model. Perhaps a better point of comparative departure would be the sectoral analysis of Kalecki (1971).
31. This proposition is empirically tested for the case of Mexico in FitzGerald (1981).
32. I refer here to the position of McKinnon (1973), although he apparently does not draw out the full structural implications of his position.
33. This approach first arose due to the very high interest rates experienced by Latin America in recent years as part of their 'liberalization' efforts: in a mark-up pricing system, higher rates feed directly into prices, bringing about stagflation. This is modelled explicitly in a structuralist framework by Taylor (1983), who makes it the central link between money and the real economy in his system. However, this effect can easily be exaggerated (see FitzGerald and Vos, 1989, ch. 2).

Chapter 5

1. This refers to the mid-1970s, when I worked as adviser to the Instituto Nacional de Planificacion (national planning office) in Peru, financed by the Ministry of Overseas Development. A key planning objective at the time was to raise the rate of domestic investment to constrain declines in the real wage, this while recognizing that the measures to increase domestic food output will take some years to have effect and that a substantial shift in the internal terms of trade in the favour of rural producers would be politically infeasible. For more details, see FitzGerald (1979c).
2. Lewis (1954) and Fei and Ranis (1964).
3. Little and Mirrlees (1974); upon which, see also FitzGerald (1987a).
4. See Harris and Todaro (1968) and Todaro (1969). Berry and Soligo (1968) develop the idea in the context of the opportunity cost of rural labour.
5. See Jolly (1973) for a useful discussion of the confusion of unemployment (or underemployment) with low-income occupations.
6. Newbery (1974).
7. The literature on this subject is voluminous. See, however, Griffin (1970) and Furtado (1970) on the overall structure, and Turnham (1971) on labour markets.
8. Clearly, this schematization is overly rigid, and ignores the 'grading' of medium-sized enterprise between the 'modern' and 'traditional' sectors. Moreover, apart from the intersectoral links provided by labour supply, wagegoods supply, and service expenditure (covered in this analysis) there is the widespread practice of 'putting-out' by large firms to small artisans, seasonal labour supply by peasant to modern farms, and direct income transfers between rural and urban areas by family members.
9. The migration process is clearly much more complex than that depicted here, factors such as educational opportunities being very important. Logically the income-equilibrium in (3) should be between peasants and the 'tail' of the urban income-distribution rather than the averages (Williamson, 1988). Moreover, the migration process usually involves movement to small towns before reaching urban areas proper. None the less, the *net* effect is similar to that described in the text.
10. If 'β' is expressed as an elasticity (that is, a marginal rather than an average propensity):

$$uL_2 = b(wL_1)^{\beta}$$

then (the neo-orthodox case, say) can be solved for:

$$dL_3 1 = \left\{\frac{\beta}{L} + \frac{1}{L}\right\} / \left\{\frac{1 - m/a}{L_3} - \frac{1}{L_2}\right\}$$

So that the condition for the general result ($dL_3 < dL_1$) holds where $\beta > \{1 - (m/a)\}L_1 L_3$. Anticipating the illustrative data in the next section, this would mean (roughly) $\beta > 0.4$, which seems reasonable.

11. The estimates given here are based on Banco Central (1974), Webb (1972) and Cebrecos (1974).
12. Newbery (1972), and also Chapter 3.
13. Griffin (1971). Little and Mirrlees (1974) do allow for a reduction in state expenditure in their formulation, but not the other variates discussed here. On this, see Chapter 4.
14. King (1971), Landau (1971) and ECLA (1972).
15. Theisenhusen (1972), Cline (1972).
16. Apart from Furtado (1970), see also Serra (1974), and Nolff (1974).
17. Such concern is expressed in Waterson (1965) and in many of the contributions to Faber and Seers (1972). Much is made of administrative inefficiency, lack of detailed information at the centre, the inflexibility of plans and shortcomings in implementation.
18. This view, to which we shall return at the end of this chapter, is well expressed by Griffin and Enos (1972) and illustrated for the case of Kenya by Leys (1975).
19. Upon which, see Marglin (1963) and Qayum (1960).
20. Davis and Whinston (1965) provide a good survey of the theory.
21. See King (1967) for examples of World Bank practice, and also UN (1958).
22. See, respectively: IBRD (1975), UNIDO (1972), ODM (1972) and OECD (1968).
23. This does not imply, of course, that the international terms of trade are in any way desirable, just that they are not determined by an individual project.
24. Alone among the four sources cited, OECD (1968, p. 92) adds to this class goods which *would* be traded under an optimal policy.
25. In fact, of the four sources cited, three recommend the use of border prices directly for traded goods (converted to the domestic currency at the official parity), while the UNIDO (1972) multiplies this by a shadow exchange rate, but this latter too – see Lal (1974) and Dasgupta (1972) – is equivalent in effect.
26. See, for example, ODM (1972).
27. This is explored further in Sen (1972).
28. UNIDO (1972) and Little and Mirrlees (1974) – this latter being a revision of OECD (1968) – all contain suggestions for this.
29. Stewart (1975).
30. Ryle (1949) pp. 17–19.
31. FitzGerald (1978b) explores the topic in the context of Latin America, and contains further references.
32. See Poulantzas (1968).
33. Harberger (1972) is the canonical statement of this approach.

Chapter 6

1. The first version of this paper 'The Problem of Financing Economic Development' (printed in Kalecki, 1976) was delivered in 1953 in Mexico: Kalecki's early work at the UN certainly had a profound effect on the 'founding fathers' of development economics in general and Latin-

American structuralism in particular. See Feiwel (1975) and Sachs (1977) on this. The first version is concerned with short-run macroeconomic adjustment and in fact contains a more rigorous and realistic model than the second 'growth' version of the paper considered here: see Chapter 3 above.

2. This 'second version' is entitled 'Problems of Financing Economic Development in a Mixed Economy' and cited here from the collection in Kalecki (1972a), although it was originally published in a *Festschrift* for Sir Roy Harrod (Eltis, 1970) which presumably accounts for the formulation in terms of a 'warranted' rate of growth.
3. Both Sawyer (1985) and Eshag (1983), for example, do this, citing the 'second version' almost verbatim and not discussing the first.
4. For a full definition of the modern category of 'basic needs', and its macroeconomic implications, see Stewart (1985).
5. That is, the 1953 version. For a detailed analysis, see FitzGerald (1987). Kalecki (1968) reaffirms his belief in the suitability of this reproduction scheme for macroeconomic analysis and growth models.
6. See Sawyer (1985); Kalecki makes an explicit argument for its applicability to developing economies, in the 'first version'. See also Taylor (1983) for the application of the mark-up principle to Computable General Equilibrium Models of developing economies.
7. This will keep the optimal industrial composition (θ) and savings rate (s) stable. It is an assumption adopted elsewhere in Kalecki's work.
8. Cornia and Jerger (1982) based on 120 surveys worldwide of household budgets, derive a value of the order of 20 per cent for s.
9. Through devaluations or adjustments in basic services prices, usually.
10. Which would then have to be redefined in terms of physical goods availability rather than by (20).
11. This argument is made on the basis of case studies, by the authors in Saith (1985) and FitzGerald and Wuyts (1988).
12. This point is developed further in Chapter 7 of this volume.
13. In passing, it is worth noting that a deterioration in the external terms of trade (E) will logically elicit an increased export orientation (that is, θ rises) to fulfil the plan – in other words, a 'backward-sloping' supply schedule. Also, the profit margin (g) in the export sector is implicitly assumed to be unaffected by variations in external prices (E), perhaps by appropriate adjustment of the exchange rate; on this, see Chapter 4.
14. Thirlwall (1972, pp. 252–7) is a good example of how this may be done with variables similar to those used here.
15. The comparison with Lewis is appealing, but not wholly appropriate. On the one hand, Kalecki specifies the dynamics of the capitalist sector itself, income distribution within it and the nature of the real wage, which Lewis does not. On the other, Lewis assumes that the food supply to the towns will increase as peasants migrate; Kalecki takes it as unaffected.
16. Kalecki distinguishes this clearly from the problem of capacity utilization in a mature capitalist economy, which depends on effective demand. In the case of a developing economy with capacity constraints, this concept seems highly appropriate.
17. He is referring here to his debate with Maurice Dobb and Amartya Sen on the 'choice of technique', on which see Sawyer (1985, ch. 11).

18. To be fair, the population of Mexico City, when Kalecki gave the first version of his paper there in 1953, was little more than two million.
19. For a fuller development of this point, see Chapter 5.
20. See Sawyer (1985, ch. 11) for a good account of Kalecki's position in these debates.

Chapter 7

1. For example, see Dobb (1970) and Bettelheim (1975).
2. For some recent work on these economies see Jameson and Wilber (1981), Spoor (1982), Wiles (1981) and White *et al.* (1983).
3. Ricardo, Marx then Kalecki (1971, 1972a, 1976).
4. I am indebted to my colleague Ken Post for this idea.
5. The technical dimensions of the internal terms of trade are discussed at length in Chapters 3 and 6 above; here we are concerned with organizational issues.
6. Guevara *et al.* (1968). Rodriguez (1983) points out, however, that Guevara never argued for the complete elimination of material incentives.
7. Rumantsiev (1979), for example, contains this inconsistency in his exposition of the 'General Law of the Socialist Economy': he emphasizes the importance of material incentives for workers, but then ignores the logically consequent positive relation between consumption and growth at the aggregate level.
8. Bettelheim (1975) argues for this, but only at the micro level.
9. This is, in the last instance, what concerns Guevara (1968); the attempt to construct an independent manufacturing economy in Cuba probably sprang from this intuition (see O'Connor, 1970).
10. For example, see Bettelheim (1975), Spoor (1982) and White (1982).
11. See Nuti (1979) for the results of this problem in Eastern Europe.
12. The obvious parallel is with small developed economies such as Denmark and New Zealand, which have achieved a high level of 'industrialization' based on agriculture and a skilled labour force.
13. Although even in the Cuban case, as Rodriguez (1983) points out, this was a theoretical distinction given that the adopted strategy was rather more of the type discussed here.
14. This is a standard result in Kalecki; see Chapter 6.
15. Nuti (1979) p. 262.

Chapter 8

1. There is insufficient space in this chapter to give proper coverage of countries' experiences, which would have to range from Cuba to China and passing through the twenty or so Third World economies outside Eastern Europe as such that might be classed as 'socialist'. Comprehensive studies are remarkably few, but the collections of case studies in Jameson and Wilber (1981), White and Croll (1983), Saith (1985) and FitzGerald and Wuyts (1988), do give some empirical basis for the stylized facts used here.

2. The introduction to Saith (1985) takes this as an empirical definition, rather than an abstract categorization of 'transition to socialism' as implied in Bettelheim (1975), and we shall do the same.
3. Hindess, in his 'Introduction to Bettelheim' (1976) argues that 'all social formations require the appropriation of surplus labour' as 'an effect of the difference between the condition of reproduction of labour and the conditions of reproduction of the economy as a whole'.
4. Kalecki (1986), which should be read in the historical context provided by Nuti (1986).
5. Chapter 6 shows how Kalecki's government decision curve might be superimposed on a 'workers' decision curve' also measuring productivity growth (based on work intensity) against consumption (that is, wage incentives). These two would have contrary slopes, and thus give determinate equilibrium indicating the maximum feasible growth rate.
6. This is a widespread view at present, as Portes (1979) indicates.
7. Nuti (1979) describes his approach as being explicitly Marxian, while Nove (1983) is implicitly non-Marxist, but they come to similar conclusions. Bettelheim's conclusions as to the emergence of a 'state bourgeoisie' point in much the same direction.
8. The phrase comes, of course, from the title of Nove (1983); although he unfortunately does not tackle the issues raised by Kalecki and Kornai, remaining in the realm of microeconomic efficiency.
9. Kornai (1980) is my main source here. For a critique, see Gomulka (1985), and the reply in Kornai (1986a). Kornai (1986b) contrasts his approach with that of other writers on 'market socialism' in Hungary.
10. Lange (1937) is the prime source; Horvat (1982) gives a recent version of a similar argument.
11. 'Central Price Determination as an essential feature of a Socialist Economy' in Kalecki (1986).
12. This approach is also taken by Kornai and Kalecki.
13. Wells (1986) is the only comprehensive study of this key sector that I am aware of.
14. This should not be read as an argument to the effect that such economies should remain raw-materials exporters; but rather as a statement of fact that they do. The proposals in Thomas (1974) for autonomous industrialization in small planned economies seem very optimistic: experience would indicate that successful small economies advance by industrializing their export base.
15. See, for example, Rumantsiev (1979) and Smirnov (1979) for recent statements of this as the orthodox socialist view on transition to socialism and development planning, respectively; although this may well be about to change.
16. Harrison (1980) gives a useful summary of this hotly-debated topic.
17. In which case, the concept of the 'working class' as a homogeneous social category (or even an ideological concept) presumably needs some reconsideration.
18. The theoretical foundations of this approach to perspective planning are to be found in Kalecki (1986). They are quite distinct from the pretended

'laws of socialist planning', propounded by Rumantsiev (1979), which were based on the maximization of the rate of accumulation.

19. This model was explored in greater depth in Chapter 6.
20. Fransman (1986) has an excellent analysis of the 'make or buy' decision in the capital goods sector. It is worth noting, in passing, that the CMEA system of aid to developing countries involves a more complete transfer of technology (albeit somewhat dated) than is customary with MNCs; see Cassen (1985).
21. Nutrition, health and education obviously raise productivity too by improving the capacity of the work-force itself. Both these points are overlooked by Kalecki and Kornai, which is surprising, given their concern for consumption.
22. Particularly in the agricultural sector; see for example, Hartford (1985).
23. Bogolomov (1983) gives an orthodox treatment of modern socialist trade theory based on world prices. Unequal exchange would in any case obtain between 'socialist centre' and 'socialist periphery' if wages and growth rates were autonomously planned in the centre.
24. I do not have the space here to discuss the problems arising in the transition from 'capitalist aid' to 'socialist aid'; but see Cassen (1985).
25. Lenin made much of this point, of course.
26. Wilczynski (1982).
27. There are other reasons too. Firstly, small producers are seen as a threat to socialism, on ideological grounds, although this seems to me to require political persuasion rather than economic repression. Secondly, they are administratively complicated to deal with, but this is an argument for co-operativization. Thirdly, state managers are logically opposed to competition in labour and product markets!
28. See the interesting debate on this issue in *Development and Change*, vol. 18 (1987).
29. Kalecki (1971) claims that this is the central issue in socialist planning.
30. Who the decision makers are is, of course, another matter; and the political consequences of high accumulation rates are profound, as the Polish experience shows. However, both Kornai and Kalecki (as well as other authors such as Nuti) see such rates as feasible, albeit undesirable.
31. National income statistics in socialist developing countries usually record only state investment and neglect household production for consumption, so neither of these phenomena will be recorded in the macroeconomic plan results.
32. This constraint is classified by Talas (1983) as a major feature of the transition to socialism in LDCs, arguing that this reduces their capacity to undertake 'primitive accumulation' by curtailing consumption in the non-state sector.
33. See 'Financing Development' in Kalecki (1986), which is set out in a formal model in Chapter 3 above.
34. Both those phenomena were discussed in depth in Chapters 3 and 6.
35. See Ellman (1979) for this argument as applied to the USSR.
36. Thirlwall (1972) expands on this point for developing countries along Kaldorian lines.

37. Griffith-Jones (1981) has this as a principal conclusion, based on the early transition experience of Russia, Czechoslovakia and Chile.
38. This point is made in Fforde (1984) who provides a fascinating microeconomic model of the labour interactions between state enterprises and the 'informal sector' in Vietnam. I would suggest, however, that in quantitative terms the seigniorage to be expected is small: if the non-state sector is 50 per cent of GDP and grows at 5 per cent per annum, its demand for money (assuming a velocity of circulation of 4) will only support a yearly budget deficit of 0.6 per cent of GDP.
39. The method is set out in Little and Mirrlees (1974). Although designed for use in OECD aid programmes, and officially adopted by the IBRD and other UN agencies, it is, in fact, more suitable for application in planned economies. Indeed the technical appendix to the manual is set out explicitly in terms of a Lewis-type dual economy where the 'modern' sector is state enterprise: see Chapter 5 of the present volume.
40. Kornai (1986b) introduces this factor, which is absent in Kornai (1980).
41. The Yugoslav experience clearly indicates the resistance of local (party) authorities to such restructuring.
42. 'Central Price Determination . . .', in Kalecki (1986).
43. This implies the application of modern 'social accounting matrix' methodology to distinguish between the accumulation balances of different institutional sectors, on which see Chapter 2 above and FitzGerald and Vos (1989).

Bibliography

ALARCON, J., J. van Heemst, S. Keuning, W. de Ruijter and R. Vos (1991) *The Social Accounting Framework for Development*, Aldershot: Avebury.

ARNDT, H. W. (1985) 'The Origins of Structuralism', *World Development*, 13 (2).

ARROW, K. (1974) 'Limited Knowledge and Economic Analysis', *American Economic Review*, LXIV, pp. 1–10.

ARTIS, M. J. (1978) 'Fiscal Policy and Crowding Out', in M. Posner (ed.), *Demand Management*, London: Heinemann.

ASIMAKOPULOS, A. (1988) *Investment, Employment and Income Distribution*, Cambridge: Polity Press.

AYALA, J. *et al.* (1979) 'La crisis ecónomica: Evolución y perspectivas', in P. González and E. Florescano (eds), *México Hoy*, Mexico City, Siglo XXI.

BANCO CENTRAL (1974) *Cuentas nacionales*, Lima: Banco Central de la Republica.

BACHA, E. (1990) 'A Three-Gap Model of Foreign Transfers and the GDP Growth Rate in Developing Countries', *Journal of Development Economics*, 32.

BAER, W. and I. Kerstenetsky (eds) (1964) *Inflation and Growth in Latin America*, Homewood, Ill.: Irwin.

BAIN, A. D. (1977) 'Flow of Funds Analysis', in *Surveys of Applied Economics II*, London: Macmillan.

BARKER, T. S. (ed.) (1976) *Economic Structure and Policy*, London: Chapman and Hall.

BELASSA, B. *et al.* (1982) *Development Strategies in Semi-industrialized Economies*, Baltimore, Md.: Johns Hopkins University Press.

BELTRAN, A. and L. R. Klein (1974) *Macroeconomic Model Building in Latin America: The Mexican Case*, New York: National Bureau of Economic Research.

BERRY, A. and R. Soligo (1968) 'Rural–urban Migration, Agricultural Output and the Supply-price of Labour in a Labour-surplus Economy', *Oxford Economic Papers*, 20 (2).

BETTELHEIM, C. L. (1975) *The Transition to Socialist Economy*, Hassocks, Sussex: Harvester Press (French original published by Maspero in 1968).

—— (1976) *Economic Calculation and Forms of Property*, London: Routledge & Kegan Paul (French original published by Maspero in 1970).

BIDELEAUX, R. (1985) *Communism and Development*, London: Methuen.

BLACKHOUSE, R. (1985) *A History of Modern Economic Analysis*, Oxford: Basil Blackwell.

BOGOLOMOV, O. (1983) *Socialist Countries in the International Division of Labour*, Moscow: Progress Publishers.

BRADFORD, C. (1987) 'Trade and Structural Change: NICs and the Next Tier NICs as Transnational Economies', *World Development*, 15 (3).

BRAUN, O. (1975) *Imperialismo y Comercio Internacional*, Buenos Aires: Siglo XXI, also published as *International Trade and Imperialism* (1983), Atlantic Heights, NJ: Humanities Press.

—— and L. Joy (1968) 'A Model of Economic Stagnation: a Case Study of the Argentine Economy', *Economic Journal*, 78 (312).

BRUNDENIUS, C. (1981) *Economic Growth, Basic Needs and Income Distribution in Revolutionary Cuba*, Lund, Sweden: Lund University Research Policy Institute.

BRUS, W. (1971) 'Kalecki's Economics of Socialism', *Oxford Bulletin of Economics and Statistics*, 39 (1).

BUKHARIN, N. (1979) *The Politics and Economics of the Transition Period*, London: Routledge & Kegan Paul.

CABALLERO, J. M. (1984) 'Unequal Pricing and Unequal Exchange between the Peasant and Capitalist Economies', *Cambridge Journal of Economics*, 8 (4).

CARR, E. H. (1972) *La Revolucion Bolchevique: El Orden Economico*, Madrid: Alianza.

CASSEN, R. H. (ed.) (1985) *Soviet Interests in the Third World*, London: Sage for the Royal Institute of International Affairs.

CEBRECOS, R. (1974) *El empleo y el desempleo en el Peru*, Lima: CISEPA.

CHAMBERLAIN, T. (1990) 'Capital Structure and the Survival of the Firm', *Journal of Post-Keynesian Economics*, 12.

CHENERY, H. (1975) 'The Structuralist Approach to Development Policy', *American Economic Review*, Oxford: Basil Blackwell.

—— and M. Bruno (1962) 'Development Alternatives in an Open Economy: The Case of Israel', *Economic Journal*, 72 (285).

——, S. Robinson and M. Syrquin (1986) *Industrialization and Growth: A Comparative Study*, New York: Oxford University Press for World Bank.

CLINE, W. R. (1972) *Potential Effects of Income Redistribution on Economic Growth*, New York: Praeger.

—— (1983) *International Debt and the Stability of the World Economy*, Washington DC: Institute for International Economics.

COLE, W. E. and R. D. Sanders (1985) 'Internal Migration and Urban Employment in the Third World', *American Economic Review*, 75.

COOPER, C. M. and E. V. K. FitzGerald (1989) *Development Studies Revisited: Twenty-five Years of the Journal of Development Studies*, London: Frank Cass.

CORBO, V., M. Goldstein and M. S. Khan (eds) (1987) *Growth Oriented Adjustment Programs*, Washington DC: International Monetary Fund and World Bank.

CORNIA, G. and G. Jerger (1982) 'Rural vs. Urban Savings Behaviour', *Development and Change*, 13 (1).

——, R. Jolly and F. Stewart (1987) *Adjustment with a Human Face: Protecting the Vulnerable and Promoting Growth*, Oxford: Clarendon Press for UNICEF.

DASGUPTA, P. (1972) 'A Comparative Analysis of the UNIDO Guidelines and the OECD Manual', *Bulletin of the Oxford University Institute of Economics and Statistics*, 34 (1).

DAVIDSON, O. (1986) 'Finance, Funding, Saving and Investment', *Journal of Post-Keynesian Economies*, IX.

DAVIDSON, P. (1978) *Money and the Real World*, London: Macmillan.

—— (1982) *International Money and the Real World*, London: Macmillan.
DAVIS, C. and W. Charemza (eds) (1989) *Models of Disequilibrium and Shortage in Centrally Planned Economies*, London: Chapman and Hall.
DAVIS, O. and A. Whinston (1965) 'Welfare Economics and the Theory of the Second Best', *Review of Economic Studies*, 32 (1).
DEANE, P. (1989) *The State and the Economic System: An Introduction to the History of Political Economy*, Oxford University Press.
DE MELO, J. (1987) 'The Macroeconomic Effects of Foreign Aid: Issues and Evidence', mimeo, Groningen University.
DERVIS, K., J. de Melo and S. Robinson (1982) *General Equilibrium Models for Development Policy*, Cambridge University Press.
DOBB, M. (1970) *Welfare Economics and the Economics of Socialism*, Cambridge University Press.
DORNBUSCH, R. (1980) *Open Economy Macroeconomics*, New York: Basic Books.
—— (1986) 'The Effects of OECD Macroeconomic Policies on Non-oil Developing Countries: A Review', *World Bank Staff Working Paper*, No. 793, Washington DC: International Bank for Reconstruction and Development.
—— and F. L. C. Helmers (1988) *The Open Economy: Tools for Policymakers in Developing Countries*, New York: Oxford University Press for World Bank.
DORNBUSCH, R. and S. Fischer (1984) *Macroeconomics*, 3rd edn, New York: McGraw-Hill.
DRAKE, P. (1980) *Money, Finance and Development*, Oxford: Martin Robinson.
DUNNING, J. (1981) 'Explaining the International Direct Investment Position of Countries: Towards a Dynamic or Development Approach', *Weltwirtschaftliches Archiv*, 117.
EATON, J. and L. Taylor (1986) 'Developing Country Finance and Debt', *Journal of Development Economics*, 7 (1) pp. 3–21.
ECLA (1972) 'The Mobilization of Domestic Resources', *Economic Bulletin for Latin America*.
EDWARDS, S. and S. van Wijnbergen (1989) 'Disequilibrium and Structural Adjustment', in H. Chenery and T. N. Srinivisan (eds), *Handbook for Development Economics*, vol. II, Amsterdam: North Holland.
EITMAN, D. K. and A. I. Stonehill (1979) *Multinational Business Finance*, Reading, Mass.: Addison-Wesley.
ELLIS, F. (1988) *Peasant Economics: Farm Households and Agrarian Development*, Cambridge University Press.
ELLMAN, M. (1973) *Planning Problems in the USSR*, Cambridge University Press.
—— (1979), *Socialist Planning*, Cambridge University Press.
ELTIS, W. A. (ed.) (1970) *Induction, Growth and Trade: Essays in Honour of Sir Roy Harrod*, Oxford University Press.
ESHAG, E. and R. Thorp (1965) 'The Economic and Social Consequences of Orthodox Economic Policies in Argentina in the Post-war Years', *Bulletin of the Oxford University Institute of Economics and Statistics*, 27, pp. 1–45.
ESHAG, E. L. (1983) *Fiscal and Monetary Policies and Problems in Developing Countries*, Cambridge University Press.
ETHIER, W. (1984) 'Higher Dimensional Issues in Trade Theory', in R. Jones

and P. Kenen (eds), *Handbook of International Economics*, 1, Amsterdam: North Holland.

EVANS, D. (1984) 'A Critical Assessment of Some Neo-Marxist Trade Theories', *Journal of Development Studies*, 20 (2).

FABER, M. and D. Seers (eds) (1972) *The Crisis in Planning*, London: Chatto and Windus.

FAGEN, R. R. (ed.) (1986) *Transition and Development: Problems of Third World Socialism*, New York: Monthly Review Press.

FEI, J. and G. Ranis (1964) *Development of the Labour Surplus Economy: Theory and Policy*, New Haven, Conn.: Yale University Press.

—— (1975) 'A Model of Growth and Employment in the Open, Dualistic Economy: The Cases of Taiwan and Korea', *Journal of Development Studies*, 11 (1) pp. 32–63.

FEIWEL, G. R. (1975) *The Intellectual Capital of Michal Kalecki*, Knoxville, Tenn.: Tennessee University Press.

FFORDE, A. J. (1984) 'Macro-economic Adjustment and Structural Change in a Low-Income Socialist Developing Economy – An Analytical Model', *Discussion Paper No. 168*, London: Birkbeck College, London University.

FITZGERALD, E. V. K. (1976) 'Peru: The Political Economy of an Intermediate Regime', in *Journal of Latin American Studies*, 8 (1).

—— (1977) 'Patterns of Saving and Investment in Mexico, 1939–76', *Working Papers*, No. 30, Cambridge, Centre of Latin American Studies.

—— (1978a) *Public Sector Investment Planning*, London, Macmillan.

—— (1978b) 'The Fiscal Crisis of the Latin American State', in J. F. J. Toye, (ed.) *Taxation and Economic Development*, London, Frank Cass.

—— (1978c) 'The State and Capital Accumulation in Mexico', *Journal of Latin American Studies*, 10 (2).

—— (1979a) 'Stabilization Policy in Mexico: The Fiscal Deficit and Macroeconomic Equilibrium, 1960–77', in R. Thorp and L. Whitehead (eds) *Inflation and Stabilization in Latin America*, London: Macmillan.

—— (1979b) 'A Note on State Capital and Industrialization in Mexico', in J. Carrière (ed.), *Industrialization and the State in Latin America*, Amsterdam: CEDLA.

—— (1979c) *The Political Economy of Peru 1956–78: Economic Development and the Restructuring of Capital*, Cambridge University Press.

—— (1981) 'Apuntes sobre el Financiamiemento de la Acumulación en México', in R. Cordero (ed.), *Lecturas sobre Crecimiento y Crisis Económica en México*, Mexico City: Fondo de Cultura Económica.

—— (1982) 'The Economics of the Revolution', in T. Walker (ed.), *Nicaragua in Revolution*, New York: Praeger.

—— (1983a) 'A Simple Kaleckian Model of Growth and Income Distribution in the Planned Peripheral Economy', *ISS Working Paper*, The Hague: Institute of Social Studies.

—— (1983b) 'The State and the Management of Accumulation on the Periphery', in D. Tussie (ed.), *Latin America and the World Economy: New Perspectives*, London: Gower.

—— (1984) 'Restructuring through the Depression: The State and Capital Accumulation in Mexico 1925–40', in R. Thorp (ed.), *Latin America in the 1930s: The Role of the Periphery in World Crisis*, London: Macmillan.

—— (1987) 'Looney and Fredriksen on Mexican Fiscal Policy: A Reply', *World Development*, 19 (4).
—— (1988) 'The Food Balance and Economic Growth: A Reply', *Development and Change*, 19 (4).
—— (1990a) 'Economic Crisis and Transition on the Periphery: The Case of Nicaragua', in Ghai, D. and C. Hewitt (eds), *Economic Crisis and the Third World: Impact and Response*, London: Zed Press for UNRISD.
—— (1990b) 'The Impact of Macroeconomic Policies on Small-scale Industry: some Analytical Considerations', in F. Stewart, H. Thomas and T. de Wilde (eds), *The Other Policy*, London: Intermediate Technology Publications.
—— and C. M. Cooper (1989) (eds) *Development Studies Revisited: Twenty-five years of the Journal of Development Studies*, London: Frank Cass.
—— K. Jansen and R. Vos (1988) 'Structural Asymmetries, Adjustment and the Debt Problem', *ISS Working Paper on Money, Finance and Development 28*, The Hague: Institute of Social Studies.
—— and R. Vos (1989) *Financing Economic Development: A Structural Approach to Monetary Policy*, London: Gower.
—— and M. Wuyts (eds) (1988) *Markets within Planning: Socialist Economic Management in the Third World*, London: Frank Cass.
FRANSMAN, M. (ed.) (1986) *Machinery and Economic Development*, London: Macmillan.
FURTADO, C. (1970) *Economic Development in Latin America*, Cambridge University Press.
GARRITSEN DE VRIES, M. (1987) *Balance of Payments Adjustment, 1945 to 1986: The IMF Experience*, Washington DC: International Bank for Reconstruction and Development.
GERSCHENKRON, A. (1962) *Economic Backwardness in Historical Perspective*, Cambridge Mass.: Harvard University Press.
GHATAK, S. (1981) *Monetary Economics in Developing Countries*, London: Macmillan.
GIBSON, B. (1985) 'A Structuralist Macromodel for Post-revolutionary Nicaragua', *Cambridge Journal of Economics*, 9 (3).
GOLDSMITH, R. W. (1969) *Financial Structure and Economic Development*, New Haven, Conn.: Yale University Press.
GOLDSTEIN, M. and M. Khan (1982) 'Effects of a Slow-down in Industrial Countries on Growth in Non-oil Developing Countries', *IMF Occasional Paper 12*, Washington DC: International Monetary Fund.
GOMULKA, S. (1985) 'Kornai's Soft Budget Constraint and the Shortage Phenomenon: A Criticism and a Restatement', *Economics of Planning*, 19 (1).
GOREAUX, L. M. and A. S. Manne (1973) *Multi-Level Planning: Case Studies in Mexico*, Amsterdam: North Holland.
GOUGH, I. (1975) 'State Expenditure in Advanced Capitalism', *New Left Review*, August.
GRIFFIN, K. (1970) *Underdevelopment in Spanish America*, London: Macmillan.
—— (ed.) (1971) *Financing Development in Latin America*, London: Macmillan.
—— and J. Enos (1972) *Planning Development*, London: Addison. New Left Review, August.
—— and J. James (1981) *The Transition to Egalitarian Development: Economic*

Policies For Structural Change in the Third World, London: Macmillan.
GRIFFITH-JONES, S. (1981) *The Role of Finance in the Transition to Socialism*, London: Pinter.
—— and O. Sunkel (1986) *Debt and Development Crises in Latin America: the End of an Illusion*, Oxford: Clarendon Press.
GRIFFITHS, B. (1971) *Mexican Monetary Policy and Economic Development*, New York, Praeger.
GUEVARA, E., E. Mandel and C. Bettelheim (1968) *La Economia Socialista: El Gran Debate*, Barcelona: Nova Terra.
GUPTA, K. L. (1984) *Finance and Economic Growth in Developing Countries*, London: Croom Helm.
HARBERGER, A. C. (1972) *Project Evaluation*, London, Macmillan.
HARNACKER, M. (1985) *La Transicion al Socialismo*, Mexico City: Siglo Vientiuno.
HARRIS, D. L. (1978) *Capital Accumulation and Income Distribution*, London: Routledge & Kegan Paul.
HARRIS, J. R. and M. P. Todaro (1968) 'Migration, Employment and Development', *American Economic Review*, 58 (3).
HARRISON, M. (1980) 'Why Did NEP Fail?', *Economics of Planning*, 16 (2).
HARTFORD, K. (1985) 'Hungarian Agriculture: A Model for the Socialist World', *World Development*, 13 (1).
HICKS, U. (1965) *Development Finance, Planning and Control*, Oxford: Clarendon Press.
HINDESS, B. and P. Hirst (1975) *Precapitalist Modes of Production*, London: Routledge & Kegan Paul.
HIRSCHMAN, A. O. (1968) 'The Political Economy of Import Substituting Industrialization in Latin America', *Quarterly Journal of Economics*, 82 (1).
HORVAT, B. (1982) *The Political Economy of Socialism*, Oxford: Martin Robertson.
IBRD (1975) *Economic Analysis of Development Projects*, Washington DC: International Bank for Reconstruction and Development.
—— (1983) *World Development Report 1983*, New York: Oxford University Press.
—— (1988) *World Development Report 1988*, London: Oxford University Press for the World Bank.
—— (1990) *World Development Report 1990*, New York: Oxford University Press.
ILO (1979) *Household Income and Expenditure Statistics 1968–76*, Geneva: International Labour Organization.
—— (1987) *World Recession and Global Interdependence: Effects on Employment, Poverty and Policy Formation in Developing Countries*, Geneva: International Labour Office.
IMF (1987) *Theoretical Aspects of the Design of Fund-supported Adjustment Programmes*, International Monetary Fund Occasional Paper, 55, Washington DC.
JAMESON, K. P. and C. K. Wilber (eds) (1981) 'Socialist Models of Development', Special Issue *World Development*, 9.
JANSEN, K. (1990) *Finance, Growth and Stability: Financing Economic Development in Thailand, 1960–86*, Aldershot: Gower.

JOLLY, R. (ed.) (1973) *Third World Employment*, London: Penguin.
JOSLIN, D. (1963) *A Century of Banking in Latin America*, Oxford University Press.
KALDOR, N. (1959) 'Economic Growth and the Problem of Inflation', *Economica*, 26.
—— (1975) 'What is Wrong with Economic Theory', *Quarterly Journal of Economics*, August.
—— (1982) *The Scourge of Monetarism*, Oxford University Press.
KALECKI, M. (1954) 'El problema del financiamiento del desarrollo económico', *El Trimestre Económico*, 4.
—— (1962) 'A Model of Hyperinflation', *The Manchester School*, 32.
—— (1968) 'The Marxian Equations of Reproduction and Modern Economics', *Social Science Information*, 7 (6).
—— (1970a) 'Problems of Financing Economic Development in a Mixed Economy', in M. Eltis *et al.* (eds), *Induction, Growth and Trade: Essays in Honour of Sir Roy Harrod*, Oxford University Press.
—— (1970b) 'Theories of Growth in Different Social Systems', *Scientia*, 5–6.
—— (1971) *Essays on the Dynamics of the Capitalist Economy*, Cambridge University Press.
—— (1972a) *Selected Essays on the Economic Growth of the Socialist and Mixed Economy*, Cambridge University Press.
—— (1972b) 'Problems of Financing Economic Development in a Mixed Economy', in Kalecki (1972a).
—— (1976) *Essays on Developing Economies*, Brighton: Harvester.
—— (1986) *Selected Essays on Economic Planning*, Cambridge University Press.
KHAN, M. S. and P. Montiel (1989) 'Growth-oriented Adjustment Programs: A Conceptual Framework', *IMF Staff Papers*, 36 (2).
—— and N. U. Haque (1990) 'Adjustment with Growth: Relating the Analytical Approaches of the IMF and the World Bank', *Journal of Development Economics*, 32.
KILLICK, T. (1981) *Policy Economics*, London: Heinemann.
—— (ed.) (1984) *The Quest for Economic Stabilization: the IMF and the Third World*, London: Heinemann for the ODI.
—— (1985) 'Twenty-five years of development: The Rise and Impending Decline of Market Solutions', *Development Policy Review*, 4 (2).
KING, J. (1967) *Economic Development Projects and their Appraisal*, Baltimore, Md.: Johns Hopkins University Press.
KING, T. 'Private saving', in Griffin (1971).
KOFI, T. A. (1981) 'Prospects and Problems of the Transition from Agrarianism to Socialism: The Case of Angola, Guinea and Mozambique', in K. P. Jameson and C. K. Wilber (eds), 'Socialist Models of Development', Special Issue *World Development*, 9.
KORNAI, J. (1980) *The Economics of Shortage*, Amsterdam: North Holland.
—— (1986a) 'The Soft Budget Constraint', *Kyklos*, 29.
—— (1986b) 'The Hungarian Reform Process', *Journal of Economic Literature*, 24 (4).
KREGEL, J. (1973) *The Reconstruction of Political Economy: An Introduction to Post-Keynesian Economics*, London: Macmillan.

KREISLER, P. (1987) *Kalecki's Microanalysis: The Development of Kalecki's Analysis of Pricing and Distribution*, Cambridge University Press.

KRUEGER, A. (1974) 'The Political Economy of the Rent-seeking Society', *American Economic Review*, 64 (3).

—— (1978) *Liberalization Attempts and Consequences*, Cambridge Mass.: Ballinger.

LACLAU, E. (1977) 'Feudalism and Capitalism in Latin America', in *Politics and Ideology in Marxist Theory*, London: New Left Books.

LAL, D. (1974) *Methods of Project Analysis: a Review*, Washington DC: International Bank for Reconstruction and Development.

—— (1983) *The Poverty of Development Economics*, London: Hobart Paperback for the Institute of Economic Affairs.

LANDAU, L. (1971) 'Savings functions for Latin America', in H. B. Chenery (ed.), *Studies in Development Planning*, Cambridge Mass.: Harvard University Press .

LANGE, O. (1937) 'On the Economic Theory of Socialism', *Review of Economic Studies* (February).

LE CHAU (1967) *Del Feudalismo al Socialismo: La Economía de Viet-Nam del Norte*, Mexico City: Siglo Veintiuno.

LEFF, N. H. (1976) 'Capital Markets in the Less Developed Countries: the Group Principle', in R. I. McKinnon (ed.), *Money and Finance in Economic Growth and Development*, New York: Marcel Dekker.

—— and K. Sato (1980) 'Macroeconomic Adjustment in Developing Countries: Instability, Short-run Growth and External Dependency', *Review of Economics and Statistics*, 62 (2).

LENIN, V. I. (1978) *Cuestiones de la Organización de la Economía Nacional*, Moscow: Editorial Progreso.

LEWIS, A. (1954) 'Economic Development with Unlimited Supplies of Labour', *Manchester School*, 22.

LEWIS, J. P. (ed.) (1986) *Development Strategies Reconsidered*, New Brunswick: Transaction Books.

LEYS, C. (1975) *Underdevelopment in Kenya*, London: Heinemann.

LITTLE, I. (1982) *Economic Development: Theory, Policies and International Relations*, New York: Basic Books.

LITTLE, I. M. D. and J. A. Mirrlees (1974) *Project Appraisal and Planning for Developing Countries*, London: Heinemann.

LLUCH, C., A. A. Power and R. A. Williams (1978) *Patterns in Household Demand and Savings*, New York: OUP for IBRD.

LOONEY, R. E. and P. C. Frederikson (1987) 'Fiscal Policy in Mexico: The FitzGerald Thesis Re-examined', *World Development*, 15 (3).

LOVE, J. (1981) 'Raul Prebisch and the Origins of the Doctrine of Unequal Exchange', *Latin American Research Review*, 16.

McEWAN, E. (1981) *Revolution and Economic Development in Cuba*, London: Macmillan.

McKINNON, R. I. (1973) *Money and Capital in Economic Development*, Washington: The Brookings Institution.

MANDEL, E. (1962) *Marxist Economic Theory*, London: New Left Books.

MARGLIN, S. (1963) *Approaches to Dynamic Investment Planning*, Amsterdam: North-Holland.

MEIER, G. and D. Seers (eds) (1984) *Pioneers in Development*, Oxford: Oxford University Press for the World Bank.

MIPLAN (1980) *Programa de Reactivacion Economica en Beneficio del Pueblo*, Managua: Ministerio de Planifacacion.

MORAWETZ, D. (1980) 'Economic Lessons from Small Socialist Developing Countries', *World Development*, 8 (5/6).

NEWBERY, D. (1972) 'Public Policy in the Dual Economy', *Economic Journal*, 82.

—— (1974) 'The Robustness of Equilibrium Analysis in a Dual Economy', *Oxford Economic Papers*, 26 (1).

NEWLYN, W. T. (ed.) (1977) *The Financing of Economic Development*, Oxford University Press.

NOLFF, M. (ed.) (1974) *Desarrollo industrial latinoamericano*, Mexico City: Fondo de Cultura Economica.

NOVE, A. (1983) *Feasible Socialism*, London: George Allen & Unwin.

NURKSE, R. (1953) *Problems of Capital Formation in Underdeveloped Countries*, Oxford: Basil Blackwell.

NUTI, D. M. (1979) 'The Contradictions of Socialist Economics: A Marxist Interpretation', in R. Miliband and J. Saville (eds), *The Socialist Register*, London: Merlin.

—— (1986) 'Michael Kalecki's Contribution to the Theory and Practice of Socialist Planning', *Cambridge Journal of Economics*, 10 (4).

O'BRIEN, D. P. (1975) *The Classical Economists*, Oxford: Clarendon Press.

O'CONNOR, J. (1970) *The Origins of Socialism in Cuba*, Ithaca, NY: Cornell University Press.

ODM (1972) *A Guide to Project Appraisal in Developing Countries*, London: HMSO for the Overseas Development Ministry.

OECD (1968) *A Manual of Industrial Project Analysis*, Paris: Organization for Economic Co-operation and Development.

PLUMTRE, A. (1947) *Central Banking in the British Dominions*, Toronto, University of Toronto Press.

PORTES, A. (1979) 'Internal and External Balance in a Centrally Planned Economy', *Journal of Comparative Economics*, 3 (4).

POULANTZAS, N. (1968) *Pouvoir politique et classes sociales*, Paris: Maspero.

PREALC (1987) *In Search of Equity: Planning for Basic Needs in Latin America*, Aldershot: Gower.

PREOBRAZHENSKY, E. (1965) *The New Economics*, Oxford University Press (originally published in Moscow: 1926).

PREST, A. (1962) *Public Finance in Developing Countries*, London: Wiedenfeld and Nicolson.

PYATT, G. and E. Thorbecke (1976) *Planning Techniques for a Better Future*, Geneva: International Labour Office.

—— and J. Round (eds) (1985) *Social Accounting Matrices: a Basis for Planning*, Washington DC: International Bank for Reconstruction and Development.

QAYUM, A. (1960) *The Theory and Policy of Accounting Prices*, Amsterdam: North-Holland.

REDDAWAY, W. (1963) 'The Economics of Underdeveloped Countries', *Economic Journal*, 73.

RODRIGUEZ, C. R. (1979) *Cuba en el Transito al Socialismo*, Mexico City: Siglo XXI.

—— (1980) *La Teoria del subdesarrollo de la CEPAl*, Mexico City: Siglo XXI.

—— (1983) *Letra con Filo*, Havana: Editorial de Ciencias Sociales.

ROE, A. (1985) 'The Flow of Funds as a Tool of Analysis in Developing Countries', in G. Pyatt and J. Round (eds), *Social Accounting Matrices: A Basis for Planning*, Washington DC: International Bank for Reconstruction and Development.

ROWTHORN, B. (1980) *Capitalism, Conflict and Inflation*, London: Lawerence and Wishart.

RUMANTSIEV, A. (1979) *The Political Economy of Socialism*, Moscow: Progress Publishers.

RYLE, G. (1949) *The Concept of Mind*, London: Hutchinson.

SACHS, I. (1977) 'Kalecki and Development Planning', *Bulletin of the Oxford University Institute of Economics and Statistics*, 39.

SAITH, A. (1985) ((ed.)) *The Agrarian Question in Socialist Transitions*, London: Cass.

SAWYER, M. (1982) *Macroeconomics in Question*, Brighton: Wheatsheaf.

SAWYER, M. C. (1985) *The Economics of Michal Kalecki*, London: Macmillan.

SAYERS, R. (1937) *Modern Banking*, Oxford University Press.

SERRA, J. (ed.) (1974) *Desarrollo latinoamericano*, Mexico City: Fondo de Cultura Economica.

SEN, A. (1972) 'Control Areas and Accounting Prices', *Economic Journal*, 82.

SHAW, E. S. (1973) *Financial Deepening in Economic Development*, Oxford University Press.

SMIRNOV, G. (1979) *Planning in Developing Countries: Theory and Methodology*, Moscow: Progress Publishers.

SPOOR, M. (1982) 'Socialist Economic Strategies in the Third World: Some Lessons from Viet Nam, Cuba and Mozambique', master's dissertation, The Hague: Institute of Social Studies.

SQUIRE, L. (1981) *Employment Theory in Developing Countries*, New York: Oxford University Press for World Bank.

STEEDMAN, I. (1977) *Marx After Sraffa*, London: New Left Books.

—— (ed.) (1979) *Fundamental Issues in Trade Theory*, London: Macmillan.

STEINDL, J. (1982) *Maturity and Stagnation in American Capitalism*, Oxford: Basil Blackwell.

STEWART, F. (1975) 'A Note on Social Cost-benefit Analysis and Class Conflict in LDCs', *World Development*, 3 (1).

—— (1985) *Basic Needs in Developing Countries*, Baltimore, Md.: Johns Hopkins University Press.

STIGLITZ, J. and A. Weiss (1981) 'Credit Rationing in Markets with Imperfect Information', *American Economic Review*, 71 (3).

STIGLITZ, J. E. and G. F. Mathewson (1986) *New Developments in the Analysis of Market Structure*, London: Macmillan for the International Economic Association.

STONE, R. (1966) 'The Social Accounts from a Consumer Point of View', *Review of Income and Wealth*, 12 (1) pp. 1–33.

—— (1971) *The Financial Interdependence of the Economy 1957–66*, London: Chapman and Hall.

SYLOS-LABINI, P. (1969) *Oligopoly and Technical Progress*, Cambridge, Mass.: Harvard University Press.

SZAJKWOSKI, B. (ed.) (1981) *Marxist Regimes*, New York: St Martin's Press.

SZENTES, T. (1971) *The Political Economy of Underdevelopment*, Budapest: Akademiai Kiado.

TALAS, B. (1983) 'Specific Prerequisites for the Transition to Socialism in the Socio-economically Underdeveloped Countries', *Development and Peace*, 4 (2).

TANZI, V. (1976) 'Fiscal Policy, Keynesian Economics and Mobilization of Savings in Developing Countries', *World Development*, 4 (10/11).

TAVARES, M. (1971) 'Financial Intermediation in Latin America', *Economic Bulletin for Latin America*, 16 (2).

TAYLOR, L. (1979) *Macro Models for Developing Countries*, New York: McGraw Hill.

—— (1983) *Structuralist Macroeconomics: Applicable Models for the Third World*, New York: Basic Books.

—— (ed.) (1988) *Varieties of Stabilization Experience*, Oxford: Clarendon Press.

THEISENHUSEN, W. (1972) 'A Suggested Policy for Industrial Reinvigoration in Latin America', *Journal of Latin American Studies*, 4 (1).

THIRLWALL, A. P. (1972) *Growth and Development: With Special Reference to Developing Countries*, London: Macmillan.

—— (1978) *Growth and Development*, London: Macmillan.

—— (1986) 'A General Model of Growth and Development on Kaldorian Lines', *Oxford Economic Papers*, 38.

—— (ed.) (1987) *Keynes and Economic Development*, London: Macmillan.

THOMAS, C. Y. (1974) *Dependence and Transformation: The Economics of the Transition to Socialism*, New York: Monthly Review Press.

THORP, R. and L. Whitehead (eds) (1979) *Inflation and Stabilization in Latin America*, London: Macmillan.

—— (eds) (1987) *Latin American Debt and the Adjustment Crisis*, London: Macmillan.

TIRADO, V. M. (1983) 'Discurso en la Ocasión del Centenario de Carlos Marx', *Barricada*, Managua, 15 March.

TODARO, M. P. (1969) 'A Model of Labour Migration and Urban Unemployment in Less Developed Countries', *American Economic Review*, 59 (1).

TOYE, J. F. J. (1978) (ed.) *Taxation and Economic Development*, London: Frank Cass.

—— (1987) *Dilemmas of Development*, Oxford: Basil Blackwell.

TURNHAM, D. (1971) *The Unemployment Problem in LDCs*, Paris: OECD.

UN (1968) *A System of National Accounts*, New York: United Nations Statistical Office.

UN (1958) *Manual on Economic Development Projects*, New York: United Nations.

UNIDO (1972) *Guidelines for Project Evaluation*, New York: United Nations Industrial Development Organization.

VADJA, I. and Simai, M. (1971) *Foreign Trade in a Planned Economy*, Cambridge University Press.

VON FURSTENBERG, G. M. and G. B. Malkiel (1977) 'The Government and Capital Formation: A Survey of Recent Issues', *Journal of Economic Literature*, 15.

VOS, R. (1990) 'Social accounts and capital accumulation', in J. Alarcon, *et al.*, *The Social Accounting Framework for Development*, Aldershot: Avebury.

—— and L. Barreiros (1990) 'Households, Firms and the State: the Distribution of Incomes and Basic Needs in a SAM for Ecuador', in Alarcon *et al.*

WATERSON, A. (1965) *Development Planning: the Lessons of Experience*, Baltimore, Md.: Johns Hopkins University Press.

WEBB, R.C. (1972) *The Distribution of Income in Peru*, Princeton, NJ: Princeton University Press.

WEINTRAUB, S. (1978) *Keynes, Keynesians and Monetarists*, Philadelphia, Pa.: University of Pennsylvania Press.

WEISSKOPF, T. (1972) 'The Impact of Foreign Capital Inflows on Domestic Savings in Underdeveloped Countries', *Journal of International Economics*, 2 (1).

WELLS, J. (1986) *The Construction Industry in Developing Countries*, Beckenham, Kent: Croom Helm.

WHEELOCK, J. (1984) *Entre la Crisis y la Agresión: La Reforma Agraria Sandinista*, Managua: Editorial Nueva Nicaragua.

WHITE, C. (1982) 'Debates in Vietnamese development policy', *IDS Discussion Paper*, 171.

WHITE, G., R. Murray, and C. White (1983) (eds) *Revolutionary Socialist Development in the Third World*, Brighton, Sussex: Harvester Press.

WHITE G. and E. Kroll (eds) (1985) 'Special Issue on Agriculture in Socialist Development', *World Development*, 13 (1).

WILCZYNSKI, J. (1982) *The Economics of Socialism: Principles Governing the Operation of the Centrally Planned Economics under the New System*, London: George Allen & Unwin.

WILES, P. (ed.) (1981) *The New Communist Third World: An Essay in Political Economy*, London: Croom Helm.

WILLIAMSON, J.G. (1988) 'Migration and Urbanization', in H. Chenery and R.N. Srinivasan (eds), *Handbook of Development Economics*, Amsterdam: North Holland.

WILLIAMSON, O.E. (1976) *Markets and Hierarchies: Analysis and Anti-trust Implications*, New York: The Free Press.

—— (1985) *The Economic Institutions of Capitalism*, New York: The Free Press.

WOLF, T.A. (1985) 'Economic Stabilization in Planned Economies', *IMF Staff Papers*, 32 (1).

WOLFSON, D.J. (1979) *Public Finance and Development Strategy*, Baltimore, Md.: Johns Hopkins University Press.

WOLPE, H. (1980) *The Articulation of the Modes of Production*, London: Routledge & Kegan Paul.

WOOD, A. (1975) *A Theory of Profits*, Cambridge University Press.

WORLD BANK (1988) *World Development Report 1988: Public Finance in Development*, New York: Oxford University Press.

WUYTS, M. (1981) 'The Mechanization of Present-day Mozambican Agriculture', *Development and Change*, 12 (1).

—— (1988) 'The Food Balance and Economic Growth: an Appraisal of FitzGerald's Reformulation of Kalecki', *Development and Change*, 19 (4).

Index